GOSPEL AND LAW:
Contrast or Continuum?

The Hermeneutics of Dispensationalism and Covenant Theology

by
DANIEL P. FULLER

Reprinted, January 1982

Library of Congress Cataloging in Publication Data

Fuller, Daniel P.
  Gospel and law: contrast or continuum?

  Bibliography: p. 198.
  Includes index.
  1. Law and gospel.   2. Dispensationalism.
  3. Covenants (Theology) I. Title.
BT79.F8   230   79-20935
ISBN 0-960-26381-0

TO MY BELOVED WIFE RUTH,
in grateful appreciation for all her work and support
in the preparation of this book.

Contents

Foreword

The origin of this book goes back to 1957 when I wrote a doctoral dissertation entitled "The Hermeneutics of Dispensationalism" for the Northern Baptist Theological Seminary. Although a number of people at that time urged me to submit it for publication, I did not feel the liberty to do so, because the writing of that dissertation involved interaction with a substantial part of what Paul must have meant by "the whole counsel of God" (Acts 20:27). It had dealt with such basic biblical themes as the covenants and the kingdom of God and had been written with so much of the haste that often accompanies meeting a deadline, that I felt I needed to wait until my thinking had matured.

In writing that dissertation I had become aware that the only difference between the old and new covenants, as Jeremiah 31:31–34 makes clear, was that the new covenant brought in a new inclination of heart to obey the commands that were already stated in the old covenant (the Mosaic law). Subsequently, I emphasized this fact in my seminary teaching.

But in the winter quarter of 1971, as I was leading an inductive exegesis course on Galatians, a perceptive student, John Piper (now Associate Professor of Biblical Studies at Bethel College in St. Paul, Minnesota), asked the fateful question, "Was the command to trust God, which is such an essential part of the new covenant, also commanded in the Mosaic law?"

Such a question had never before entered my mind, and I was unable to give a satisfactory answer. As I look back now, I realize that the reason I had never entertained such a question was because all my previous Christian teaching had been from the vantage point of what is, generally speaking, covenant theology. There the conditional promises of the Bible echo "the covenant of works" into which God supposedly entered with Adam and Eve when, according to Genesis 2:17, he made the enjoyment of eternal life conditional upon their refraining from eating of the tree of the knowledge of good and evil. The covenant of grace, on the other hand, was the good news of God's promise to give eternal life to those who trusted in Christ's death and resurrection for the forgiveness of sins. Even though faith was regarded as essential for receiving these blessings, faith was also thought of as "a gift of God" (a false interpretation of Ephesians 2:8), so that this covenant of grace, unlike the covenant of works, was based on an *un*conditional promise. Since faith was the "condition" for enjoying the covenant of grace, one did not think of it as being one of the conditions required by the covenant of works.

The dispensationalism and the notes of the *Scofield Reference Bible* upon which I had been raised had always emphasized that one was saved simply by faith and not by works, although the man who was saved by faith would be indwelt by the Holy Spirit, who would produce good works in his life by the power of God. Like covenant theology, dispensationalism taught that good works always accompanied genuine faith. But it looked to the Holy Spirit rather than to faith as providing the impulse resulting in good works.

In the 1957 dissertation I was critical of dispensationalism because it applied so much of Scripture to the Jew rather than to the Church. In revolt I championed covenant theology because it regarded God as working with only one people throughout redemptive history. As recently as the spring of 1972 I regarded myself as holding essentially to covenant theology, even though the previous year John Piper had asked a question whose answer, when it finally became clear to me, would make it impossible for me to hold to that system any longer. Thomas Provence, presently one of my doctoral students, provided immense help by asking a crucial question about Romans 9:31–32. In this passage Paul writes, "Israel who pursued the righteousness which is based on law did not succeed in fulfilling that law. Why? Because they did not pursue it through faith, but as if it were based on works." In response to this passage Tom asked, "Then did not the Mosaic law enjoin the obedience of faith and fully reject all works calculated to merit blessing from God?" At that time I agreed with him completely. But it was not until the summer of 1972 that I realized the implication of Tom's question: I was no longer a covenant theologian. I realized that if the law is, indeed, a law of faith, enjoining only the obedience of faith and the works that proceed therefrom (I Thess. 1:3; II Thess. 1:11), then there could no longer be any antithesis in biblical theology between the law and the gospel. I then had to accept the very drastic conclusion that the antithesis between law and gospel established by Luther, Calvin, and the covenant theologians could no longer stand up under the scrutiny of biblical theology.

Six and one-half years have passed since that fateful summer, and what is written in the following pages is the fruit of two fifteen-month-long sabbaticals and several summers. In addition, I have worked through both Romans and Galatians twice in Greek exegesis classes. I wish to take this occasion to thank the Fuller Seminary Board of Trustees for making the first, and half of the second, sabbatical possible. I also want to thank my dear friend and colleague, Dr. Calvin Schoonhoven, for his generous contribution which made the latter half of the second sabbatical possible.

As a result of this study I have concluded that proper exegesis of Romans 10:4 is that Christ is the *telos* of the law, not in the sense of being its termination, but as climaxing it as the One who is in a continuum with it. I have also concluded that the "law of faith" in Romans 3:27 is not the principle of justification by faith alone, as Charles Hodge and other covenant theologians affirm, but that it is the very Mosaic law itself. I have further concluded that compliance with the Mosaic law is an "obedience of faith" (Rom. 1:5; 16:26). But perhaps my most radical conclusion is that in Pauline and other biblical theology, true faith is not merely accompanied by good works as something coordinate with it, but that faith itself is the mainspring for producing good works. I have had to regard as Galatianism any teaching that sees faith as merely giving one the assurance of salvation, and the Holy Spirit and the law as impelling good works. Sanctification, like justification, must be by faith *alone*.

Many people helped to bring this work to completion. First and foremost is my wife, Ruth, who encouraged me so often and was ready and willing to criticize my writing as well as type the finished draft of each chapter. She also spent many hours working to achieve stylistic consistency and helped to gather all the details necessary for the footnotes and bibliography. Next in importance is Dr. John Piper, who set aside several days from a busy schedule as a writer and teacher to read the final draft with care and then pose searching queries regarding various parts of the manuscript. Ronald Ganzer, a student at Fuller Seminary, should receive a special word of recognition for suggesting a change in title from "The Hermeneutics of Dispensationalism" to its present form. Steven Waterman, also a student at Fuller, gave valuable assistance in wording the most sensitive part of this book, namely, that covenant theology, dispensationalism, or any system of doctrine that does not see faith as the cause for good works is teaching a virtual Galatianism.

I also want to thank the eighty or so members of the class in "Gospel and Law," who received these chapters piecemeal in the fall quarter of 1978, for their interaction.

All scriptural quotations in this book are taken from the Revised Standard Version except where I felt I could supply a better translation directly from the original languages.

Pasadena, California   DANIEL P. FULLER
February 20, 1979

Abbreviations
of Oft-Cited Works

ACP John F. Walvoord, "The Abrahamic Covenant and Premillennialism"

CP John F. Walvoord, *The Church in Prophecy*

D Lewis S. Chafer, "Dispensationalism"

DT Charles C. Ryrie, *Dispensationalism Today*

MK John F. Walvoord, *The Millennial Kingdom*

NSB *Holy Bible*. New Scofield Reference Edition

RSB Charles C. Ryrie, *The Ryrie Study Bible*

SB *The Scofield Reference Bible*. Edited by C. I. Scofield

ST Lewis S. Chafer, *Systematic Theology*, 7 vols.

CHAPTER ONE
Dispensationalism's Basic Concern

The system for biblical interpretation which is known as "dispensationalism" exercises a rather widespread influence in American evangelicalism. An indication of this influence today is the sales figures for two books about this system. Hal Lindsey's *The Late Great Planet Earth* has sold more than thirteen million copies since its first publication in 1970, and still sells forty to fifty thousand copies a month. A movie version of the book appeared in January 1979.

The *New Scofield Reference Edition* of the Bible has sold over one million copies since it appeared in 1967. That is about half what the older *Scofield Reference Edition* sold in the thirty years between 1915 and 1945.[1] It is particularly significant that this new edition, based largely on the old King James Version, should have achieved such sales when a number of newer English translations are also enjoying great popularity.

Why has dispensationalism been so influential in American evangelicalism during much of the twentieth century? The answer lies in the strong ties between today's evangelicals and the fundamentalist movement which peaked during the 1920s. That movement, whose beginnings are evident as early as 1878,[2] arose to counteract the inroads that theological liberalism was making into many old-line denominations and their seminaries. The original purpose of the fundamentalist movement was certainly not

---

[1] According to Oswald T. Allis, *Prophecy and the Church* (Philadelphia: Presbyterian and Reformed Publishing Company, 1945), p. 267, "More than 2,000,000 copies of this Reference Bible have been printed in this country."

[2] Ernest R. Sandeen, *The Origins of Fundamentalism,* Facet Books, historical series 10 (American Church), ed. Richard C. Wolf (Philadelphia: Fortress Press, 1968), p. 11.

to advance some new theological position. Instead its objective was to form a rallying point for biblical Christianity. But after the turn of the century, and especially after World War I, the leadership of this movement somehow came to be dominated by those holding to a dispensational way of interpreting Scripture. As a result those who remained in that movement came to feel that being a dispensationalist was essential to being a fundamentalist.

What happened to Philip Mauro at the 1928 World Fundamental Conference in Chicago is a concrete example of how dispensationalism had come to be regarded as an implicit requirement of fundamentalism by that time. Mauro had been one of the most prominent leaders in the movement for several years, and he was scheduled to speak at this conference. But at the last minute his invitation was withdrawn because he had just published a book criticizing the postponed kingdom theory of dispensationalism and the *Scofield Reference Edition* of the Bible.[3] An editorial in *The King's Business,* the official organ of the Bible Institute of Los Angeles, said that Mauro

> sent out a "Letter to the Household of Faith" stating that after making all preparations to take his part [in the 1928 conference], he was notified at a late hour by the president of the association that it had been thought best to eliminate him from the program because of the fact that he had expressed disagreement with some of the notes of the Scofield Bible.[4]

The editorial then asked, "Must one now subscribe to the 'postponed kingdom theory' in order to fellowship with the fundamentalist group? If so, scores of loyal ministers and teachers, among them some of the greatest living expositors of Scripture, will find themselves—like Mr. Mauro—ostracized."

Many of today's staunchest evangelicals can trace their spiritual pilgrimage back to this mood that welcomed only those in wholehearted concurrence with the dispensationalist view. In 1936, Lewis Sperry Chafer, the founder of Dallas Theological Seminary, argued that one evidence upholding the truth of dispensational-

---

[3]Philip Mauro, *The Gospel of the Kingdom* (Boston: Hamilton Bros., 1928).
[4]John MacInnis, "Is Fundamentalism Being Redefined?" *The King's Business* (September, 1928), p. 517.

ism was the number and vitality of the Christian leaders who espoused its tenets. Concluding a forty-page article on "Dispensationalism," Chafer said, "There is reason why churches are filled, souls are saved, and the interest in missionary work thrives, where the whole Bible, *with its vital distinctions,* is faithfully preached."[5]

These "vital distinctions" of dispensationalism are the physical versus the spiritual seed of Abraham; the earthly, Messianic kingdom of God versus the timeless, spiritual kingdom; Jesus' coming again "for" his saints in distinction to his coming again "with" his saints; and the absolute distinction between Israel—God's earthly people, and the Church—God's heavenly people. Chapters five through seven of this book will consider the arguments dispensationalism advances for making these distinctions.

This book is an inquiry into underlying principles of interpretation which lead dispensationalists to make these distinctive emphases in their exposition of the Bible. Its thesis is that dispensationalism draws a sharp distinction between Israel and the Church in order to keep the teachings of grace in Scripture free from the teachings of the law. In a paragraph entitled "Dispensations" in the introduction to the *New Scofield Bible,* the editors affirm that "although not all Bible students agree in every detail of the dispensational system presented in this Reference Bible, it is generally recognized that the distinction between law and grace is basic to the understanding of the Scriptures."[6] One of dispensationalism's best-known slogans is the need to "rightly divide the Word" (cf. II Tim. 2:15). C. I. Scofield entitled one of his guides for studying the Bible "Rightly Dividing the Word of Truth." He affirmed that "the Word of Truth has right Divisions," and "any study of that Word which ignores those Divisions must be in large measure profitless and confusing."[7] In beginning the chapter entitled "Law and Grace" Scofield declared:

The most obvious and striking division of the word of truth is that

[5]Lewis Sperry Chafer, "Dispensationalism," *Bibliotheca Sacra,* 93 (October 1936), 447. Italics added.
[6]*The New Scofield Reference Edition,* E. Schuyler English, chairman of the editorial committee (New York: Oxford University Press, 1967), p. vii. Henceforth this edition will be signified by the letters NSB.
[7]C. I. Scofield, *Rightly Dividing the Word of Truth* (Findlay, Ohio: Fundamental Truth Publishers, 1940), p. 5.

between Law and Grace. Indeed, these contrasting principles *characterize* the two most important dispensations—Jewish and Christian. ... Scripture never, in *any* dispensation, mingles these two principles. Law always has a place and work distinct and wholly diverse from that of grace. Law is God prohibiting and requiring; grace is God beseeching and bestowing.[8]

Reformation theology from the outset, both in its Lutheran and Calvinistic branches, was also greatly concerned to distinguish properly between law and grace. In fact, Luther himself used the slogan "rightly divide the word" to stress the need for distinguishing between law and gospel. In his *Commentary on Galatians* (1533) he said:

both the word of grace and of wrath must be rightly divided, according to the Apostle [II Tim. 2:15f.]. ... He that teacheth that men are justified before God by the observation of the law, passeth the bounds of the law, and confoundeth these two kinds of righteousness, active and passive, and is but an ill logician, for he doth not rightly divide. Contrariwise, he that setteth forth the law and works to the old man, and the promise of forgiveness of sins and God's mercy to the new man, divideth the Word well.[9]

Likewise, Article V of the Lutheran *Formula of Concord* (1573) begins:

We believe, teach, and confess that the distinction of the Law and of the Gospel, as a most excellently clear light, is to be retained with special diligence in the Church of God, in order that the Word of God, agreeably to the admonition of St. Paul [II Tim. 2:15], may be rightly divided.[10]

Lutheranism today is considerably agitated over the question of just how this "distinction" should be applied. Because of criticism, notably from Karl Barth, that Luther's way of separating law and grace made it easier for people to submit to the rule of Hitler, Lutherans in Germany reexamined Luther's distinction between

---

[8]Ibid., p. 34.

[9]Martin Luther, *Selections from His Writings,* ed. John Dillenberger (Garden City, New York: Doubleday & Company, 1961), p. 103.

[10]Philip Schaff, ed., "The Formula of Concord," *The Creeds of Christendom* (3 vols., 4th ed.; New York: Harper & Brothers, 1877), III, 126–127.

law and gospel, and his correlative distinction between the two kingdoms in which a Christian dwells.[11] The resulting debate in Lutheranism has centered on the question of whether Luther meant "law" to represent a system of propositions which sum up all of God's righteous demands, or whether he meant it to represent primarily all (whatever its source) that accuses a person, in distinction from the gospel, which announces God's forgiveness.[12] This also seems to be the nub of the debate on law and gospel in American Lutheranism today. Missouri Synod Lutherans, under the leadership of J. A. O. Preuss, stress that "law," as the antithesis to the gospel, signifies "the expression of God's immutable will." Another group of Lutherans contends that the "Statement" issued by Preuss "understands the Law of God merely as legislation, as divine commands, and thus omits the reality of the wrath of God against sin from consideration, [and] it comes to moralistic conclusions about the Law, conclusions which betray its fundamental failure to observe the *due* distinction between the Law and the Gospel."[13]

The Calvinistic side of Reformation theology has also been concerned about this question. In III, 2, 29 of the *Institutes,* Calvin sharply distinguished between "the conditional promise" of the law "that sends us back to our own works," and the "freely given promise" of the gospel which is "the proper goal of faith." But Calvin's heirs continued to experience difficulty on this subject. Writing in 1749 Jonathan Edwards said, "There is perhaps no

[11]See Karl Barth, "Gospel and Law," *God, Grace, and Gospel,* trans. J. S. McNab, Scottish Journal of Theology Occasional Papers No. 8 (London: Oliver and Boyd, 1959), pp. 1–28. This famous monograph was read (in absentia) in Barmen, Germany in 1935 after Barth left his professorship in Muenster. He then became the professor of theology at the University of Basel for the remainder of his life. In a letter written in December, 1939, Barth explained more of what was behind this paper: "The German people are suffering from the legacy of the greatest Christian German, from the error of Martin Luther in regard to the relationship between law and gospel, between secular and spiritual regulations and authority. Through this distinction of Luther's, Germany's inbred paganism is not so much limited and reduced, but rather receives ideological clarification, confirmation, and strength." Quoted by Hermann Diem, "Luthers Predigt in den zwei Reichen," *Theologische Existenz heute,* N.F. 6, 1947.

[12]See Gerhard O. Forde, *The Law-Gospel Debate* (Minneapolis: Augsburg Publishing House, 1969), esp. chs. 10 and 11.

[13]Walter E. Keller, et al., "A Review Essay of *A Statement of Scriptural and Confessional Principles,*" *The Cresset* (May 1973), p. 11.

part of divinity attended with so much intricacy, and wherein orthodox divines do so much differ as stating the precise agreement and difference between the two dispensations of Moses and Christ."[14] From the time of Johannes Coccelus (1603–1669) the Calvinistic tradition in Reformed theology has taken the shape of what is called "covenant theology," in which the "covenant of works" reflected in the law of Moses is contrasted with the "covenant of grace" set forth in the gospel. But recently a leading spokesman for this tradition has opined that "covenant theology ... needs recasting."[15]

We have seen how dispensationalism is concerned, along with Lutheranism and covenant theology, to make and maintain the proper distinction between the law and grace. But what chiefly distinguishes dispensationalism from these streams of Reformation theology is its contention that *the only way* to maintain properly this distinction is to understand that, according to Scripture, God's dealings with Israel are totally separate from his dealings with the Church. Dispensationalism is convinced that covenant theology is unable to keep law and grace separate because it insists on maintaining a continuity between God's dealings with Israel and with the Church. It argues[16] that covenant theology, in insisting upon this continuity, must mix the law, which characterizes God's dealings with Israel, with the message of grace and the gospel, which is a unique characteristic of God's dealings with the Church. But if covenant theology were to "rightly divide the Word" not only by distinguishing between the legal and gospel messages of Scripture, but also by seeing the absolute distinction between Israel and the Church, then its message would lead people into the full joy and freedom of serving God simply out of gratitude for what he has done for them in Christ.

So a consideration of the hermeneutic of dispensationalism must assess the validity of this system's argument that the Bible intends to teach a complete separation between God's dealings with Israel and with the Church. But since dispensationalism's

---

[14]Jonathan Edwards, "Inquiry Concerning Qualifications for Communion," *The Works of President Edwards* (4 vols., 8th ed.; New York: Leavitt & Allen, 1858), I, 160.

[15]John Murray, *The Covenant of Grace* (London: Tyndale Press, 1953), p. 5.

[16]See below, pp. 25-26.

basic reason (it will be argued) for stressing this separation is to
free the teachings of grace from the works of the law, an evalua-
tion of dispensationalism's hermeneutic must also consider what
the Bible intends to teach about the relation between the gospel
and the law. In fact, we must achieve a conclusion regarding this
relationship (in chapter four) before proceeding to assess dispensationalism's distinctive ways of interpreting such crucial biblical
themes as the Abrahamic and Mosaic Covenants (chapter five),
the kingdom of God (chapter six), and the Church (chapter seven).

Since dispensationalism's more recent history is chiefly characterized by its conflict with covenant theology over the relationship between law and Israel, and grace and the Church, a
consideration of this conflict in chapters two and three will help
us understand dispensationalism's distinctive hermeneutic. There
we shall see how its chief proponents handled certain key passages of Scripture in contrast to the way the advocates of covenant
theology did. It will become clear that both felt impelled to honor
the apostle Paul's apparent antithesis between law and works, and
the gospel and faith, such as seems to exist in Romans 10:5–8 and
Galatians 3:12, the two passages (others could be adduced) which
Calvin felt set forth this antithesis "most clearly"[17] (*Institutes* III,
11, 17). Chapter four will consist of a reexamination of these
passages within their immediate contexts. After demonstrating
that the way in which both dispensationalism and covenant theology handle these passages is incorrect, the chapter will conclude with a proposal for a new approach which should have far-
reaching implications for our understanding of the covenants, the
kingdom of God, and the Church.

Before we proceed to a consideration of dispensationalism's
conflict with covenant theology, however, something should be
said about the origin of dispensationalism and its distinctive emphasis on a complete separation between God's dealings with

___

[17]We approach the question of law and the gospel deliberately by way of
covenant theology and Calvin rather than by Luther's interpretation of Paul,
since a consideration of the history of dispensationalism in chapters two and
three indicates that its proponents were mostly from a generally Calvinistic
background. Furthermore the revision that dispensationalism has recently
undergone stems from a conflict with covenant theology and not with
Lutheranism.

Israel and his dealings with the Church. By itself the term "dispensationalism" evokes the idea of the different ways, or dispensations, in which God has administered redemptive history from age to age. But other systems of biblical interpretation which deny such a separation have also divided redemptive history into several dispensations. So in order to learn about the origins of dispensationalism we must first consider the problem of nomenclature.

I. *The Problem of Nomenclature*

Dispensationalists make it very clear that the basic tenet of their teaching is the complete distinction between Israel and the Church. In his book entitled *Dispensationalism Today,* Charles Ryrie says:

> A dispensationalist keeps Israel and the Church distinct.... This is probably the most basic test of whether or not a man is a dispensationalist, and undoubtedly it is the most practical and conclusive. A man who fails to distinguish Israel and the Church will inevitably not hold to dispensational distinctions; and one who does, will.[18]

A generation before Ryrie, Lewis Sperry Chafer also cited this distinction as essential to dispensationalism:

> The dispensationalist believes that throughout the ages God is pursuing two distinct purposes: one related to the earth with earthly people and earthly objectives involved, while the other is related to heaven with heavenly people and heavenly objectives involved. ... Over against this, the partial dispensationalist, though dimly observing a few obvious distinctions, bases his interpretation on the supposition that God is doing but one thing, namely, the general separation of the good from the bad, and, in spite of all the confusion this limited theory creates, contends that the earthly people merge into the heavenly people; that the earthly program must be given a spiritual interpretation or disregarded altogether; and that there is nothing in eternity but heaven and hell.[19]

Dispensationalists acknowledge, though usually with some reluctance, that J. N. Darby (1800–1882), one of the prime movers

---

[18]C. C. Ryrie, *Dispensationalism Today* (Chicago: Moody Press, 1965), pp. 44f. Henceforth this book will be signified by the letters DT.

[19]Chafer, "Dispensationalism," p. 448.

in what is known as the Plymouth Brethren movement, was the first to develop dispensationalism by stressing this distinction between Israel and the Church. Chafer, for example, after citing Jonathan Edwards' allusion to dispensational distinctives,[20] goes on to say:

> Similarly, a worthy and scholarly research of the Bible with dispensational distinctions in view was made during the last century in England by J. N. Darby, Charles H. Mackintosh, Wm. Kelly, F. W. Grant and others who developed what is known as the Plymouth Brethren movement. These men created an extended literature of surpassing value which is strictly Biblical and dispensational, which literature, however, has been strangely neglected by many conservative theologians.[21]

According to this statement Darby was the first to develop that "strictly Biblical" dispensationalism which Chafer himself championed a century later. Linking Darby to Edwards with the adverb "similarly" could mislead one to think that Darby simply developed more completely the essential idea of dispensationalism which Edwards had implicitly held. An examination of Edwards' writings, however, and in particular his *History of Redemption*, shows that he affirmed the unity of God's purpose throughout redemptive history and regarded God's work with the Church as a continuum of his work with Israel. So this statement, while acknowledging Darby as the originator of dispensationalism, fails to stress the radical difference between Darbyism, with its emphasis on God's two purposes in history, and what Chafer calls the "partial dispensationalism" which regards God as doing "but one thing."

Ryrie also admits that "[informed dispensationalists] recognize that as a *system* dispensationalism was largely formulated by Darby . . ." (DT 66, ital. added). But like Chafer, he wants to stress that some aspects of this teaching are heard in others who lived before Darby. So Ryrie considers many Christian thinkers from Justin Martyr, Irenaeus, Clement of Alexandria, and Augustine to such post-Reformation theologians as John Edwards (1639–1716) and Isaac Watts (1674–1748), who had developed some way of dis-

[20]Edwards, "Inquiry. . .," p. 160.
[21]Chafer, "Dispensationalism," pp. 392–393.

tinguishing between different dispensations in redemptive history. From this Ryrie concludes that "neither Darby nor the [Plymouth] Brethren originated the concepts involved in the *system* [of dispensationalism]" (DT 74, ital. added). He also says, "Although we cannot minimize the wide influence of Darby, the glib statement that dispensationalism originated with Darby, whose system was taken over and popularized by Scofield, is not historically accurate" (DT 76).

But how is it that Ryrie can affirm "the wide influence of Darby" in formulating dispensationalism as a *system* and yet say that "Darby did not originate the concepts involved in this system," and that the dispensational system did not originate with Darby? He can make such apparently contradictory statements because he uses the word "dispensationalism" in two different ways. Ryrie is saying that Darby did largely formulate the system of dispensationalism that is based on the complete distinction between Israel and the Church. But he did not originate the "system" of dispensationalism that has to do simply with dividing redemptive history into several periods, for an examination of the history of Christian thought shows that this idea has been held from Irenaeus on.

So it is not proper for Ryrie to use the words "dispensationalism" and "system" to represent any and all schemes for dividing redemptive history into various periods. These schemes are so diverse, to say nothing of the systems of thought of which they happen to be parts, that they cannot be lumped together and called a "system" of "dispensationalism." But the interpretation of Scripture which Darby developed, on the basis of a complete distinction between Israel and the Church, does have a coherence and a distinctiveness for which the word "system" is entirely appropriate. Ryrie often uses the word "dispensationalism" to represent this "system" that was, as he says, "largely formulated by Darby." Yet in his book *Dispensationalism Today,* he should not have confused the issue by using the word "dispensationalism" in two senses, describing the teaching of each as a "system" when one is such a conglomerate that it simply cannot bear such a predication.

Part of the problem is, to be sure, that the system of biblical interpretation formulated by Darby came to be called "dispensationalism," not because this word calls attention to what is distinctive about this teaching but simply as a matter of historical accident. Darby himself used the word "dispensation" quite often in his writings.[22] The very nature of his system of thought required this. To affirm that God, in founding the Church at Pentecost, left off dealing with his earthly people Israel and will resume the completion of his purpose for them only after he raptures the Church away from the earth, implies radical changes in God's management of redemptive history. Such fundamental changes require one to think of God as administering redemptive history in one way *before,* and in another way *after,* these changes occur. Since one meaning that the word "dispensation" can have in conventional English is the ordination and administration of a certain policy, it was only natural for Darby to speak of how a prior dispensation differed from a succeeding one. With his speaking often about such radical dispensational changes, it is understandable how this system picked up the name "dispensationalism," in distinction from other systems whose changes in dispensations are much less pronounced and hence use the word "dispensation" only infrequently. For example, in Article VII, 6, the Westminster Confession (1647) speaks of the one covenant of grace as being administered throughout redemptive history "under various dispensations." But since the dispensational changes envisioned there do not, like Darby's, imply complete disjunctures at Pentecost and the rapture of the Church, relatively little is said about them; thus there was never any reason to call the theology of the Westminster Confession "dispensationalism."

It is unfortunate that Darbyism picked up the name "dispensationalism," since this word does not, by itself, direct one's attention to Darby's basic premise but rather to an idea that comes into prominence only as a corollary of this premise. Much confusion would have been avoided if this system had received a name that, instead of calling to mind some chart outlining "God's

---

[22]Following are some of the titles of Darby's essays in which the word "dispensation" appears: "The Apostasy of the Successive Dispensations," *The Collected Writings of J. N. Darby,* ed. Wm. Kelly (34 vols., London: Morrish, 1867–c.1900), I, 192–202; "The Character of Office in the Present Dispensation," I, 140–170; "The Dispensation of the Kingdom of Heaven," II, 80–96.

Plan of the Ages," could have signified dispensationalism's basic distinctive of the radical separation between Israel and the Church.

To be sure, dispensationalism is well known for its graphic representations of how God administers redemptive history from "creation to the consummation." But dispensationalists are really quite unconcerned with the number of dispensations there are in redemptive history or what they are called. According to Ryrie, "the number of dispensations in a dispensational scheme and even the names of the dispensations are relatively minor matters. Presumably one could have four, five, seven or eight dispensations and be a consistent dispensationalist" (DT 48). They must, however, insist on at least three dispensations in order to assert the idea of the Church as a parenthesis between God's dealings with Israel. If Pentecost marks the time when God stops dealing with Israel and founds the Church, and if the rapture of the Church signals the resumption of God's dealings with Israel, then there must be a dispensation before the Church age, one during the Church age, and one afterward. Thus these are the only dispensations that Dallas Seminary regards as essential. "The doctrinal statement of the Dallas Theological Seminary," Ryrie notes, "mentions only three [dispensations] by name (the Mosaic Law, the present dispensation of grace, and the future dispensation of the millennial kingdom)" (DT 50).

Dispensationalists would alleviate much confusion in relating their history if they would include in their discussion only those who have stressed the need for these three dispensations, and would stop including all Christian thinkers who have divided redemptive history into epochs. They could affirm, without reluctance, that their teaching originated with Darby, for limiting their history to such a recent antecedent as Darby would not affect in the least the question of the truth or falsehood of their teaching. The answer to that question is determined simply by the exegesis of Scripture.

It is refreshing, therefore, to hear one dispensationalist fully endorse Darby as the man who rediscovered the apostolic teachings which had been lost to the Church during the sixteen-hundred-year interval. Dr. Harry Ironside, for years the pastor of the Moody Memorial Church in Chicago, declared concerning the concept of the parenthesis Church:

until brought to the fore through the writings and preaching and teaching of a distinguished ex-clergyman, Mr. J. N. Darby, in the early part of the last century, it is scarcely to be found in a single book or sermon through a period of sixteen hundred years! If any doubt, let them search, as the writer has in a measure done, the remarks of the so-called Fathers, both pre- and post-Nicene; the theological treatises of the scholastic divines; Roman Catholic writers of all shades of thought; the literature of the Reformation; the sermons and expositions of the Puritans; the general theological works of the day.[23]

We must now take a closer look at the life and teachings of Darby, whom dispensationalists themselves either concede (Ryrie and Chafer) or forthrightly affirm (Ironside) as the one who first advocated the distinctive premise of their system of interpretation.

II. The Formation of Darby's View

Born in Ireland in 1800, Darby received his education first at Westminster School and later at Trinity College, Dublin, where he graduated as Classical Gold Medalist. He started into the law profession but after several years began to undergo a period of deep religious anxiety. In later life, when counseling by correspondence a woman who was greatly troubled, he recounted this early experience by way of encouragement. "I went through deep exercise of soul," Darby related, "before there was a trace of peace, and it was not until after six or seven years that I was delivered."[24]

In 1823 he forsook the law profession, and two years later was ordained as a priest in the Church of England. He commenced his ministry among the Irish Catholics who were settled in a wild, mountainous district. In the following quotation taken from a letter written between 1855 and 1860 to Professor Tholuck at Halle, he recounts the motives that led him to forsake law for the ministry:

> I was a lawyer; but feeling that, if the Son of God gave Himself for me, I owed myself entirely to Him, and that the so-called Christian world was characterized by deep ingratitude toward Him, I longed

[23]Harry A. Ironside, *The Mysteries of God* (New York: Loizeaux Brothers, 1908), pp. 50–51.

[24]*Letters of J. N. D.* (3 vols., Kingston-on-Thames, England: Stow Hill Bible and Tract Depot, n.d.), II, 310.

for complete devotedness to the work of the Lord; my chief thought was to get round amongst the poor Catholics of Ireland. I was induced to be ordained. I did not feel drawn to take up a regular post, but, being young in the faith and not yet knowing deliverance [later defined as coming to the realization of Christ's all-sufficiency both to give him a holy standing before God and to impart a new life by which he would have victory over sin], I was governed by a feeling of duty towards Christ, rather than by the consciousness that *He* had done *all* and that I was redeemed and saved; consequently it was easy to follow the advice of those who were more advanced than myself in the Christian world. As soon as I was ordained, I went amongst the poor Irish mountaineers, in a wild and uncultivated district, where I remained two years and three months working as best I could.[25]

He goes on to relate how during this time he became disturbed over the disparity between the way his work was being carried out and the biblical picture concerning the Church and Christianity. At the end of two years and three months (1827) he suffered an injury to his leg which required that he go to Dublin for surgery and a long period of convalescence. It was during this time that his six or seven years of anxiety ended as he experienced deliverance through the knowledge of Christ's all-sufficiency. Concerning this deliverance he says:

During my solitude, conflicting thoughts increased; but much exercise of soul had the effect of causing the scriptures to gain complete ascendancy over me. I had always owned them to be the word of God. When I came to understand that I was united to Christ in heaven, and that, consequently, my place before God was represented by His own, I was forced to the conclusion that it was no longer a question with God of this wretched "I" which had wearied me during six or seven years, in presence of the requirements of the law.[26]

The insight that he was united with Christ in heaven brought Darby to a new understanding of the Church. Further on in his letter to Tholuck he said, "It then became clear to me that the church of God, as He considers it, was composed only of those who were so united to Christ, whereas Christendom, as seen externally, was really the world, and could not be considered 'the

---

[25]Ibid., III, 297.
[26]Ibid., III, 298.

church'. ...."[27] Because of this view of the Church, he came to feel that ordination by any church of Christendom or by dissenting groups, was done too often apart from the authority of Christ. So he was convinced that the only thing to do was to join with other believers without any organization, but simply on the basis of Matthew 18:20, "Where two or three are gathered together in my name, there am I in the midst of them." Leaving Anglicanism, Darby began to meet with others who shared his view of the prevailing apostasy in the visible Church. This group, along with similar groups in Ireland and England, grew into what later became known as the "Plymouth Brethren."

The conviction that he was united with Christ affected not only Darby's view of the Church but also his understanding of eschatology. In a letter written in 1868 he said:

> The coming of the Lord was the other truth which was brought to my mind from the word, as that which, if sitting in heavenly places *in* Christ, was alone to be waited for, that I might sit in heavenly places *with* Him. Isaiah xxxii brought me to the earthly consequences of the same truth, though other passages might seem perhaps more striking to me now; but I saw an obvious change of dispensation in that chapter, when the Spirit would be poured out on the Jewish nation, and a king reign in righteousness.[28]

In the letter to Tholuck, he told more about this new understanding of prophecy:

> In my retreat, the 32nd chapter of Isaiah taught me clearly, on God's behalf, that there was still an economy to come of His ordering; a state of things in no way established as yet. The consciousness of my union with Christ had given me the present heavenly portion of the glory, whereas this chapter clearly sets forth the corresponding earthly part. I was not able to put these things in their respective places or arrange them in order, as I can now; but the truths themselves were then revealed of God, through the action of His Spirit, by reading His word.[29]

These statements, which Darby himself singles out as the basic ideas which controlled his thinking, show the importance he attached to distinguishing between Israel and the Church. God does

[27]Ibid.
[28]Ibid., I, 516.
[29]Ibid., III, 298–299.

have a plan for Israel which would be consummated upon the earth in the future. But he purposed that the Church should have a heavenly destiny and enjoy the closest possible relationship to himself in that it would constitute the body of Christ. On the basis of this distinction between Israel and the Church, Darby found support for making a sharp distinction between the grace of God which is for the Church and the law which is for Israel:

> Prophecy throws a great light upon the dispensations of God; and, in this sense, it does much as regards the freedom of our souls toward Him. For what hinders it more than the error so often committed, of confounding the law and the gospel, the past economies or dispensations with the existing one? If, in our internal fighting, we find ourselves in the presence of the law, it is impossible to find peace; and yet if we insist on the difference which exists between the position of the saints of old, and that of the saints during the actual [present] dispensation, this again troubles the minds of many. Now the study of prophecy clears up such points, and at the same time enlightens the faithful as to their walk and conversation; for whilst it always maintains free salvation by the death of Jesus, prophecy enables us to understand *this entire difference* between the standing of the saints now and formerly, and lights up with all the counsels of God the road along which His own people have been conducted, whether before or after the death and resurrection of Jesus.[30]

This passage makes it clear that the problem between the supposed law-passages and the grace-passages of Scripture is to be resolved by insisting on "*this entire difference* between the standing of the saints now and formerly." Through understanding that Isaiah 32 and other similar passages referred only to God's purposes for Israel upon the earth, Darby could distinguish his heavenly standing with Christ (cf. Eph. 2:6–7) to be part of God's wholly distinct purpose for the Church. Since the gospel of grace was presently revealed for the benefit of the Church, the laws that had been revealed in connection with God's purposes for Israel were of no direct concern for the Christian. Consequently, Darby renounced all efforts to serve Christ out of duty (law), and henceforth rejoiced in Christ's having done all for him.

Thus dispensationalism joins with Lutheranism and with the

[30]J. N. Darby, "The Hopes of the Church of God," *The Collected Writings of J. N. Darby*, II, 563.

covenant theology of Calvinism in seeking to draw a sharp distinction between the law and the gospel. But it distinguishes itself from these two streams of Reformation theology by its insistence on a complete disjuncture between God's workings with Israel and his workings with the Church. When dispensationalism began to exercise its widespread influence in American evangelicalism through the great popularity of the *Scofield Reference Bible,* this distinctive aroused strong protest from the proponents of covenant theology. Did this limiting of grace to the Church age mean that Israelites in the dispensations preceding and following were saved by trying to fulfill the works of the law? As the following chapter will show, this protest from covenant theology has caused contemporary dispensationalists, and particularly the notes in the *New Scofield Bible,* to speak more guardedly than Darby, Scofield, and Chafer of the distinction between Israel and the Church to enforce the contrast between law and the gospel.

CHAPTER TWO
The Dialogue with Covenant Theology

In contrast to the Christians who held to dispensationalism's basic emphasis of sharply distinguishing between Israel and the Church, there were other Bible-believing Christians who regarded this emphasis to be at variance with the teachings of Scripture. Generally these were leaders in the Presbyterian or Reformed Churches, whose heritage stemmed from Calvin and the "covenant theology" of his successors. Dispensationalism's recent history is best understood by listening carefully to its dialogue with covenant theology.

I. Covenant Theology's Protest
Albertus Pieters of the Reformed Church in America became aware of the great influence the Scofield Bible was having when he returned from Japan in 1923:

> when I was beginning my work as Bible teacher and College Pastor in Hope College, Dr. John E. Kuizenga, then one of the professors in our seminary, remarked to me that no one could be a teacher of the Bible, in these days, without reckoning with the Scofield Bible, since it was so widely used, and so highly esteemed by many Christian people. ... Upon Dr. Kuizenga's advice, I procured a copy, and made myself acquainted with its contents.[1]

He went on to describe this Bible's vast influence and the serious problems its teachings posed for covenant theology. In light of these problems, Pieters made the following statement to the min-

[1]Albertus Pieters, *A Candid Examination of the Scofield Bible* (Swengel, Pennsylvania: Bible Truth Depot, n.d.), p. 3.

18

isterial association of the Christian Reformed Church assembled at Calvin College on June 1, 1936:

> The importance of the problem [presented by the Scofield Bible] is accentuated by the fact that those who use this work are, in other respects, among the best Christians in our churches, those with the deepest faith in the Holy Scriptures and with the most sincere devotion to the Lord. These good people do not lack faith and zeal, but they sadly lack knowledge; and the tragedy of the situation lies just here, that this is the very thing they think they have obtained from the Scofield Bible![2]

Pieters was bothered by what he regarded as Scofield's "excessive typology," the apparent inconsistency of his dispensational framework, and the flimsy foundation upon which so much of his eschatological system was based.[3] But Scofield's biggest departure from covenant theology was the distinction he drew between Israel and the Church.[4]

In addition to Pieter's remarks, which were on the popular level, other covenant theologians outlined some of the deeper implications of this distinction.

Oswald Allis' objections

Dr. Oswald T. Allis of Westminster Theological Seminary, Philadelphia, wrote two articles in the *Evangelical Quarterly* which laid bare the root of the tension between covenant theology and dispensationalism.[5] In the first article he emphasized the hermeneutical tensions existing between these two systems of biblical interpretation. From the covenant theologian's viewpoint, the basic hermeneutical error in dispensationalism was its insistence on dividing and compartmentalizing the Scriptures, with the result that a most important distinction was made between those Scriptures relating to Israel and those relating to the Church.[6] In the second article he cited what he considered to be the most serious

---

[2]Ibid., p. 5.
[3]Ibid., pp. 10–22.
[4]Ibid., p. 23.
[5]Oswald T. Allis, "Modern Dispensationalism and the Doctrine of the Unity of Scripture," *The Evangelical Quarterly,* VIII (January 1936), 22–35; and "Modern Dispensationalism and the Law of God," ibid. (July 1936), 272–290.
[6]Allis, "Modern Dispensationalism and the Unity of Scripture," p. 35.

theological error arising from this hermeneutical starting point: "Closely related to this fundamental error [of hermeneutics] and partly responsible for it, partly the result of it, is a serious misunderstanding of the true nature and purpose of the law of God."[7] This error is the antithesis dispensationalism makes between law and grace, so that the two can never simultaneously work together to bring about the salvation of man. Allis declared:

> The fundamental error in the attitude toward the Sinaitic covenant which is shown in the Scofield Bible is the failure to distinguish between the law as a covenant of works and the law as a ministration or dispensation in the covenant of grace, in other words in the failure to recognize that the Sinaitic covenant belongs to the covenant of grace.[8]

To grasp the significance of this observation, it is necessary to understand what Allis means by "the covenant of works" and "the covenant of grace." According to the Westminster Confession:

> The first covenant made with man was a covenant of works, wherein life was promised to Adam, and in him to his posterity, upon the condition of perfect and personal obedience.
> Man by his fall having made himself incapable of life by that covenant, the Lord was pleased to make a second, commonly called the covenant of grace: wherein he freely offered unto sinners life and salvation by Jesus Christ, requiring of them faith in him that they may be saved. . . .[9]

From the fall onward, the covenant of grace spelled out the terms by which sinful man could come to enjoy life and salvation. Nevertheless the covenant of works continued to play a role in the fulfillment of God's plan of redemption. The Westminster Confession says:

> God gave to Adam a law, as a covenant of works, by which he bound him and all his posterity to personal, entire, exact, and perpetual obedience; promised life upon the fulfilling, and threatened

---

[7]Allis, "Modern Dispensationalism and the Law of God," p. 272.
[8]Ibid., p. 280.
[9]"The Westminster Confession of Faith A.D. 1647," *The Creeds of Christendom*, ed. Philip Schaff (3 vols., 4th ed.; New York: Harper & Brothers, 1877), III, VII, 2,3.

death upon the breach of it. . . . This law, after his fall, continued to be a perfect rule of righteousness; and as such was delivered by God upon Mount Sinai in the ten commandments. . . . The moral law doth forever bind all, as well justified persons as others, to the obedience thereof. . . . Christ in the gospel [does not in] any way dissolve, but much strengthens this obligation. . . . Although true believers be not under the law as a covenant of works, to be thereby justified or condemned, yet it is of great use to them . . . in that, as a rule of life informing them of the will of God and their duty, it directs and binds them to walk accordingly. . . . (XIX, 1, 2, 5, 6)

Once men had become guilty before God they were no longer in a position to merit and gain eternal life, as Adam had once been, by fulfilling the law expressed in the covenant of works. As sinners, they could not repair the injury they had inflicted upon the glory of God. Nevertheless God reiterated the law in wording much like the original covenant of works. The Mosaic law said, "You shall therefore keep my statutes and my ordinances, by doing which a man shall live" (Lev. 18:5). Jesus also said, in answering the question of what a man must do to inherit eternal life, "You shall love the Lord your God with all your heart . . . and your neighbor as yourself. . . . Do this, and you shall live" (Luke 10:27–28).

According to covenant theology, God has continued to give such statements to sinful men in order that they might always be held responsible to do the right thing, and that "examining themselves [by the law] they might come to a further conviction of, humiliation for, and hatred against sin; together with a clearer sight of the need they have of Christ" (West. Conf. XIX, 6). But even after men have come to Christ, the law—with its conditional promises and threats—continues to have a very salutary function in one's Christian life:

[The law] is likewise of use to the regenerate, to restrain their corruptions, in that it forbids sin; and the threatenings of it serve to show what even [the Christian's] sins deserve, and what afflictions in this life they may expect for [their sins], although freed from the curse thereof threatened in the law. The promises [of the law], in like manner, show them God's approbation of obedience, and what blessings they may expect upon the performance thereof; although not as due to them by the law as a covenant of works. . . . (West. Conf. XIX, 6)

In covenant theology the law fulfills all these functions for men without eclipsing the fact that salvation for sinners is always by grace through faith in Christ. Indeed, biblical revelation, notably from Moses to Christ, has many statements worded like the covenant of works in that blessings (even the blessing of salvation itself) are conditioned on obedience. But then it also has statements, notably in the New Testament and particularly in John's Gospel and Paul's epistles, which affirm that God's blessings come simply by grace, through faith. Despite this apparent polarity, the Westminster Confession declares that "there are not ... two covenants of grace different in substance but one and the same [covenant of grace] under various dispensations [of the Old and New Testaments]" (VII, 5–6).

In contrast with covenant theology, dispensationalism taught that in the period from Moses to Christ, God put the Jewish nation under a virtual covenant of works. In his famous note on John 1:17 Scofield said:

> [Grace] is ... constantly set in contrast to law, under which God demands righteousness from man, as, under grace, he gives righteousness to man. ... Law is connected with Moses and works; grace with Christ and faith. ... Law blesses the good; grace saves the bad. ... Law demands that blessings be earned; grace is a free gift. ...
>
> As a dispensation, grace begins with the death and resurrection of Christ. ... The point of testing is no longer legal obedience as the condition of salvation, but acceptance or rejection of Christ, with good works as a fruit of salvation. ...[10]

In commenting on Habakkuk 2:4 and on the change that occurred when Israel as a nation was set aside and the Church called into being, Scofield also said:

> This opening of life to faith alone, makes possible not only the salvation of the Gentiles during the dispersion of Israel ... but also makes possible a believing remnant in Israel while the nation, as such, is in blindness and belief, with neither priesthood nor temple, and consequently unable to keep the ordinances of the law. Such is Jehovah! In disciplinary government His ancient Israel is cast out of the land and

---

[10]*The Scofield Reference Bible*, ed. C. I. Scofield (new ed., New York: Oxford University Press, 1917), p. 1115. Henceforth references from this work will simply be SB followed by a page number.

judicially blinded, but in covenanted mercy the individual Jew may resort to the simple faith of Abraham. (SB 956)

It was on the basis of such statements that Allis charged that dispensationalism denied one covenant of grace and taught instead that God set forth two ways for saving men at different periods in redemptive history. Noting Scofield's distinction between the gospel of the kingdom and the gospel of grace, Allis said:

> The Gospel of the grace of God—in a word, the Cross—belongs to the Church age; the Gospel of the kingdom was preached before the Church was founded and is to be preached after the Church is "raptured." But it is a different Gospel. It is the Gospel of the Crown, not the Cross. This is consistent Dispensationalism. "Grace" and "the Kingdom" belong to two distinct dispensations which are definitely set in contrast, and each has a Gospel of its own. Salvation clearly will be on quite a different basis in the Kingdom age from what it is today in the Church age.[11]

Such a distinction, Allis argued, stemmed from dispensationalism's hermeneutical premise that God's workings with Israel and the Church were always distinct. Allis thought that dispensationalism divided the Scriptures so sharply on this basis that it was

> divisive and holds a doctrine of Scripture which tends to be and is in many respects as destructive of that high view of Scripture which its advocates assert as it is disastrous to some of the doctrines most precious to the hearts of those that hold it. In a word, despite all their differences Higher Criticism and Dispensationalism are in this one respect strikingly similar. Higher Criticism divides Scripture up into documents which differ from or contradict one another. Dispensationalism divides the Bible up into dispensations which differ from or even contradict one another, and so radical is the difference as viewed by the extremist* that the Christian of today who accepts the Dispensational view finds his Bible (the part directly *intended* for him) shrunk to the compass of the Imprisonment Epistles [Ephesians, Philippians, Colossians].[12]

[11]Allis, "Modern Dispensationalism and the Unity of Scripture," pp. 29–30.

[12]Ibid., p. 24. *By the "extremist" position, Allis meant the radical (but consistent) views of E. W. Bullinger, *The Foundations of Dispensational Truth* (1931).

In replying to Allis' charges,[13] L. S. Chafer agreed that it was dispensationalism's hermeneutical presuppositions, in contrast to those of covenant theology, which made it necessary to assert two ways of salvation. Chafer repeatedly affirmed Darby's foundational premise that the Bible reveals how God works with two distinct peoples, the earthly people of Israel and the heavenly people comprising the Church. The following quotation shows how the Church's unique standing as a heavenly people implies a similarly unique way of being saved:

> The heavenly people, by the very exalted character of their salvation being "made" to stand in all the perfection of Christ ... have no burden laid on them of establishing personal merit before God. ... No meritorious system, such as was the Law, could possibly be applied to a people who by riches of divine grace have attained to a perfect standing, even every spiritual blessing *in Christ Jesus.* (D 415)

As for Israel, the earthly people, Chafer declared:

> The essential elements of a grace administration—faith as the sole basis of acceptance with God, unmerited acceptance through a perfect standing in Christ, the present possession of eternal life, an absolute security from all condemnation, and the enabling power of the indwelling Spirit—are not found in the kingdom administration. [The essential elements are] declared to be the fulfilling of "the law and the prophets" ... and [there is] an extension of the Mosaic law into realms of meritorious obligation which blast and wither as the Mosaic system could never do (Matt. 5:20–48). These [future] kingdom injunctions ... could perfect no one as men in Christ are now perfected. ... (D 416)

He summarized his position by saying that "... with the call of Abraham and the giving of the Law and all that has followed, there are two widely different, standardized, divine provisions, whereby man, who is utterly fallen, might come into favor with God" (D 410).

Chafer made these statements because he felt that this was the

---

[13]L. S. Chafer, "Dispensationalism," *Bibliotheca Sacra,* 93 (October 1936), 390–449. Henceforth this article will be referred to as D with a page number following.

only way to honor the intended meanings of all the passages of Scripture and to submit truly to the authority of the Bible. He rejected the interpretational procedure called the analogy-of-faith hermeneutic, whereby one part of Scripture, supposedly the clearer part, provided the basis for interpreting the more obscure part. He was therefore convinced that all the prophecies of a glorious future for Israel found in the Old Testament prophets were not "spiritually fulfilled" in the Church of today, but would be literally fulfilled in the future dispensation of the millennium, or kingdom age:

> These systems [of law and grace] do set up conflicting and oppos-ing principles. But since these difficulties appear only when an attempt is made to coalesce systems, elements, and principles which God has separated, the conflicts really do not exist at all outside these unwar-ranted unifying efforts; in fact they rather demonstrate the *necessity* of a due recognition of all God's different and distinct administrations. The true unity of the Scriptures is not discovered when one blindly seeks to fuse these opposing principles into one system. ... A plan of interpretation which, in defense of an ideal unity of the Bible, con-tends for a single divine purpose ... is doomed to confusion when confronted with the many problems which such a system imposes on the text of Scripture. (D 416–417)

He concluded his article by saying:

> Those who pursue an idealism as to the unity and continuity of the Bible ... must, if sincere, face the problem their method of interpre-tation generates. ... Though dispensationalism does ... departmental-ize the message of the Word of God according to its obvious divisions, [it] does also discover the true unity of the Bible. The outstanding characteristic of the dispensationalist is ... that he *believes* every statement of the Bible and gives to it the plain, natural meaning its words imply. [Dispensationalism] has changed the Bible from being a mass of more or less conflicting writings into a classified and easily assimilated revelation of both the earthly and heavenly purposes of God, which purposes reach on into eternity to come. (D 446–447)

It is evident that Allis and Chafer did not differ over some triviality or technicality in theology. Rather, they differed over the nature of the Bible's unity—a question which is second in im-portance only to that of the truth of Scripture. Both men were deeply committed proponents of the truth of Scripture, but each felt that the way the other viewed the Bible as a unity seriously threatened its truth. Naturally the truth of the Bible and the unity of the Bible are indissolubly linked, for that which is true cannot be contradictory but must cohere.

Because Allis and covenant theology in general saw the Bible as a unity by having the passages that taught grace subordinate the passages that taught law, Chafer claimed they were guilty of not allowing each passage in the Bible to set forth its own intended meaning. Dispensationalism, on the other hand, avoided this pitfall. As Chafer put it, "The outstanding characteristic of the dispensationalist is that he believes every statement of the Bible and gives to it the plain, natural meaning its words imply" (D 446–447).

According to Allis, however, dispensationalism's departmentalizing of Scripture bore too much similarity to Higher Criticism. Then too, by departmentalizing the Bible, the dispensationalist had removed almost all significance from the term "unity." Indeed, the Bible set forth the workings of *one* God, but his workings with Israel and the Church were so coordinate that they remained separate and distinct on into eternity. The human mind, in its deep-seated quest for seeing how two things are finally resolved into one, chafes at that which must ever remain essentially two. But according to Chafer that was just the trouble with covenant theology. It allowed the mind, in its desire to see oneness, to ride roughshod over some of Scripture's intended meanings and arbitrarily make agreement between the antithesis of law and grace by forcing law to be seen as playing a subordinate role or even by forcing law passages to read as though they were really teaching grace.

In making this criticism of covenant theology, Chafer was not guilty of battling against some straw man that he had set up. Charles Hodge (1797–1878), a leading covenant theologian in America during the last century, did use that hermeneutical procedure to which Chafer objected—that of interpreting one part of Scripture in terms of another:

> From the Scriptures, therefore, as a whole, from the New Testament, and from the Old as interpreted *by infallible authority* in the

and 18:18–30, where Jesus, in response to the query of what one must do to inherit eternal life, replied that men must keep the Ten Commandments and love God with all their hearts and their neighbors as themselves. In Hodge's understanding, Jesus answered this question by stating the covenant of works rather than the gospel because he discerned that the questioners had already rejected the gospel. "If a man will not ... accede to the method of salvation by grace, he is of necessity under law," Hodge said in commenting on these passages (II, 375). In his answers to the lawyer and the rich young ruler, Jesus was simply affirming that "the eternal principles of justice are still in force. If any man can present himself before the bar of God and prove that he is free from sin ... he will not be condemned" (II, 122).

But Chafer saw these passages in quite a different light. Even though it is expressly said in Luke 10:25 and 29 that the lawyer's questioning was insincere (so that it is at least plausible that he was not willing to accede to the gospel), Chafer declared that surely for the rich young ruler and even for the lawyer, Jesus' answer was the proper one to be given during what was still the Mosaic dispensation:

> Dr. Charles Hodge states: "The Scriptures know nothing of any other than two methods of attaining eternal life: the one which demands perfect obedience, and the other which demands faith" (*Systematic Theology*, Vol. II, p. 117). That offer of eternal life which depends on obedience is thought by Dr. Hodge and others to be hypothetical and unattainable by anyone, and therefore serves to enforce the fact that there is but one practical way to secure eternal life—by faith alone. [But] there are two important factors often omitted from this discussion: (a) Eternal life, if offered on the ground of obedience at all, is offered only to those who are Israelites, and (b) they had the continuing animal sacrifices which, when faithfully offered, maintained for them a righteous position before God and became the ground of forgiveness for every failure. Because of this forgiveness, the standing of a Jew before God could not have been hypothetical. ... The final standing of any Jew before God was not based on law observance alone, but contemplated that Jew in the light of the sacrifices he had presented in his own behalf. ... (D 423, note)
>
> A very clear and comprehensive body of Scripture bears on eternal life as related to Judaism. However, it is there contemplated as an *inheritance* [in contrast to the present possession of eternal life which the Church enjoys]. The doctrine as related to Judaism is found in

well-identified passages. . . . Luke 10:25–29, in which passage the lawyer asks as to how he may *inherit* eternal life and is told by Christ
in the most absolute terms that eternal life for him is gained by the
keeping of the Mosaic Law. Luke 18:18–27, where it is likewise reported that a young ruler made the same inquiry, namely, "What shall
I do to inherit eternal life?" and to this sincere man our Lord quoted
the Mosaic commandments; but when the young man declared that
these things had been kept by him from his youth, Christ did not
chide him for falsehood but took him on to the ground of complete
surrender of all he was and all he had as the way into the state which
Christ termed "perfect." (D 422–423)

Thus Chafer believed that the answers Jesus gave were directly
pertinent to the question, "What must I do to inherit eternal life?"
Indeed, the perfect keeping of the law was impossible for men of
that day, but Jesus answered as he did because in thatdispensation,
striving to keep the whole law was as essential to inheriting eternal life as was the faithful offering of sacrifices to atone for one's
inevitable failure to keep the law perfectly. Chafer felt he was
honoring Scripture by understanding Jesus' replies as expressions
of the Mosaic dispensation during which they were uttered. In
Chafer's view, to say, like Hodge, that Jesus replied as he did to
the lawyer in order to consign him to the condemnation he was
calling down upon himself, or to confront him with what was
impossible so that he would humbly turn and accept salvation by
grace through faith, was an example of how covenant theology
"blindly seeks to fuse these opposing principles [of law and grace]
into one system."

Chafer's statements make it clear that, depending on the dispensational period out of which a biblical book was speaking,
there were two ways of salvation set forth in Scripture. For the
Jew under the Mosaic dispensation, salvation came by trying to
keep the law and by faithfully offering sacrifices; for the Christian
under grace, salvation is simply by faith in Christ's finished work.
Oswald Allis had not misunderstood Chafer when he charged him
with believing that the Bible taught two real ways of salvation. In
fact Chafer had spoken out with such unmistakable clarity and
was having such a powerful influence that the Southern Presbyterians officially charged him with heresy.

The Southern Presbyterians versus Chafer

In July, 1938, Professor James E. Bear of the Union Seminary, Richmond, Virginia, published an article showing, like Allis, the various points at which dispensationalists were decidedly at odds with the Westminster Confession.[15] Three years later he became the chairman of a committee of the General Assembly of the Presbyterian Church in the United States, which in 1944 made the following recommendation:

> It is the unanimous opinion of your Committee that Dispensationalism ... is out of accord with the system of doctrine set forth in the Confession of Faith, not primarily or simply in the field of eschatology, but because it attacks the very heart of the Theology of our Church, which is unquestionably a Theology of one Covenant of Grace. As Dr. Chafer clearly recognizes, there are two schools of interpretation here which he rightly designates as 'Covenantism' as over against 'Dispensationalism.'[16]

In the preamble to the final recommendation, it was stated that President Chafer taught "a dispensational view of God's various and divergent plans of salvation for various groups in various ages."[17]

Chafer's response to this statement lacked the confident tone with which he had answered Allis. He declared that there was no excuse on the Committee's part "for this libelous statement,"[18] because for the past year he had tried to meet with some of the members of Bear's committee to explain his statements. Had he been given the chance to explain himself, he would have interpreted his statements as follows:

> the Editor [Dr. Chafer] has never held such views [that there are divergent plans of salvation] and ... he yields first place to no man in

[15]James E. Bear, "Dispensationalism and the Covenant of Grace," *The Union Seminary Review,* XLIX (July 1938), 285–307.

[16]"Report of the Ad Interim Committee on Changes in the Confession of Faith and Catechisms," *Minutes of the Eighty-Fourth General Assembly of the Presbyterian Church in the United States, 1944* (Richmond, Virginia: Presbyterian Committee for Publication, 1944), pp. 123–124.

[17]*Minutes of the Eighty-Fourth General Assembly of the Presbyterian Church in the United States, 1944,* quoted by L. S. Chafer, "Dispensational Distinctions Denounced," *Bibliotheca Sacra,* 101 (July 1944), 259.

[18]Chafer, "Dispensational Distinctions Denounced," p. 259.

contending that a holy God can deal with sin in any age on any other ground than that of the blood of Christ. The references cited by the Committee from the Editor's writings have no bearing on salvation whatever, but concern the rule of life which God has given to govern His people in the world. He has addressed a rule of life to Israel on the ground that they are His covenant people. Observing the rule of life did not make them a covenant people. In like manner God has addressed a rule of life with heavenly standards to the believers of this age; not as a means of salvation but because they are saved.[19]

Thus Chafer advanced two arguments to support his contention that the committee headed by James Bear had libeled him. One was that he had always believed that it was only on the basis of the death of Christ that a holy God could deal with sin in any age. The second argument was that his statements about the need for a Jew to strive to keep the law in the Mosaic era had "no bearing on salvation whatever."

With regard to the first argument, it should be pointed out that there was a sense in which Chafer believed in one way of salvation for all ages. In the article replying to Allis' criticism, Chafer had said that whatever the conditions a man must meet in any dispensation in order to be saved, salvation was a possibility only because of the death of Christ:

> whatever God does for sinful man on any terms whatsoever, being made possible through the death of Christ, is, to that extent, an act of divine grace; for whatever God does on the ground of Christ's death is gracious in character, and all will agree that a divine covenant which is void of all human elements is more gracious in character than one which is otherwise. . . . On the human side . . . the human requirements which the divine covenant imposes may be either absolutely lacking, or so drastically imposed as to determine the destiny of the individual. (D 430)

According to this statement, even where human requirements are "drastically imposed" (as in the Mosaic and kingdom dispensations), salvation was available only because Christ died. But this emphasis on "human requirements" that are "drastically imposed" in some dispensations was what the Southern Presbyterians were

[19]Ibid.

objecting to. They were *not* claiming that Chafer had taught that in some ages salvation came apart from Christ's death.

With regard to the second argument (that the Jews' keeping of the law had "no bearing on salvation whatever"), Chafer did believe that Israel was already God's people when the law was given to them, so that they did not need to keep it in order to become what they already were. But this sense in which they were already God's people *excluded* eternal acceptance with God. In his reply to Allis, Chafer stated that such acceptance came only to those who faithfully strived to keep the law and offered sacrifices for their failure to do so. Chafer believed that inheriting eternal life is central to salvation. How he could then say that for the Jew "keeping the law had no bearing on salvation whatever" is not at all clear.

In fact a few months before Bear's committee divulged its conclusions Chafer had argued:

> a one-covenant theory precludes any distinctly new undertaking upon the part of God and hence the omission of that which the Apostle elevates to the place of highest doctrinal import. This new creation [the Church] is not a second chapter in Judaism, but is a wholly new and specifically intended demonstration of divine grace—"That in the ages to come he might show the exceeding riches of his grace." And again, respecting a distinction between Israel and the Church, the question may be asked: Why did Nicodemus, the flower of Judaism, need to be born again, if Israel and the Church constitute one continuous purpose of God as Covenantism teaches? Why did the Apostles need to be saved? Why was Saul of Tarsus saved, who had lived "blameless before the law"? And why should three thousand Jews, many of them priests, be saved on the day of Pentecost? Were all of these utter failures under Judaism, or was God introducing a new thing for which Judaism had prepared no one?[20]

But even though this paragraph implies that vast numbers of Israelites possessed the particular kind of salvation that was for the Jews during the Mosaic dispensation, it seems incredible that Chafer would argue that every one in Israel lived up to the "drastic requirements" of (1) trying to keep all the law, and (2) faithfully offering the sacrifices for their failure to do so. But if some

[20]Lewis Sperry Chafer, "Dispensational Distinctions Challenged," *Bibliotheca Sacra*, 100 (July 1943), 342–343.

Jews did not live up to these "drastic requirements," then the keeping of the law was crucial to whether or not a Jew enjoyed his particular kind of salvation. It was this insistence that salvation for the Jew depended, in part, on striving to keep the law that clashed with the historic teaching from the Reformation onward that salvation is always by faith alone.

Further evidence that the Southern Presbyterians had not libeled Chafer came from a number of statements that appeared in his *Systematic Theology,* which was published three years after the Southern Presbyterians had charged him with heresy:

> the law stands as the representation of the merit system—that divine arrangement which, according to the New Testament, is held as the antipodes of God's plan of salvation by grace. Beyond the one truth that both systems are ordained of God for application in such ages as He may elect, they set up contrasts at every point.[21]
>
> Under grace the fruit of the Spirit *is,* which indicates the present possession of the blessing through pure grace; while under the kingdom, the blessing *shall be* to such as merit it by their own works. (ST IV, 219)
>
> In this age, God is dealing with men on the ground of His grace as it is in Christ. His dealings with men in the coming age are based on a very different relationship. At that time, the King will rule with a rod of iron. There is no word of the cross, or of grace, in the kingdom teachings. (ST IV, 222)

With such statements, which apparently follow the same line of thinking as Chafer's predecessor, C.I. Scofield,[22] going on record as late as 1947, it is no wonder that John Wick Bowman of San Francisco Theological Seminary argued a few years later that dispensationalism did teach two ways of salvation:

> if any man is saved in any dispensation other than those of Promise and Grace, he is saved by *works* and not by faith! ... [The dispensationalist] is clearly left with two methods of salvation on his hands— *works* for the majority of the dispensations, *faith* for the rest—and we have ... to deal with a fickle God who deals with man in various ways at various times.[23]

---

[21] Lewis Sperry Chafer, *Systematic Theology* (7 vols., Dallas: Dallas Seminary Press, 1948), III, 343. Henceforth quotations will be designated as ST with a volume and page number.

[22] Supra, p. 22.

[23] John Wick Bowman, "Dispensationalism," *Interpretation,* X (April 1956), 178.

II. Dispensationalism's More Recent Replies

It is significant that leading dispensational thinkers did not try to defend Scofield's and Chafer's teaching of two ways of salvation. Although no one seemed to be troubled by covenant theology's teaching that before he had sinned, Adam could have been confirmed in righteousness only if he, by his own efforts, merited this blessing by keeping the law for a limited probationary period, there was something in the Christian conscience that balked at saying that a sinful Israelite's salvation, during the Mosaic and kingdom eras, depended in part on his striving by his unaided efforts to keep the law.

E. Schuyler English and the New Scofield Bible

Since 1940 Dr. E. Schuyler English had been consultant to the Oxford Press as it continued to reprint the *Scofield Reference Bible,* which had been selling so well for more than thirty years. In 1948 he edited the "Pilgrim Bible," whose format and teaching made it a young people's version of the *Scofield Bible.* In the notes of this Bible, English clearly affirmed (in contrast to Scofield) that "the Old Testament saints ... are saved through faith in God's Word, and by the Blood. ..."[24]

But as long as the *Scofield Bible* could be construed to teach that an Israelite was saved by works during the Mosaic and kingdom eras, then such charges as Allis, Bear, and Bowman had made would continue to trouble the proponents of this system. Thus in 1954 the revision of the *Scofield Bible* was begun by a committee of nine men, chaired by E. Schuyler English. According to English, the purpose of the new edition was to offer a *Scofield Bible* with more legible type and additional marginal notes, headings, and footnotes. There was also need for a revision of certain inaccuracies, as well as an updating of archaeological information, and some of the archaic words of the King James text.[25]

One of the inaccuracies that needed clarification was Scofield's famous note on John 1:17, which stated that the Jews were saved

---

[24]E. Schuyler English, ed., *Holy Bible,* Pilgrim edition (New York: Oxford University Press, 1948), p. 1240.

[25]"E. Schuyler English Looks at Dispensationalism," *Christian Life,* XVIII, 5 (September 1956), p. 25.

by works during the Mosaic era. In 1956, two years after the work of revision had commenced, English replied to Bowman's charge:[26]

> [That dispensationalism teaches that man has been saved by different means in different ages] is wholly contrary to fact. Dispensationalism teaches that man is saved by grace, and grace alone in any age. The divinely-given tests of the different dispensations are to show man his failure and complete helplessness alone and turn him to God's grace in salvation through the blood of His beloved Son.[27]

When the *New Scofield Reference Bible* was published in 1967, English cited that among its various accomplishments, it clarified a misunderstanding:

> Scofield's note on grace at John 1:17 needs clarification. Although nowhere else in his writings [*sic?*] does Scofield imply such a thing, this footnote says, "The point of testing [in the Church age] is no longer legal obedience as the condition of salvation, but acceptance or rejection of Christ with good works as a fruit of salvation (refs.)." This misleading statement has been corrected. As in the footnote at Genesis 1:28 ... the fact that salvation has been and always will be, whatever the age or dispensation, by grace through faith in God's redemptive position in Christ and His sacrificial death, has been stressed.[28]

Not only is this affirmation made in the footnote at Genesis 1:28, which introduces the whole subject of dispensations, but the foreword also says, "a recognition of the dispensations is of the highest value, so long as it is clearly understood that throughout all the Scripture there is only one basis for salvation, i.e. by grace through faith."[29]

The Dallas Seminary Statement of Faith

In 1952, Dallas Seminary, the school founded by Chafer, published a statement of faith whose fifth article sought to clarify how dis-

---

[26]Supra, p. 34.

[27]"E. Schuyler English Looks at Dispensationalism," p. 25.

[28]E. Schuyler English, "The New Scofield Reference Bible," *Bibliotheca Sacra*, 124, 2 (April–June 1967), 130. In his note on Habakkuk 2:4 Scofield said virtually the same thing as in his note on John 1:17. See above, p. 22. This note remained unchanged in the *New Scofield Bible*.

[29]*The New Scofield Reference Bible*, ed. E. Schuyler English (New York: Oxford University Press, 1967), p. vii. Henceforth references from this revised edition will be denoted by NSB followed by the page number.

pensationalism affirms that salvation in every age is simply by faith through grace. The following is a quotation of the entire article, since it constitutes a landmark in the history of dispensationalism:

> We believe that the dispensations are stewardships by which God administers His purpose on the earth through man under varying responsibilities. We believe that the changes in the dispensational dealings of God with man depend upon changed conditions or situations in which man is successively found with relation to God, and that these changes are the result of the failures of man and the judgments of God. We believe that different administrative responsibilities of this character are manifest in the Biblical record, that they span the entire history of mankind, and that each ends in the failure of man under the respective test and in an ensuing judgment from God. We believe that three of these dispensations or rules of life are the subject of extended revelation in the Scripture, viz.: the dispensation of the Mosaic Law, the present dispensation of grace, and the future dispensation of the millennial kingdom. We believe that these are distinct and are not to be intermingled or confused, as they are chronologically successive.
>
> We believe that the dispensations are not ways of salvation nor different methods of administering the so-called Covenant of Grace. They are not in themselves dependent on covenant relationships but are ways of life and responsibility to God which test the submission of man to His revealed will during a particular time. We believe that, if man does trust in his own efforts to gain the favor of God or salvation under any dispensational test, because of inherent sin his failure to satisfy fully the just requirements of God is inevitable and his condemnation sure.
>
> We believe that according to the "eternal purpose" of God (Eph. 3:11) salvation in the divine reckoning is always "by grace, through faith," and rests upon the shed blood of Christ. We believe that God has always been gracious, regardless of the ruling dispensation, but that man has not at all times been under an administration of grace as is true in the present dispensation. (I Cor. 9:17; Eph. 3:2; 3:9, R.V.; Col. 1:25; I Tim. 1:4, R.V.).
>
> We believe that it has always been true that "without faith it is impossible to please" God (Heb. 11:6), and that the principle of faith was prevalent in the lives of all the Old Testament saints. However, we believe that it was historically impossible that they should have had as the conscious object of their faith the incarnate, crucified Son, the Lamb of God (John 1:29), and that it is evident that they did not comprehend as we do that the sacrifices depicted the person and work of Christ. We believe also that they did not understand the redemptive significance of the prophecies or types concerning the sufferings of Christ (I Peter 1:10–12); therefore, we believe that their

faith towards God was manifested in other ways as is shown by the long record in Hebrews 11:1-40. We believe further that their faith thus manifested was counted unto them for righteousness (cf. Rom. 4:3 with Gen. 15:6; Rom. 4:5–8; Heb. 11:7).[30]

In a letter written in 1956, the President of Dallas Seminary, Dr. John F. Walvoord, said, "I feel that our statement on dispensations is much nearer the norm among contemporary dispensationalists than some of Dr. Chafer's explanations." Walvoord felt that "in many places [Dr. Chafer] does seem to overemphasize the legal character of the Mosaic dispensation as well as the millennial kingdom and to put a similar stress on grace in the present age." Declaring himself to be in general harmony with Chafer's teachings, Walvoord said he believed "it is fair to state that Dr. Chafer should be regarded somewhat in the role of a creative thinker who, like all other creative thinkers, states things somewhat differently than others and sometimes overstates distinctions in an effort to make his point." According to Walvoord, Dr. Chafer himself had not drafted Dallas Seminary's statement of faith on dispensations, yet he had read it and given it his personal approval. Then Walvoord concluded, "I would recommend that you study this statement very carefully as I think you will find it a remarkable condensation of dispensational teaching, which has freed dispensationalism of some of the aspects which have caused criticism."[31]

Creeds are notorious for the way they compress complex ideas into succinct and terse statements, and even though Dallas Seminary's statement of faith is much longer than the creeds of most schools, one question remains unanswered. When it declares, "We believe that ... salvation in the divine reckoning is always 'by grace through faith,' " it seems that the words "in the divine reckoning" are reminiscent of how Chafer could say that even the salvation which came to the Jews as a reward for keeping the law in the energy of the flesh was by grace because apart from the death of Christ, not even a salvation by such works would have been possible.[32] Such a statement could harmonize quite well

[30]Dallas Theological Seminary, *Doctrinal Statement* (Dallas, Texas: Dallas Theological Seminary, 1952), Article V.

[31]Letter from Dr. John F. Walvoord, President, Dallas Theological Seminary, to the author, November 23, 1956.

[32]Supra, pp. 30–31.

with Chafer's affirmation that God was "more gracious"[33] to men in the present Church age than in the previous law and future kingdom ages, because the condition for receiving salvation today is simply faith without works. So the question remains whether or not Dallas Seminary was now really affirming that in all dispensations, the only condition men had to meet in order to be saved was faith in God's gracious promise.

This creed, however, goes on to say that "we believe that, if man does trust in his own efforts to gain the favor of God or salvation under any dispensational test ... his failure to satisfy fully the just requirements of God is inevitable and his condemnation is sure." Chafer had taught that when human requirements were stipulated in the ages of the law and the kingdom, "... no mention is made of a provision of divine enablement for their fulfillment." But in the age of grace, "both supernatural standards of action are announced and complete ability by the Spirit is provided for their fulfillment" (ST, IV, 156). To the extent that men must depend on their own powers to do God's will, they do not depend upon God. How then could Dallas' statement that any dependence on one's own efforts in any dispensation would lead to condemnation harmonize with Chafer's teaching that a Jew would indeed inherit eternal life when, by his own efforts, he zealously kept the law? Perhaps Chafer made peace with his seminary's statement of faith at this point by saying, "To be sure, the Jew in the Mosaic age who tried to be saved simply by a zealous keeping of the Mosaic law but who did not offer any sacrifices to atone for his failure to do so and thus assumed that he kept the law perfectly—such a Jew would not inherit eternal life but be condemned." Those, however, who offered sacrifices acknowledged that more than their own efforts was needed in order to be saved.

Thus while Dallas' creed laid great stress on the grace of God as being essential for salvation in all dispensations, it did not explicitly deny what Chafer had taught. In fact, its insistence, in the usual dispensational manner, that "man has not at all times been under an administration of grace as is true in this present dispensation" raises the question as to whether dispensationalism could

---

[33]Supra, p. 31, and the quotations designated by footnote 21 on p. 33.

ever clearly affirm that men are always saved by grace alone. Therefore, while writing my dissertation on dispensationalism in 1956 with only Dallas' creed and Chafer's theology to explain dispensationalism, I objected to the Dallas creed as follows:

> What distinction is to be made between the grace manifested in this age and that of other ages? If, as it is declared, God is always gracious, then it is confusing to distinguish a particular age by a term that characterizes all ages. If, however, there is a difference between the grace administered in this age and that of other ages, the semantical problem is replaced by a theological problem. The theological problem arises because the Biblical concept of grace conceives of God as acting absolutely gratuitously.* If there is any thought of God's bestowing his blessing in reciprocation for what man has done, then His actions cannot be characterized as gracious, for Paul says, "If it is by grace, it is no more of works; otherwise grace is no more grace" (Rom. 11:6). Hence it is impossible to think of varying degrees of grace, for God either is or is not gracious. Yet [Dallas Seminary's] doctrinal statement implies a difference between the grace manifested in this and in other ages. Does this mean, then, that room is again made for Chafer's statement that God is "more gracious" in the administering of some covenants than in others, depending on whether human requirements enter in?[34]

I also complained that dispensationalists were long on making protestations that they believed in salvation by grace through faith in all ages, but short on explaining how they could consistently affirm this along with their other essential affirmations. Several years later Charles Ryrie, the Dean at Dallas Seminary, wrote that my complaint about dispensationalism was justified:

> [Fuller's] questioning is fair. Dispensationalism does need to show in a systematic way how grace was displayed under the Mosaic Law. We need not more brief statements that we believe in only one way of salvation ... but we need to expound the doctrine of salvation under the law. (DT 116)

Ryrie's explanation
Ryrie believed that my problem with dispensationalism's teaching about law and grace would vanish had I "distinguished the basis

---

[34]Daniel P. Fuller, "The Hermeneutics of Dispensationalism," Unpublished Doctoral Dissertation, Northern Baptist Theological Seminary, 1957, pp. 164–165.
    *See Addendum on p. 46 for remarks on "acting absolutely gratuitously."

of salvation (which is by grace) from the content of revelation (which was not the same under the law as it is today)" (DT 124). According to Ryrie, God saves men in all dispensations by grace made possible by the death of Christ, but the content of the revelation of this grace, which a man must believe to be saved, changes from dispensation to dispensation. Since the content of that revelation changes, the conscious object of faith and the experience of believers also changes from age to age.

Ryrie's handling of grace in the Mosaic dispensation illustrates what he means. In the Levitical sacrificial system of the age of law, men could find that revelational content which signified that somehow God would graciously forgive sin. Striving to be docile to the exegetical data regarding those sacrifices, Ryrie affirms that "the bringing of the sacrifices restored the offender to his forfeited position as a Jewish worshiper and restored his theocratic relationship" (DT 128). But for one to be restored to God as a member of the theocratic state did not necessarily effect an eternal acceptance before him. The passages in the Pentateuch which established the manner in which sacrifices were to be offered make it clear that restoration to mere temporal acceptance as a member of the theocratic state was not necessarily dependent on the faith or the spiritual state of the person offering the sacrifices. "The face value interpretation of these passages," says Ryrie, "assigns a genuine atonement for sins [to provide theocratic restoration] to the sacrifices simply because they were offered and not because the offerer was either worthy in himself or perceptive of something which the sacrifices pictured" (DT 128).

But theocratic restoration was not the only purpose of the sacrifices. "There seemed to have been in the offerings that which could point a believing worshiper to a better sacrifice which would deal finally with the entire sin question" (DT 129). This "ulterior efficacy in the sacrifices ... did not belong to them as sacrifices but as prefigurations of a final dealing with sin" (DT 129). That they had to be offered repeatedly was one indication that they were imperfect and that there was something better that they prefigured. It was the revelation involved in this "something better" that provided people living during the Mosaic dispensation with the possibility of being saved by grace through faith. Naturally, for one to receive this eternal acceptance with

God on the basis of this ulterior efficacy of the sacrifices, it was necessary for him to exercise faith in what the sacrifices prefigured.

Thus, the content of revelation that opened the door to eternal acceptance with God was very different then from what it is today in the age of grace. Today we know of the incarnation, death, and resurrection of Jesus Christ, so we understand quite clearly how God is able to remain just while he justifies the ungodly person who simply entrusts himself to Christ as Savior and Lord. But those living in the Mosaic age did not have such a clear revelation. "By comparison with the grace of Christ [revealed to us today], all previous revelations of grace were as nothing" (DT 125). So there was a revelation of grace in the Mosaic age, but the contrast between the dimness of that revelation of grace and the clarity of its revelation in this present age is so great that John was justified in drawing an antithesis between the two ages by saying that "law came by Moses but grace and truth came by Jesus Christ" (John 1:17). By basing the contrast on the clarity by which grace is revealed, Ryrie has no need to say, as did Scofield and Chafer, that salvation during the Mosaic age depended in part upon works.

But while grace was dimly revealed in the Mosaic age, law was revealed then with unmistakable clarity, and this makes it understandable why the Bible characterizes that period as the age of law (e.g., Rom. 5:20–21; II Cor. 3:7–11; Gal. 3:23–24). Of course all of the law, so clearly revealed then, could not by itself show a man how to be saved. "The law could not save," Ryrie affirms (DT 126). Knowledge of how to be saved was dimly visible only in the typological features of that era's sacrificial system. But knowledge of how to be saved was there; thus, two revelations existed side by side in that era. Ryrie argues that the revelation of grace was antithetical to the revelation of law by citing several passages in the New Testament where grace and law are contrasted (e.g., Rom. 4:14–16; 6:14–15; Gal. 2:21).

In accordance with the usual dispensational teaching, Ryrie believes that the essential thing about each of the several dispensations is the particular test with which it confronts men. In each dispensation God singles out one aspect of what men must do to please him and confronts them with this. Man's complete failure to please God is thus shown, facet by facet, in the successive dispensations. In the Mosaic era men demonstrate their failure by disobeying the law, and in the Church age they demonstrate it by their unwillingness to exclude all boasting and accept full salvation made possible purely on the basis of Christ's finished work. But Ryrie goes one step farther than his dispensational predecessors in that he affirms that in *every* dispensation God confronts men in some way with the test of whether or not they will accept by faith a salvation made possible by grace:

> There was a way of salvation revealed in each dispensation, and man's response to that particular revelation was *a* test of that economy. But there are many other tests in every dispensation. Every bit of revelation carries with it a test of whether men will respond positively or negatively to the particular thing revealed. (DT 125)

It seems that all the "other tests" of each dispensation are some form of the law which, by itself, functions only to expose man's sinfulness, failure, and deserved condemnation. These "other tests" arise from revelations which are directly antithetical to those which, while testing a man, also show him how to be saved. Thus in connection with the Mosaic era Ryrie affirms:

> Men were saved under the law economy but not by the law. ... And yet the law [i.e., all the revelation during the age of law] contained the revelation which brought men to a realization that their faith must be placed in God the Saviour. How did it do this? Primarily through the worship which it instituted through the sacrificial system. The sacrifices were part of the law [word used in same sense as previously]; the keeping of them did not save; and yet a man could respond to what [the sacrifices] taught so as to effect eternal salvation. (DT 126)

Ryrie makes it clear by the title of his book, *Dispensationalism Today,* that he regards his explanation as an elaboration on the basic concepts implied in dispensationalism which hitherto have not been thought through very carefully or explained very precisely. In the foreword, Frank E. Gaebelein declares that Ryrie's book "is the first book-length contemporary apologetic for dispensationalism to be written by a recognized scholar" (DT 7). Significantly, this book defends dispensationalism not by supporting the statements of Scofield and Chafer which drew such criticism from the exponents of covenant theology, but by modifying these statements. Whereas these older spokesmen left themselves vulnerable to the charge that dispensationalism taught that Israelites were saved by works during the Mosaic era, Ryrie has made it unmistakably clear that men were always to seek salvation on the basis of the gracious revelation given in each dispensation. These gracious revelations are to be sharply distinguished from revelations in every dispensation, which fall generally in the category of law rather than grace, since they function only to show man his failure and deserved condemnation. Covenant theology, therefore, can no longer be so disturbed by dispensationalism, since it now teaches that gracious revelations *always* appear alongside legal ones, and covenant theology, in its own way, also regards God as confronting men with two antithetical revelations throughout redemptive history.

That Ryrie has given a more definitive exposition of dispensationalism is borne out by the fact that the *New Scofield Bible* also sets up grace and law as paralleling each other throughout redemptive history. The editors affirm that in every dispensation there is sufficient revelation for a man to be saved by grace through faith:

> During each of [these dispensations] man is reconciled to God in only one way, i.e. by God's grace through the work of Christ that was accomplished on the cross and vindicated in His resurrection. Before the cross man was saved in prospect of Christ's atoning sacrifice, through believing the revelation thus far given him. Since the cross man has been saved by believing on the Lord Jesus Christ in whom revelation and redemption are consummated. (NSB 3)

But like Ryrie, the editors affirm that not all the revelation given during any one dispensation is directly suitable for engendering faith so that a man can be saved. In each dispensation,

> On man's part ... the continuing requirement is obedience to the revelation of God. This obedience is a stewardship of faith. ... The purpose of each dispensation ... is to place man under a specific rule of conduct, but such stewardship is not a condition of salvation. In every past dispensation unregenerate man has failed, and he has failed in this present dispensation [the sixth dispensation, the Church] and

will in the future. But salvation has been and will continue to be available to him by God's grace through faith. (NSB 3)

In their note on the Church dispensation, the editors state:

> The point of testing in this dispensation is the Gospel of our Lord Jesus Christ. . . . The continuing, cumulative revelation of the previous dispensations combines with this fuller revelation to emphasize the utter sinfulness and lostness of man and the adequacy of the historically completed work of Christ to save by grace through faith all who come unto God by him. (NSB 1162)

It would seem that part of this revelation, which should show a man "his utter sinfulness and lostness," would thus be suited to encourage him to turn to that revelation, available in every dispensation, which is itself suited to awaken faith.

The commandments of the Mosaic law are surely a part of this "continuing, cumulative revelation of the previous dispensation," which emphasizes "the utter sinfulness and lostness of man." The editors say that "the . . . law utterly condemns even the best man . . ." (NSB 1067), and surely the commandments which did this in the preceding Mosaic dispensation would continue to emphasize man's lostness in the present one, since "the deposit of truth in the earlier time-periods is not discarded; rather it is *cumulative* [italics added]" (NSB 3).[35]

Then too, before the Mosaic dispensation there had been the age of conscience, and although it continued as a dispensation only from the Fall to the Flood, the editors affirm that conscience is a part of the deposit of truth which is not discarded. "Thus conscience (moral responsibility)," they declare, "is an abiding truth of human life" (NSB 3). They also affirm that in the Gentile world conscience continued to be the norm whereby men were either accused or excused even during the dispensation of human government. Furthermore, when Gentiles became exposed to the

---

[35]To be sure, the editors affirm that "the Mosaic law has been 'done away' in that it has been superseded by another law, i.e., the standards of grace revealed in the N[ew] T[estament]." But they go on to say, "The Mosaic law still constitutes a revelation of the righteousness of God and remains as a part of Scripture which 'is profitable for doctrine, for reproof . . .' " (NSB 1254).

Mosaic law, that law "was to them, as to Israel, 'a ministration of death,' a 'curse' " (NSB 18).[36]

Though the disparate notes in the *New Scofield Bible* are not ideally suited to set forth the complete and continuous explanation that Ryrie has provided, it seems clear from these citations that the editors, like Ryrie, see all revelation in every dispensation as a test, but only part of this revelation as a test which is also suited to awaken faith so a man can be saved by grace. But since the rest of the revelation in any given dispensation is a test which, like the law, simply condemns, there are in every age two opposite kinds of revelation: a message of salvation by grace, and a message of the law. In comparing these contemporary statements of dispensationalism with covenant theology, we conclude that there is no longer any substantive difference between the two on the subject of the law and the gospel. Both regard God as confronting men with what is generally a legal revelation so that they will despair of their ability to save themselves and respond to revelation setting forth salvation by grace.[37]

But this does not mean that all is well with dispensationalism. Dispensationalists are as insistent as ever upon maintaining the sharp distinction between Israel and the Church and upon rejecting the hermeneutic of a theological, or an analogy-of-faith interpretation of Scripture, in which one passage is interpreted in terms of another. There is also evidence that dispensationalists

---

[36]In this note the editors say that "a wholly new responsibility arises when either Jew or Gentile knows the Gospel," which is to believe on Christ and to be saved. But in speaking of the revelation which gives this "wholly new responsibility," they cannot mean that the moral law set forth in conscience or in the Mosaic law is no longer binding in this dispensation, since they have been so emphatic in saying that "the deposit of truth in earlier time-periods is not discarded; rather it is cumulative" (NSB 3).

[37]Ryrie says, however, that "although both dispensational and covenant theologies teach salvation by grace, the way each explains it is entirely [!] different. The dispensationalist sees grace in the context of the tests of the various dispensations, whereas the covenant theologian grounds it in the covenant of grace." C. C. Ryrie, *The Grace of God* (Chicago: Moody Press, 1963), pp. 44–45. The only substantive difference that Ryrie cites, however, is that covenant theologians like Hodge (supra, pp. 26–27) said that Old Testament saints had to exercise faith *in Christ* in order to be saved, whereas the dispensationalist says that an Old Testament believer simply believed God's gracious revelation given at that time. This is a difference, but not enough to warrant Ryrie's claim that there is an *entire* difference.

have not fully grasped how their more recent explanations entangle them in covenant theology's problems, which their predecessors thought dispensationalism alone could solve.

Addendum to asterisked footnote on p. 39:
    In speaking in 1957 about grace as an absolutely gratuitous act of God, I had not yet learned to make the distinction between the gratuitous grace involved in *un*conditional election that Romans 11:5f. is speaking about, and unmeritorious conditionality involved in receiving and persevering in grace that is discussed below on pp. 106–109.

CHAPTER THREE

Sharing Covenant Theology's Problems

We recall that J. N. Darby emphasized that dispensationalism's foundational tenet was a radical distinction between Israel and the Church because this distinction kept the revelation of grace in the Bible separate from the revelation of the law. Understanding this distinction helped to free him from the legalism (allegedly learned from the Church of England) of thinking he should be "governed by a feeling of duty toward Christ...," and Darby subsequently concluded that he was controlled "by the consciousness that *He* [Christ] had done all."[1] He also said, "What hinders [the freedom of our souls toward Christ] more than the error so often committed of confounding the law and the gospel, the past economies or dispensations with the present one [?]"[2] It was understanding God's grace to him as a member of Christ's heavenly body, the Church, in distinction from the way God dealt with Israel, that freed his soul from legalism. He spoke of how "facts are addressed to the Jewish church ... as to a people with whom God had *direct* dealings on earth.... On the other hand, the church is a system of *grace* and heavenly hopes."[2a]

But now that Ryrie and the *New Scofield Bible* affirm that alongside the revelation of the law there is also a revelation of God's grace to Israel, they remove the primary reason that led to Darby's decision. Darby had seen Israel all tied up with law, and in order to remove himself from the bondage of law so that he could enjoy the freedom of grace as a member of the Church, he declared that the distinction between Israel and the Church was fundamental to enjoying grace and freedom from law. However,

[1]Supra, page 14.
[2]Supra, page 16.
[2a]J. N. Darby, "On 'Days' Signifying 'Years' in Prophetic Language," *Collected Writings*, II, 54. Italics added.

47

when Ryrie and the *New Scofield Bible* regard Israel and the
Church to be saved on the basis of gracious revelations given in
each dispensation, this distinction between Israel and the Church
is no longer needed to facilitate the separation between law and
grace which was Darby's reason for making this distinction in the
first place.

But Walvoord (as one of the editors of the *New Scofield Bible*)
does not seem to understand how this new emphasis (in distinction from that of Chafer and Scofield) of a gracious revelation
in every dispensation destroys the basic reason dispensationalism
once had for distinguishing between Israel and the Church. He
contends that dispensationalism is far better equipped than covenant theology for the task of protecting the Church from the
legalism and Galatian error of mixing works with faith:

> The Roman Church builds much of its claim for sovereignty on the
> inheritance from Israel of the combined political and religious au-
> thority revealed in the Old Testament. The concept of the church is
> enhanced, and ecclesiastical organization and authority are given
> Scriptural sanction. By so much, also, the New Testament revelation
> of the church as essentially a spiritual organism rather than an orga-
> nization is often slighted and in effect denied. The great contrast be-
> tween the legalism as found in the Mosaic dispensation and grace as
> revealed in the present age is usually ignored. The effect is often a
> repetition of the Galatian error.[3]

He also argues that Augustinianism, which originated the amillen-
nial idea that the Old Testament prophecies regarding Israel's future kingdom have been fulfilled by the Church, tends to ". . .
enhance legalism and human effort and to subtract from the divine grace immediately bestowed apart from sacraments by a
work of the Holy Spirit."[4] According to Walvoord, "One of the
serious errors of the covenant theologians is their disregard of
the essentially legal and nongracious rule provided by the Mosaic
covenant."[5]

But dispensationalism, Walvoord affirms, with its emphasis that
the Church and Israel are always distinct, avoids the legalistic
error to which covenant theology exposes the Church. By quar-

---

[3]John F. Walvoord, *The Millennial Kingdom* (Findlay, Ohio: The Dunham
Publishing Company, 1959), p. 81.
    [4]Ibid., p. 85.
    [5]Ibid., p. 91.

antining the Church from God's dealings with Israel in the Mosaic era and the future millennial era, he believes that dispensationalism, rather than covenant theology, can protect the Church from the lethal virus of legalism and Galatianism which (apparently) is central to God's dealing with Israel in the dispensations bracketing the Church age.

But how can Walvoord regard God's dealings with Israel as "essentially legal and nongracious," when the *New Scofield Bible*'s revision committee, of which he was a member, affirmed that in both the Mosaic and kingdom dispensations salvation was by faith in the gracious part of the revelations comprising the tests for those dispensations? And how can he talk of "the great contrast between the legalism as found in the Mosaic dispensation and grace as revealed in the present age,"[6] when the *New Scofield Bible* declares that law is part of the revelation of the Church age, because the legal revelation both in the age of conscience and in the Mosaic law is not discarded but is cumulatively part of the deposit of truth that confronts men now? When the *New Scofield Bible* makes such an affirmation, and when Ryrie, in saying that "there are *many* other tests [besides those which save] in *every* dispensation" (DT 125, ital. added), is stating that there is a legal revelation *to* (and not just "for") the present Church age, then all efforts to quarantine the Church from the legalism of other dispensations is futile. The virus of legal revelation is now as much in the isolation ward for the Church as it is for the wards of the Mosaic and kingdom ages. If the Church was put in the isolation ward to keep it away from such a virus, and now this virus is in the isolation ward, the great reason for placing the Church into that ward no longer exists.

In affirming that law is part of the revelation to the Church, dispensationalists, of course, are not saying that believers are back "under the law." But they are now saying something very similar to covenant theology. The Westminster Confession states that "although true believers be not under the law as a covenant of works ... yet it is of great use to them ... informing them of the will of God ..." (XIX, 6). And, like covenant theology, this cumulative revelation of law helps men see their own sinfulness so they gain "a clearer sight of the need they have of Christ" (XIX, 6).

[6]Supra, p. 48.

But we recall Ryrie's saying that "by comparison with the grace of Christ [revealed to us today], all previous revelations of grace were as nothing" (DT 125). Thus our objection might be answered by his saying that separating the Church from Israel enforces God's grace to the Church because it removes her from that body of revelation in which grace was so dimly perceived. If the Church tries to get her theology as much from the Old Testament as from the New (Ryrie and Walvoord might argue), then she is going to expose herself to the noxious virus of Galatianism, not because there was no gracious revelation in the Mosaic era, but because of the *preponderance* there of legal revelation over gracious revelation.

If this is the case, though, how terribly difficult it would have been for any Jew to find eternal acceptance with God on the basis of revelation given through to the end of the Mosaic age! Although Ryrie acknowledges that grace was revealed in several ways then (more will be said about these ways later in this chapter), a Jew would have had to have been extraordinarily bold if he learned to trust in God's eternal acceptance of him not by the legal revelation that God was shouting at him, but rather by listening only to God's whisper of these ways. To the extent that there is stress on the dimness of grace in that age because of the preponderance of legal revelation, it will become difficult to affirm that God would hold Jews responsible to be saved by grace during the Mosaic era. Paul holds the heathen responsible because of the *clarity* with which God can be seen from creation (Rom. 1:20), but a man's responsibility during the Mosaic era to own up to gracious revelation diminishes in direct proportion to the dimness of that revelation.

Yet if it is argued that Ryrie's emphasis on the dimness of grace in the Mosaic age means only to point out that while God clearly promised the forgiveness of sins at that time, he did not then reveal how Christ's atonement enabled him to be just in forgiving the sinner, then Walvoord is not helping the Church to understand grace by warning her to regard herself as separate from this people to whom God plainly promised forgiveness and with whom God's dealings comprise three-quarters of our Bible. Neither can the Church learn about grace by distinguishing herself from God's dealings with Israel in the future millennium, for then knowledge of Christ's atonement would show how God forgave sin. So making the Church a parenthesis between God's dealings with Israel in the past and in the future does not help her to understand grace when gracious and legal revelations are given to her just as they were and will be given to Israel.

Therefore, although today's dispensationalism explains the relationship between law and grace in wording that is different from that of covenant theology, there is no substantial difference in meaning. But in making this rapprochement with covenant theology—which would have brought the strongest protests from Scofield and Chafer—dispensationalism has not only eliminated the chief reason for making a distinction between Israel and the Church but has involved herself in two of the problems which the older dispensationalism, Chafer argued, neatly avoided. These are the problems of (1) mixing law and grace and of (2) imposing an analogy-of-faith, theological interpretation on Scripture.

I. Mixing Law and Grace

Two exponents of covenant theology, Oswald Allis and James Bear, criticized Scofield and Chafer for teaching that the way of salvation for Israel during the Mosaic and future kingdom eras is essentially different from the way of salvation in the present Church age.[7] Scofield's fundamental error, Allis charged, was "the failure to distinguish between the law as a covenant of works and the law as a ministration ... in the covenant of grace. ..."[8]

It is extremely difficult to grasp covenant theology's explanations of how a line of thought, which has the structure of the covenant of works, nevertheless functions as part of the covenant of grace. We have already seen something of this difficulty when Charles Hodge said the Bible consisted of a revelation of a "legal element" alongside the revelation of the "gospel,"[9] and how the only way one could really know that salvation was by grace in the Old Testament was by interpreting the Old by the infallible authority of the New Testament.[10] The following compilation of what older covenant theologians have said in their attempt to explain the problem of law and gospel gives additional evidence that covenant theology is as vulnerable to criticism at this point

[7]Supra, pp. 19–20, 26–27, 30.
[8]Supra, p. 20.
[9]Supra, p. 27.
[10]Supra, pp. 26–27.

as Scofield and Chafer were vulnerable to the criticisms of Allis and Bear.

Johann Heidegger (1633–1698) said:

> The word of God, the rule of our sanctification, belongs to both law and gospel. ... As to the manner in which law and gospel enjoin sanctification [the law] sets God forth to be worshipped as Creator, [while the gospel sets forth the same God], especially in Christ, as the Redeemer. As to the end, because the law enjoins sanctification for the sake of acquiring life, the gospel enjoins it as a duty of gratitude for life and salvation acquired.[11]

Here is an example of how covenant theology teaches that the one God sets forth one rule for his people, which rule, however, consists of such opposites that God himself becomes bifurcated into a Creator in one and a Redeemer in the other. It is startling how such a statement resembles statements by Marcion, the famous heretic of the second century. Concerning Marcion, Tertullian said (all direct statements by Marcion have been destroyed):

> [Marcion's] whole aim ... centers in this, that he may establish a diversity between the Old and New Testaments, so that his own Christ may be separate from the Creator, as belonging to this rival god, and as alien from the law and the prophets. ... Marcion has laid down the position that Christ ... is a different being from Him who was ordained by God the Creator for the restoration of the Jewish state, and who is yet to come. Between these he interposes the separation of a great and absolute difference—as great as lies between what is just and what is good; as great as lies between the law and the gospel, as great (in short) as is the difference between Judaism and Christianity.[12]

Although covenant theology affirms that the God of the Old Testament is the same God as in the New, a striking example of how it makes a single pronouncement from God affirm opposites comes from Leonard Riissenius (c. 1695), who declared,

> The law of works contained in the decalogue is distinguished from the law of faith and the promise of grace in Paul, Rom. 3:27; Gal. 3:17–18. But we do not say this as though we would deny that a

---

[11]Quoted from Heinrich Heppe, *Reformed Dogmatics*, ed. E. Bizer, trans. G. T. Thompson (London: George Allen & Unwin Ltd., 1950), p. 569.

[12]Tertullian, *Against Marcion*, IV, 6.

covenant of grace was then made with the Israelites ... or as though
we thought that the decalogue had nothing in common with a covenant of grace and was nothing else than the covenant of works itself.
... [Rather] ... God willed that there should be strictures of the covenant of grace in the decalogue, as is pretty openly shown by the
prefix annexed to it, where He professes Himself His people's
God ... and by the promises annexed to the second and fifth
commandments.[13]

And in more recent times Louis Berkhof has stated:

The Sinaitic covenant included a service that contained a positive
reminder of the strict demands of the covenant of works. The law was
placed very much in the foreground, giving prominence once more
to the earlier legal element. But the covenant of Sinai was not a re-
newal of the covenant of works; in it the law was made subservient
to the covenant of grace. This is indicated already in the introduction
to the ten commandments, Ex. 20:2; Deut. 5:6 [where God emphasizes
that he is already Israel's God].[14]

But if there really is a mixture of a virtual covenant of works
in the decalogue itself with grace in the introduction to it, it is
no wonder that Berkhof then goes on to say that "the Jews lost
sight [of the covenant of grace] aspect, and fixed their attention
on the [covenant of works] aspect. They regarded the covenant
ever increasingly, but mistakenly, as a covenant of works, and saw
in the symbols and types [which emphasize grace, according to
Berkhof] a mere appendage to this."[15]

But how can anyone then blame the poor Jews for trying to
be saved by works, if God is really saying such opposite things in
adjacent sentences? If, as Berkhof says, the "covenant of works"
and the "legal element" were given prominence as the "law was
placed very much in the foreground" at Sinai, then Jesus should
never have condemned the Jews for their legalism, for they were
simply following the Old Testament where, to use Hodge's words,
"the law predominated over the gospel."[16]

[13]Quoted from Heinrich Heppe, *Reformed Dogmatics,* p. 570.
[14]Louis Berkhof, *Systematic Theology* (3rd ed., Grand Rapids: Wm. B. Eerdmans Publishing Co., 1946), p. 298.
[15]Ibid.
[16]Supra, p. 27.

Another objection is the extreme implausibility of saying, as does Berkhof (and Riissenius), that whereas grace is taught in the introduction to the Ten Commandments ("I am the Lord your God who brought you up out of the land of Egypt"—Exod. 20:2), the commandments themselves that follow in verses 3–17 conform to the thought structure of the covenant of works. It is asking too much to expect people to believe that God shifts from one kind of revelation to its opposite as he goes from one sentence to another in a paragraph that has every evidence of being a single literary unit. But because covenant theology is so deeply convinced that Scripture itself draws the sharpest contrast between the law and the gospel, it has no alternative but to state such an implausibility.

Dispensationalism from Darby to Chafer was convinced that it could solve this problem in a more plausible manner than covenant theology: instead of having the same God speak opposites within the same paragraph to the same people, it understood God as having two separate purposes for two separate peoples, and a revelation for one that was distinct from the revelation for the other. Dispensationalism, Chafer argued, "has changed the Bible from being a mass of more or less conflicting writings [as in covenant theology] into a classified and easily assimilated revelation of both the earthly and heavenly purposes of God, which purposes reach into eternity to come."[17]

Although older dispensationalists thought that this way of handling the problem of law and the gospel avoided the extreme implausibility that God would speak out of both sides of his mouth in the same breath, it did create the equal implausibility that God's purpose for any people could ever involve salvation by works. But as today's dispensationalism has reverted to a virtual covenant theology in the way it handles the law-gospel problem, it must now, more than ever, regard God as shifting from a legal to a gospel revelation in the same breath. We cite two examples of this, one from the Dallas Seminary Statement of Faith and one from the notes of the *New Scofield Bible* on Matthew's teaching on forgiveness.

[17]Supra, p. 25.

The Dallas Seminary Statement of Faith

According to the last few sentences of the fifth article of this statement,[18] the examples of faith set forth in Hebrews 11 denote "other ways" (than seeing the redemptive significance of the sacrifices) by which men, in Old Testament times, could exercise *saving* faith. An examination of Hebrews 11, however, shows that a number of the revelations to which men responded—as the Dallas creed affirms—with a genuine and saving faith consisted of a command from God, accompanied by promised blessings for obedience, and/or threats of doom for disobedience. To illustrate, "By faith Noah, being warned by God concerning events as yet unseen, took heed and constructed an ark for the saving of his household; by this he ... became an heir of the righteousness which comes by faith" (Heb. 11:7). Thus the revelation to which Noah responded in saving faith was the command to build an ark, enforced by the knowledge that this was the only way for him to escape the impending judgment upon the world.

Abraham provides another example. "By faith Abraham obeyed when he was called to go out to a place which he was to receive as an inheritance" (Heb. 11:8). From this single verse we see that the revelation to Abraham consisted of (1) a command and (2) a promise. He had to obey the command to leave his homeland *in order to* gain the inheritance God had promised.

The same pattern of revelation was the basis for the genuine faith of Moses. He knew (1) that God had a far greater wealth in store for him and his people than all the treasure of Egypt and (2) that the pleasures of sin would last only for a time. Then too, Moses forsook Egypt because he endured "as seeing him who is invisible." As he enjoyed fellowship with the invisible God, it became clear to him that he could continue to enjoy this only if he left Egypt. In other words, Moses' knowledge of God came to involve a command from him to leave Egypt, which was enforced both by the promise of greater treasures that could be enjoyed forever and by the threat that Egypt's pleasures would soon vanish. Thus Moses obeyed God *in order to* gain the greater riches of Christ and avoid the misery to which sin soon leads.

In the summary statement of Hebrews 11:32–38 we read (verse

---

[18]Supra, pp. 36–37.

35) that "some were tortured, refusing to accept release, that [*in order that—hina* in the Greek] they might rise again to a better life." Thus these people through revelation had the *promise* that they would be raised from the dead if they *persevered* in their hope of God's promise even unto death. So they obeyed God *in order that* they might enjoy such a promise.

From these examples, it is clear that faith in Hebrews often consisted in an obedience to God that was induced by promises and/or threats. According to this chapter, men obeyed God *in order that* blessings might be obtained and disasters averted, and the Dallas Seminary creed affirms that the faith resulting from such revelations was genuine.

Ryrie speaks of six "other ways" besides the grace prefigured in the sacrifices by which people in the Mosaic era could know that God was gracious and thus believe and gain eternal acceptance with him: (1) God elected Israel to be his peculiar people when, in comparison with other nations, they sorely lacked any distinctive to merit such a favor; (2) God kept restoring Israel despite her repeated rebellions which indicated that she deserved nothing but judgment; (3) at the very time Jerusalem was being destroyed by the Babylonians for having disobeyed the law, God promised that he would make a new covenant with Israel—and this meant that God was gracious to them on a basis totally separate from anything they had done; (4) God imparted his Holy Spirit to *in*dwell some people in Israel, people who, by themselves, had done nothing to deserve such a blessing, and this indicated that God saved men through grace by faith apart from themselves; (5) throughout Israel's long history of rebellion against God, he nevertheless continued to manifest himself to them and graciously afforded them benefits which were opposite from what their works deserved. Finally, (6) God swore both by the Abrahamic and Davidic Covenants that, apart from any conditions Israel would have to meet, he would permanently establish her as a nation with a glorious kingdom (DT 119ff.). If any Israelite reflected on one of these revelational facets or on the revelation of grace prefigured in the sacrifices, he could have known that God saved men by grace, and if he believed God, he would have eternal acceptance with him. But none of these "other ways" provides a category for those revelations of Hebrews 11 which fall into the command-promise/threat structure.

It is plausible that Ryrie does not include them in his list because he regards such revelations as unsuited for providing a basis for faith in God's grace. Instead, they function only to give dispensational tests which cannot save a man. Such revelations fit the category of the law rather than that of the gospel.

> The law said, "Do *in order to* be blessed"; i.e., "Do because you have to." Grace says, "Do because you have been blessed"; i.e., "Do because you want to." A "have to" motive will never produce genuine sanctification. In reality such a motivation will actually stir up sin. . . . Only by believing that we are free from the law with its "have to" requirements can we begin to be sanctified in God's way and meet God's high requirements under grace.[19]

Because the Mosaic law consists of commands enforced by promises and/or threats, Ryrie believes that it sets forth a merit principle that is antithetical to those revelations in which God shows men they can be saved by grace through faith:

> The basic principle by which the law was operative in the lives of men was a merit principle.[20]

> Under law the order was blessing for merit, but under grace it is grace instead of merit and then blessing in addition. Grace by its very nature can involve no merit.[21]

> [The motive for correct conduct under law] was this: If you obey, you will be blessed. . . . Under the law of Christ the order has been completely reversed. . . . The motive for obeying the law of Christ under grace is because we have been blessed rather than *in order to* be blessed.[22]

[19]C. C. Ryrie, *The Grace of God,* p. 104. Italics added.
[20]Ibid., p. 35.
[21]Ibid., p. 57. In saying this Ryrie is not denying that God's impartation of the law to Israel was a gracious act. The Mosaic law "was given as an act of gracious election" (ibid., p. 35). The commands of this law brought blessing to Israel in that they are "for the ungodly to point them to Christ" (ibid., p. 103) and also they provided a cohesiveness for the nation as a whole (DT 117).
[22]C. C. Ryrie, *The Grace of God,* p. 115. Italics added. Ryrie is differentiating between law and grace in exactly the same way as did the covenant theologian, Johann Heidegger, supra, p. 52.

For Ryrie, revelations of grace have the structure of "Do, be-cause God has blessed," while the legal revelations, because they have the structure of "Do in order to be blessed," set forth the merit principle. Ryrie would naturally omit any revelation having the structure of the merit principle from his list of "other ways" in which revelation in the Mosaic era could engender saving faith. But then at least some of the revelations in Hebrews 11 which evoked faith could not, according to his premises, evoke the sav-ing faith that his seminary's creed says they did. Several of these "faith" responses had to be something different from "saving faith." This, however, would involve one in the extreme implausibility that such opposite revelations would produce what the writer of He-brews calls "faith" and regards as essentially the same in every instance.

The New Scofield Bible and Matthew's teaching on forgiveness (Matt. 18:23–35)

This passage from Matthew relates Jesus' parable of the Unforgiv-ing Servant. This servant owed his master the enormous sum of ten million dollars. Initially the master planned to settle the debt by selling the servant, his wife, and children. But when the servant knelt before him and pled for time to repay the debt, the master had compassion on him and exonerated him from all obligation to repay the money.

There was another servant who owed only a few cents to this servant whose ten million dollar debt had just been cancelled. When this other servant asked for a little more time in which to repay his debt, the first servant did not forgive as he had been forgiven but threw the other into debtors' prison. When the mas-ter heard about this, he called in the servant whose large debt he had cancelled and said, "You wicked servant! I forgave you all that debt because you besought me; and should you not have had mercy on your fellow servant, as I had mercy on you?" The editors of the *New Scofield Bible* see this as an example of how Paul taught people (Eph. 4:32; Col. 3:13) to forgive on the basis of the fact that God had forgiven them in Christ: "Human forgiveness [one man forgiving another] rests upon and results from divine forgiveness. ... [This] principle is stated in Mt. 18:32–33 [the quotation cited just above]; Eph. 4:32" (NSB 1039).

The parable concludes (Matt. 18:34–35) by relating how the master withdrew his forgiveness from the unforgiving servant and threw him into prison until he should repay the entire amount. The lesson Jesus wanted men to learn from this is "so also my heavenly Father will do to everyone of you, if you do not forgive your brother from the heart" (Matt. 18:35). But the editors comment only on verse 34, saying, "Here is justice on the ground of law. Compare the grace of God offered to sinners . . ." (NSB 1024), and they cite several passages relating to this.

That Jesus should climax this parable with "justice on the ground of law" presents the editors of the *New Scofield Bible* with a "problem." This comes out in their comment on the fifth petition of the Lord's Prayer in Matthew 6:12, where Jesus teaches his disciples to pray, "And forgive us our debts, as we also have forgiven our debtors." In verses 14–15, Jesus expatiates on this petition: "For if you forgive men their trespasses, your heavenly Father also will forgive you; but if you do not forgive men their trespasses, neither will your Father forgive your trespasses." Concerning Matthew 6:12 the editors say, "The *problem* [italics added] raised by the conditional nature of this petition for forgiveness may be explained as follows." They then proceed to interpret the fifth petition so that it means the restoration to fellowship that a child receives after he has been punished for some misbehavior.

It would seem that their comment on the ending of the parable of the Unforgiving Servant also indicates a problem for them, in distinction from the earlier verses of the parable where the master's forgiveness of an enormous debt would constitute an example of God's grace to sinners. The editors are unwilling to take at face value Jesus' teaching that God's forgiveness comes only on the condition of forgiving the wrong that another has inflicted. They need to explain this problem, but in so doing they would have to concede that Jesus taught both grace and law in the course of one parable.

This way of interpreting the fifth petition of the Lord's Prayer is an attempt, like that of the Westminster divines, to make a legal statement in Scripture read like a gracious one. In their Shorter Catechism's answer #105 they said:

> In the fifth petition, which is "And forgive us our debts as we forgive our debtors," we pray that God, for Christ's sake, would freely

pardon all our sins; which we are the rather encouraged to ask, because by his grace we are enabled from the heart to forgive others.

Covenant theology would agree with Ryrie that the thought structure of Matthew 6:12, 14–15 accords with "do *in order to* be
blessed."[23] Those from a Reformed tradition do not want people
to relate to God in a legalistic fashion any more than the dispensationalists do, and so they composed answer #105 in a way
which revises these verses in the Lord's Prayer to fit the thought
structure of "do (be forgiving) *because* of all that Christ has
done."

Lewis Sperry Chafer complained that covenant theology had
no right to make this fifth petition into a grace statement: "It is
this assumed freedom to soften the elements of Law with Grace
and to vitiate Grace with Law which leads to confusion and which
blinds good men to the most imperative and vital distinctions in
the Word of God" (D 447). It seems that he would also level this
complaint against the way his successors have handled the fifth
petition in the *New Scofield Bible*. His basic complaint was that
covenant theology superimposed the grace thought structure on
a legal thought structure in the Bible. For this reason C. I. Scofield
said forthrightly, in commenting on the fifth petition, that "this is
legal ground. . . . Under law forgiveness is conditioned upon a like
spirit [of forgiveness] in us" (SB 1002). For him as well as for
Chafer, all one needed to do to make the Bible coherent was to
"rightly divide" its passages into those for the Jew and those for
the Church.

But today's dispensationalists have veered away from their earlier generation of spokesmen, because dividing things in a straightforward manner made it very hard not to affirm that the Jews
were saved on the grounds of legalism and works. Dispensationalism does not have that problem now because it has espoused
the analogy-of-faith hermeneutic of covenant theology. Thus like
covenant theology, which must separate the grace of Exodus 20:2
from the law of verses 3–17, and must impose an allegedly Pauline
idea on the fifth petition of the Lord's Prayer, dispensationalists
have resorted to a theological hermeneutic for handling the prob-

[23]Supra, p. 59.

lem of forgiveness in Matthew. They have also blundered in that they have regarded the examples of Old Testament faith in Hebrews 11 as nonlegalistic, when the thought structure of these statements fits in very well with their understanding of what constitutes legalism.

II. *Imposing a Theological Interpretation*[24]

Covenant theology has argued that the hermeneutical procedure of interpreting one portion of Scripture in terms of another is quite legitimate. Hodge was following this procedure when he said that "from the Old [Testament] as interpreted by the infallible authority in the New, we learn that the plan of salvation has always been one and the same," even though "under the Old Testament, the law predominated over the gospel."[25] The Westminster Confession gave credal authority to this method when it affirmed in I, 9:

> The infallible rule of interpretation of Scripture is the Scripture itself; and therefore, when there is a question about the true and full sense of any Scripture (which is not manifold, but one), it must be searched and known by other places that speak more clearly.

Today's dispensationalists have clearly switched over to an analogy-of-faith hermeneutic. We have noted how they regard the conditionality for receiving forgiveness in the fifth petition of the Lord's Prayer to be a "problem."[26] Their method of solving this "problem" is stated at the end of the note on Matthew 6:12: "The ultimate motive for forgiving our debtors is based on the grace of God, and appears later in the progress of revelation (Eph. 4:32; Col. 3:13)" (NSB 1001). They are anxious to avoid anything that seems to make salvation conditional on works. But it just may be

---

[24]The term "theological interpretation" is borrowed from Louis Berkhof, *Principles of Biblical Interpretation* (2nd ed.; Grand Rapids: Baker Book House, 1952), pp. 133–166, to denote understanding one passage of Scripture in terms of another. Theological interpretation is another way of designating the analogy-of-faith principle found in Reformation hermeneutics. "Analogy-of-faith" is the term Bernard Ramm, *Protestant Biblical Interpretation* (2nd ed.; Boston: W. A. Wilde, 1956), pp. 125–128, approves to represent this mode of interpretation.

[25]Supra, pp. 26–27.

[26]Supra, pp. 58–60.

that the Bible teaches that God's forgiveness is conditioned not only on Christ's dying for our sins, but also on our repentance, which would include forgiving those who have wronged us. The editors of the *New Scofield Bible* believe that Paul's teaching, rather than Jesus' words in Matthew 6:12, constitutes the supposed foundation stone upon which they build their understanding of all that the Bible teaches about forgiveness. That they interpret Matthew 6:12 in the light of Ephesians 4:32 and Colossians 3:13 is evident in that they view "forgiving our debtors" (Matthean terminology) from the vantage point of the "later revelation" of Paul.

Certainly every Bible student wants to gather together all that the Bible teaches about various matters. But it would seem that we should allow each relevant passage to retain and contribute its own intended meaning for what Scripture teaches on a given doctrine. Otherwise one resorts to the arbitrariness of singling out a "later" or "simpler" teaching as the control for building the doctrine. This is the great objection to an analogy-of-faith hermeneutic. Chafer, we argue, was right when he declared that such a hermeneutical procedure vitiates biblical authority.[27]

Charles Ryrie was correct in taking me to task for espousing a "theological" hermeneutic in my unpublished doctoral dissertation of 1957 (DT 93–95). In these pages he strongly argues for a hermeneutic that admits only a "literal" or "normal" interpretation of a given passage, and which never allows a passage from later revelation to invalidate the meaning of a passage in earlier revelation. In the intervening years I have come to agree with him. But now to my dismay I find that today's dispensationalism has reverted to the hermeneutic of covenant theology, even though it means suppressing the explicit statements of Matthew 6:12, 14–15. Ryrie himself, in the comment in his *Ryrie Study Bible* on Matthew 6:14–15, where Jesus makes God's forgiveness of a man's sins conditional upon his willingness to forgive others, repeats essentially the same interpretation given by the editors of the *New Scofield Bible*:[28] "This is a forgiveness which affects fellow-

[27]Supra, p. 25.
[28]Supra, pp. 58–60.

ship in the family of God, not the forgiveness that leads to salvation."[29]

So it would seem that we are placed on the horns of a dilemma. On the one hand, we may divide the Bible into specific passages for the Jew or for the Church, but then we encounter the problem of a holy God telling some men how they can be saved if they work hard enough. On the other hand we can take the course of covenant theology and today's dispensationalism and see law and grace as appearing side by side throughout the entire Bible, and even alternating within a single literary unit, as between Exodus 20:2 and 3–17, or between Matthew 18:33 and 34–35. It is difficult to believe that the biblical writers expected their original readers to sense when these shifts took place right in the middle of a passage with the earmarks of being a literary unity. There is much to be said in favor of the complaint of a recent writer that covenant theology (and today's dispensationalism) has a "dualism between law and grace," a "junction of opposites in which God is seen as operating doubly in his encounters with men, now on the basis of law, now on the basis of grace, a double dealing which if not schizophrenic is at least polar and ever in paradoxical tension."[30]

Neither the path of the older dispensationalism nor that of its contemporary form and covenant theology seems promising. In the next chapter, we will examine the two passages where Calvin thought that Paul clearly made an antithesis between grace and faith on the one hand, and law and works on the other. These passages are the root cause of all the law-grace difficulties in Lutheranism, Calvinism, covenant theology, and the dispensationalism of yesterday and today. We will conclude that the antithesis is only apparent and not real. This, then, will make the enjoyment of grace dependent on faith and good works. That this conditionality of grace does not therefore open the door to human en-

---

[29]Charles C. Ryrie, *The Ryrie Study Bible,* New American Standard Translation (Chicago: Moody Press, 1978), p. 1454. Henceforth this work will be designated as RSB.

[30]Holmes Ralston, III, *John Calvin versus the Westminster Confession* (Richmond: John Knox Press, 1972), p. 37. Contrary to Ralston, we would argue that this tension is in John Calvin as well as the Westminster Confession.

deavor in which a man may boast will be demonstrated in the second half of the next chapter.

CHAPTER FOUR
Paul's View of the Law

Dispensationalism and covenant theology affirm that there are both conditional and unconditional promises in Scripture. If asked to justify this conclusion, they would probably argue as does John Calvin, in his *Institutes* and elsewhere, that a number of passages in Paul clearly declare that biblical revelation contains an antithesis between law and works on the one hand, and the gospel, grace and faith on the other. Our purpose in this chapter is to reexamine Paul's teaching on this matter by focusing on the two passages in Paul which Calvin thought "most clearly" set forth the distinction between the "faith righteousness and the law righteousness" (*Inst.* III, 11, 17).[1] These passages are Romans 10:5–8 and Galatians 3:10–12.

We quote Romans 10:5–8 from the Revised Standard Version and designate the Old Testament verses with quotation marks and references:

> [5]Moses writes that "the man who practices the righteousness which is based on the law shall live by it" (cf. Lev. 18:5). [6]But [*de* in the Greek] the righteousness which is based on faith says, "Do not say in your heart, 'Who will ascend into heaven?' (that is, to bring Christ down) or 'Who will descend into the abyss?' (that is, to bring Christ up from the dead)." [8]But what does it say? "The word is near you, on your lips and in your heart (that is, the word of faith which we preach)" (cf. Deut. 30:11–14).

According to Calvin this "important passage" shows that "righ-

---

[1]This citation and the following from the *Institutes* will be documented in this manner: The English translation is from John Calvin, *Institutes of the Christian Religion,* 2 vols., trans. F. L. Battles; The Library of Christian Classics, ed. John T. McNeill, vols. XX, XXI (Philadelphia: The Westminster Press, 1967). The Latin for the crucial statements appearing in brackets after those statements comes from Iojanne Calvino, *Institutiones Christianae Religionis* (Geneva: Apud Iohannem, le Preux, 1606).

teousness which is given through the gospel has been freed of all conditions of the law. ... The gospel promises are free and dependent solely upon God's mercy, while the promises of the law depend on works" (III, 11, 17).

Then in III, 11, 18 Calvin says, "The second passage is this: 'It is evident that no man is justified before God by the law. For 'the righteous shall live by faith' [Hab. 2:4]. But the law is not of faith; rather, [Lev. 18:5] 'the man who does these things shall live in them' [Gal. 3:11–12]." From this passage Calvin also argues for a complete distinction between a "law righteousness" and a "faith righteousness":

> How would this argument be maintained otherwise than by agreeing that works do not enter the account of faith but must be utterly separated? The law, [Paul] says, is different from faith. Why? Because works are required for law righteousness. Therefore it follows that [works] are not required for faith righteousness. (III, 11, 18)

I. An Examination of Paul's Purported Antithesis between the Law and the Gospel

(We commence with Romans 10:5–8, but acknowledge that it belongs to the larger literary unit that runs from Romans 9:30—10:10.)

Romans 10:5–8

On the surface it would seem that the "but" introducing verse 6 ("But the righteousness based on faith says ...") is a strong adversative. The terms "righteousness of the law" and "righteousness of faith," which are used respectively in verse 5 and verses 6–8, are also used in Philippians 3:8–9, where they are unmistakably antithetical to each other. In that passage Paul says, "For [Jesus'] sake I have suffered the loss of all things and count them as refuse, in order that I might gain Christ and be found in him, not having a righteousness of my own, based on law, but that which is through faith in Christ, the righteousness from God that depends on faith. ..." From this passage one could plausibly infer that Paul intended these same sets of words to be construed antithetically in Romans 10:5–8. But when one scrutinizes this passage and its immediate context beginning back at Romans 9:30, two considerations emerge which present difficulties in accepting such an understanding.

The first difficulty emerges from the consideration that Paul cites passages from the Pentateuch to support both what he meant by "the righteousness based on faith" (v. 6; cf. Deut. 30:12–14) and also what he meant by "the righteousness based on law" (v. 5; cf. Lev. 18:5). If one regards the *de* ("but" or "and") as introducing a contrast to the righteousness mentioned in the preceding verse, then one must either (1) concede that the Pentateuch can state such opposites, or (2) that Paul, while holding to the intended meaning of Leviticus 18:5 in Romans 10:5, nevertheless ignored the intended meaning of Deuteronomy 30:11–14 when he used the wording of those verses to describe the righteousness of faith in Romans 10:6–8. The Greek word for the "but" introducing Romans 10:6 is *de* and not *alla*. Lexicographers generally agree that "very frequently [*de* is used] as a transitional particle pure and simple without any contrast intended."[2] Liddell and Scott point out that *de,* when used with *men,* can have a strongly adversative force. But when, as in Romans 10:5–8, there is no preceding *men,* then *de* is "used merely to pass from one thing to another."[3]

To escape these two unpleasant alternatives, the attempt has been made to understand Leviticus 18:5 as directed to unregenerated people, while Deuteronomy 30:11–14 is directed to those who have had the circumcision of heart (regeneration) spoken about in Deuteronomy 30:6. Calvin used this approach. Likewise Everett Harrison affirms that "[Deut. 30:11–14] presupposes a heart attitude of loving obedience (Deut. 30:6–10) rather than a legalistic attempt to attain righteousness."[4]

The problem with this line of interpretation, however, is that Deuteronomy 30:6 speaks about Israel's *future* regeneration, whereas verses 11 through 14 are talking about what was true at that present time. Verse 11 says, "This commandment which I command you *this day* is not too hard for you, neither is it far

[2] William F. Arndt and F. Wilbur Gingrich, *A Greek-English Lexicon of the New Testament and Other Early Christian Literature* (4th ed.; Cambridge: at the University Press, 1952), p. 170.
[3] *An Intermediate Greek-English Lexicon,* Founded upon the 7th edition of Liddell and Scott's Greek-English Lexicon (Oxford: at the Clarendon Press, 1964), p. 175.
[4] E. F. Harrison, *Romans,* The Expositor's Bible Commentary, 12 vols., ed. Frank E. Gaebelein (Grand Rapids: Zondervan, 1974–), X, 111.

off." Likewise, verse 15 says, "See, I have set before you *this day* life and good, death and evil." So verses 11 through 14 apply to unregenerate people, and according to verse 6, the great majority of Israel will not be circumcised in heart until a later time (Deut. 30:1–10, esp. v. 6). Many commentators contend that Paul molded the wording of Deuteronomy 30:11–14 so that it no longer conveyed the meaning it had in its own immediate context but conformed instead to Paul's understanding of justification by faith. Zahn, Lagrange, Leenhardt, Michel, Käsemann, Hodge, and Denney are among those who argue that in using this Deuteronomy passage, Paul simply took Moses' words and gave them another meaning from that intended by Moses. Denney states, "The apostle is not thinking in the least what the writer of Deuteronomy meant. . . . Paul is putting his inspired convictions into a free reproduction of these ancient inspired words." F. F. Bruce holds this same view but confesses that it is not as easy for us moderns, as it was for Paul, to pit Deuteronomy (in Romans 10:6–8) against Leviticus (in Romans 10:5).

There are, however, a few expositors who argue that it is impossible to suppose that Paul would turn the meaning of Deuteronomy 30:11–14 completely around so that it would support his teaching about a righteousness of faith, in contrast to a righteousness of the law. One reason for this implausibility is that Paul was concerned about demonstrating his great loyalty to the Old Testament and to the Mosaic Law while writing his letter to the Romans. In the salutation of Romans 1:1–7 he emphasizes that the gospel, which he is about to expound, is that promised by the Old Testament prophets. He also stresses that Jesus Christ, the center of the gospel, is the descendant of David (Rom. 1:3). In Romans 3:1 and 9:1–5 Paul lists the great advantages which the Jews have had, and in 3:31 he stresses, as though answering an objector, that he teaches to uphold the law. In Romans 7:1 he says, "I am speaking to those who know the law." He declares in Romans 8:4 and 13:8 that men continue to be responsible to fulfill the law. With such loyalty to the Old Testament and the law, it would be difficult to assume that Paul could be so indifferent to the intended meaning of Deuteronomy 30:11–14.

Another reason for this implausibility is that much of Romans was written in a debating style (e.g., sections introduced by rhetorical questions, etc.). Paul did not resort to this style because he felt compelled to combat heresy in Rome. He did not regard the church at Rome to be threatened, like the churches of Galatia, with the heresy of the Judaizers, for he said in Romans 15:14, "I myself am satisfied about you [Romans] that you yourselves are full of goodness, filled with all knowledge, and able to instruct one another." Why, then, is so much of Romans structured as though Paul were debating with the Judaizers? One plausible answer is that Romans, written at the conclusion of the third missionary journey, is a summary of how Paul had been preaching during those journeys. He wanted the Roman church to welcome him so that he might be able to use it as a base for missionary operations in the western half of the Mediterranean. Therefore he wrote Romans to summarize the gospel which he had been preaching. But Paul also wanted his readers to get a sample of how he had preached. Since much of his preaching up until then had been carried on in conflict with Judaizers, that style carried over into his letter to the Romans.

But if this dialectical style echoes dozens of real-life debates with Judaizers over the past decade or so, it is inconceivable that Paul would be proposing interpretations of the Old Testament which arose from his own Christian presuppositions. If he had expected to make any headway against the Judaizers, he obviously would have been careful to use the Old Testament in a way that accorded with their understanding of it. Therefore if Deuteronomy 30:11–14 was, like Leviticus 18:5, speaking of the righteousness of the law, Paul would not have reinterpreted it in the supposedly opposite terms of the righteousness of faith. Had he done such a thing, he certainly would have "undone every effort to persuade either friend or foe of his positive attitude toward the law."[5] It is far more plausible that Paul, in quoting Deuteronomy 30:11–14, was giving the meaning to that passage which its own words required.

Furthermore, Felix Flückiger has pointed out that making Romans 10:6–8 an antithesis to Romans 10:5's citation of Leviticus

---

[5]M. Jack Suggs, " 'The Word is near you,': Rom. 10:6–10," *Christian History and Interpretation: Studies Presented to John Knox*, W. R. Farmer et al., eds. (Cambridge: at the University Press, 1967), p. 229.

18:5 would contradict Paul's custom of quoting the Old Testament as a positive support for what he was saying. "It was not the custom of Paul," Flückiger observes, "to seek out contradictions in the scripture and to quote the Old Testament as meaning that one of its statements is no longer valid."[6] He argues that in quoting Deuteronomy 30:11–14 after Leviticus 18:5, Paul is waging warfare against the difficult life-style which the Pharisees said men must emulate in order to be saved. By wording Deuteronomy 30:11–14 as a command so that it reads, "Do not say in your heart, 'Who will ascend into heaven?' ... or 'Who will descend into the abyss?' ... ," Paul is rebuking the Pharisees for misconstruing the law of Moses and, to use the words of Peter at the Jerusalem Council, "putting a yoke on the neck of the disciples which neither our fathers nor we have been able to bear" (Acts 15:10). If Paul is affirming in Romans 10:6–8 that Deuteronomy 30:11–14 should not be misinterpreted in the Pharisaic manner, then he is affirming that Leviticus 18:5 should be understood in a way that differed radically from the interpretation held by mainstream Judaism. As Flückiger puts it:

> To be sure, Moses required that a man must do the righteousness required by the law, in order to live. But this requirement is not fulfilled by superhuman achievements ("to climb into heaven," "to climb down into the abyss," which was Paul's way of expressing the impossible task which the Jews, through their zeal for the righteousness of works, wanted to produce and fulfill by their own efforts). [The righteousness required by the law] is fulfilled rather through the Word which is in the heart and in the mouth—which according to [Rom.] 10:10 is faith and confessing the Lord: "for with the heart one believes (and this leads) to righteousness, and with the mouth one confesses (and this leads) to salvation." The life which Moses promises according to [Rom.] 10:5 is therefore to be enjoyed by those who believe and confess. The obedience of faith thus becomes the proper fulfilling of the law, which requires righteousness and promises life to those who do righteousness.[7]

There is, then, another plausible way of interpreting Romans 10:5–8, which avoids the difficulties of Calvin's purportedly "most

[6]Felix Flückiger, "Christus, des Gesetzes *telos*," *Theologische Zeitschrift*, 11 (1955), 155.
[7]Ibid.

clear" understanding of these verses. Flückiger's construction avoids having Deuteronomy 30:11–14 clash with Leviticus 18:5, or having Paul impute a meaning to the Deuteronomy passage which directly contradicts its intended meaning. But a second difficulty in Calvin's way of understanding Romans 10:5–8 emerges from a consideration of Romans 9:30–32a, which begins the train of thought climaxing at 10:10. (Chapter 10 of Romans should have begun at 9:30!)

The following is a literal translation of Romans 9:30–32a with additional words deemed essential to the proper understanding of it enclosed in brackets:

> [30]What shall we say then? [We say] that the Gentiles, who followed not after righteousness, attained it, even the righteousness which is of faith; [31a]but Israel, [although] she pursued [the] law of righteousness, [31b]did not arrive at [that] law. [32a]Why? Because [Israel pursued the law of righteousness] not by faith, but, as it were, by works.

We observe that the function of verse 32a is to supply the *reason for* the failure of Israel asserted in verse 31b. This reason is represented merely by the adverbial modifier "not by faith, but, as it were, by works." Since these are the words which Paul makes explicit in reprimanding Israel's action, we understand this failure to consist not in a wrong action (in the verb to be supplied) nor in the wrong goal of that action (in the direct object to be supplied), but in the *manner* in which she sought the proper goal. Like any author, Paul left out the verb and the direct object in verse 32a because they could be supplied so easily from what he had just said. All expositors agree that the verb "pursue," taken from 31a, should be supplied in answering the question of why "Israel failed to attain [that] law" (9:31b).

As for the direct object to be supplied, the majority of Protestant expositors feel impelled to supply the abstract principle of "righteousness" or "justification by faith." This is taken from the second "law" of 9:31, and is not to be understood as the concrete Mosaic law after which Israel strove in the first half of 9:31. They argue that if the Mosaic law was to be supplied as the direct object in the clause of 9:32a, then Paul would be saying that Israel failed to fulfill the Mosaic law because she failed to respond to it in faith. But most Protestant exegetes contend it would have been impossible for Paul to have implied that the response called for by the Mosaic law is faith and the works of faith (cf. I Thess. 1:3; II Thess. 1:11). There are too many places where Paul seems to regard the Mosaic law as enjoining what is opposite from faith (Rom. 4:13; 10:5–8; Gal. 2:16; 3:2, 5; 3:11–12). Consequently these exegetes understand the "law" (*nomos*) which Israel failed to attain to refer to a principle, namely, the principle of justification by faith. (Romans 7:21, 23; and 8:2 are three places where Paul uses *nomos* to represent an abstract principle rather than something concrete like the Mosaic law.)

For example, Charles Hodge argued that "justification" should be supplied as the direct object in 9:32a because that was what the Jews were really seeking as they pursued the concrete Mosaic law (v. 31a).[8] When verse 31 goes on to say that "the Jews did not attain law," Hodge understands this failure to consist of not attaining the *principle* of justification. To support this he appealed to Romans 3:27, where Paul says that justification comes not through a "law of works, but a law of faith." Since it would be impossible for the covenant theologian Hodge to understand Paul to regard the Mosaic law as teaching faith and its consequent works of faith, he argues that Paul uses "law" (*nomos*) at 3:27 and here in 9:31 to represent a principle, namely, that of justification. Consequently the direct object for the clause declaring the cause for Israel's failure in 9:32a would be "justification." Hodge's translation of 9:32a reads, "Because they sought it [justification] not by faith, but, as it were, by the works of the law."

Two difficulties, however, arise from this interpretation. For one thing, it is arbitrary for Hodge to impose the abstract idea of "justification" on the two "law"s in verse 31. Elsewhere in Romans the context demands that *nomos* means "a principle" (Rom. 7:21, 23; 8:2). But in Romans 9:31, 32a there is a strong argument that the concrete Mosaic law is represented by the first, and therefore the second, *nomos.* Surely the Jews regarded their law to exist

---

[8]Charles Hodge, *Commentary on the Epistle to the Romans* (new ed.; Grand Rapids: Wm. B. Eerdmans Publishing Company, 1953 [reprint of 1886 ed.]). Ad loc.

in the most concrete terms and gloried in their possession of it in contrast to other peoples.

The second difficulty with Hodge's understanding of Romans 9:31–32a is that he ignores the implication of "as it were" (*hōs*). He translates the sentence as follows: "[Israel failed] because they sought justification not by faith, but, *as it were*, by the works of the law [italics added]." In commenting on the "as it were" (*hōs*) in this verse, the grammarian Georg Winer said, "the expression *ek pisteōs* ["by faith"] [in Romans 9:32] denotes the objective standard; [and] *hōs ex ergōn* ["as of works"], the purely subjective standard."[9] But in seeking justification by zealous attention to the Mosaic law, Israel was working with something very objective and concrete. So the way she sought to fulfill the law, namely, by serving God with works in which she thought she could boast (as the "as it were" [*hōs*] demands), was totally fanciful and subjective. This way was *not* prescribed at all by the concrete Mosaic law but was in fact proscribed by it. The "as it were" (*hōs*) signified that the idea of serving God by works in which men could boast stemmed from a subjective, fanciful notion which the Jews read into the Mosaic law without the slightest encouragement to do so from the law itself.

Since faith, as the grammarian Winer pointed out, was to be inferred from an objective standard, and since the Mosaic law was that objective standard which received all of Israel's zealous attention, the conclusion is therefore inescapable that that standard taught nothing but faith and the obedience which flows from faith. This sort of obedience, as we shall see, gives no occasion for men to boast over their works before God, others, or themselves.

Had Hodge allowed the inescapable implication of the "as it were" (*hōs*) to figure in his exposition of Romans 9:31–32a, he could have followed the normal exegetical procedure of regarding the second *nomos* ("law") in 9:31 to represent, like the first one, the concrete Mosaic law. The direct object in the clause in 9:32a explaining why Israel failed to attain that concrete law would be that very law. The reason for her failure was that she

[9]Georg B. Winer, *Grammar of the Idiom of the New Testament*, trans. H. Thayer (7th ed.; Andover: Warren F. Draper, 1897), p. 619. Other commentators who call attention to this meaning of the phrase *hōs ex ergōn* as pointing to "the purely subjective standard" are Sanday-Headlam, Lagrange, Lenski, and Godet.

tried to fulfill that law through her own fanciful notion of works in which she could boast, whereas the objective standard of the Mosaic law itself taught nothing but the obedience of faith which excludes all boasting. But Hodge allowed covenant theological considerations to supersede grammatical considerations found in these verses.

H. A. W. Meyer similarly interpreted 9:31–32a in that he regarded the two "law"s in 9:31 to refer to justification by faith, rather than the concrete Mosaic law.[10] But he stressed that the *hōs* in 9:32 adds emphasis to the Jews' seeking justification by works, rather than calling attention to the subjective and fanciful nature of seeking justification in this way. Meyer argued that the "as" is used here in the same way in which it is used in John 1:14: ". . . and we have beheld his glory, glory *as* of the only Son from the Father." His argument is that just as the "as" in John 1:14 shows how truly glorious Jesus was, so the "as" in Romans 9:32a shows just how much the Jews were given over to seeking justification by meritorious works.

But John 1:14 is not analogous to Romans 9:32a. Jesus' glory in John 1:14 is connected with that of the Father to show how truly glorious Jesus was. Since the "as" in 9:32 does not connect "works" with anything, the works are subjective and fanciful, and not prescribed by any objective norm.[11]

In distinction from Hodge and Meyer, Theodor Zahn regarded the first *nomos* to represent the concrete Mosaic law, whereas the second was the abstract principle of justification.[12] But he used the first *nomos* to supply the chief object in 9:32a. Zahn construed Paul's answer to the question of why Israel failed to attain the law to be "because Israel pursued the concrete, Mosaic

[10]H. A. W. Meyer, *The Epistle to the Romans,* trans. by J. C. Moore et al. (5th ed.; New York: Funk & Wagnalls, Publishers, 1884), p. 392. Also Ulrich Wilckens, *Rechtfertigung als Freiheit* (Neukirchen: Neukirchener Verlag, 1974), p. 98, n. 47.

[11]This is the sense given to *hōs* in Romans 9:32 in Arndt and Gingrich's *Greek-English Lexicon of the New Testament.* Under *hōs,* see III, 3. Other commentators who advocate this meaning of the *hōs* ("as") are C. K. Barrett, Matthew Black, and E. J. Leenhardt (cf. note 9).

[12]D. Theodor Zahn, *Der Brief des Paulus an die Römer* (2nd ed.; Leipzig: A. Deichert, 1910).

law of righteousness." He affirmed that this Mosaic "law of righteousness" after which Israel strove

> *should* [italics added] not be denoted as that which imparts righteousness or brings it with itself, for such a thought is never attached [by Paul] to it (Gal. 2:21; 3:11, 21). Rather the Mosaic law *should* [italics added] be denoted as that which demands righteousness from its subjects (Rom. 10:5; cf. Eph. 2:15).[13]

Like Hodge, however, Zahn declared that the "law" which Israel failed to attain (9:31b) was not the Mosaic law but the "law" or "principle of justification by faith" that Paul had supposedly mentioned in Romans 3:27.

In answering the question of why Israel was guilty of a misdeed when she was simply following the Mosaic law, Zahn said:

> As the revelation that was imparted to Israel through Moses was attached to the promise given to the patriarchs (Exod. 3:15; 6:3–4), and as all the Ten Commandments *were based on* [italics added] God's gracious redemption of the people out of Egypt, so Israel, like her founders, *should* [italics added] have held fast to God's gracious promises and deeds as the starting point of conduct that would be pleasing to God.[14]

Israel, however, bracketed the law off from its gracious promises:

> More and more as time passed by Israel proceeded from the *erroneous* [italics added] presupposition that works, which she had to produce, were the foundation of her religion and privileged position, and the very essence of the good conduct required by God.[15]

For Zahn to understand Romans 9:31–32 this way, however, is to make Paul as disobedient as Israel in misunderstanding the nature of the Mosaic law. Zahn said that according to Paul, the Mosaic law "should" be designated as that which demands righteousness rather than that which imparts righteousness. If this is the way the law "should" be designated, then Israel was right in bracketing the Ten Commandments off from "God's gracious

[13]Ibid., p. 470.
[14]Ibid., p. 471.
[15]Ibid.

promises and deeds," and they were certainly not guilty of holding an "erroneous presupposition" in affirming that works were the foundation of their standing before God. Zahn cannot have it both ways: Paul cannot be right in understanding the law to demand perfect righteousness, when the Ten Commandments "should" be construed as of a piece with "God's gracious promises and deeds."

As to the *hōs* in the clause *"as it were,* by works" (9:32a), Zahn affirmed that the " 'out of works' introduced by 'as' is a presupposition existing simply in the head of the Israelites."[16] But then he proceeds to say that "the works, by which the Jews intended to achieve the goal [of righteousness] were nevertheless what the Mosaic law *actually* [italics added] required." Again, Zahn cannot have it both ways. "The righteousness of works" cannot "exist simply in the head of the Israelites" and at the same time be "what the Mosaic law actually required."

The Calvinist Frederic Godet (1812–1900), much like the Lutheran Zahn, affirmed:

> law may [!] be regarded in two aspects, [1] according as we take the Mosaic institution in its fulness, comprehending there the elements of grace which belonged to it in view of a previous justification and a real sanctification, or [2] as we lose these elements of grace out of view to fasten only on the commandment and turn it to the satisfaction of human pride.[17]

But if the "elements of grace" really belonged to the law, then they should always figure in the interpretation of it, and we should not overlook these elements which alter the law and thus bolster people's pride.

Most Protestant commentators, as we have said, construe Romans 9:31–32a generally as do Hodge, Zahn, and Godet. We have examined the thinking of these three commentators of the last century because they devoted considerable space to a discussion of these verses. Many recent expositors have reached the same conclusions but cast no new light on the subject.

There are, however, at least three recent commentators who

---

[16]Ibid., p. 471, note.

[17]F. Godet, *Commentary on the Epistle to the Romans,* A. Cusin and T. Chambers, trs. and eds. (Grand Rapids: Zondervan, 1970), p. 378. The first translation from the French was made in 1883.

avoid the contradiction inherent in saying that the law can have
two meanings. These commentators insist that the intent of the
Mosaic law, in both the Pentateuch and in Paul's interpretation of
it, is to enjoin obedience stemming from faith and therefore
excludes all boasting. They supply "Mosaic law" as the direct
object in the answer to the question in Romans 9:32a. In commenting on Romans 9:31–32a, Felix Flückiger says:

> If Israel did not attain the law, because she wanted to be righteous
> not by faith but by works, then "the attainment of the law," or in other
> words, "the attainment of the righteousness made known *by the law*
> [italics added]," can only be by the righteousness of faith, and the
> Jewish works-righteousness is not at all what God intends by the
> law—the Jewish concept stands upon a misunderstanding of the law.[18]

What a radical departure from the usual way of construing these
verses! We argue, however, that such an interpretation is correct
because (1) it regards the direct object in the answer of Romans
9:32 as the concrete Mosaic law, and (2) while Flückiger does
not strengthen his position by an explicit reference to the *hōs*
("as") in 9:32a, his declaration that "the Jewish works-righteousness ... stands upon a misunderstanding of the law" affirms that
the way the majority of the Jews sought to attain righteousness
was purely a subjective idea and enjoyed no backing from the
Old Testament itself.

Earlier we saw that Flückiger construes Paul's meaning in Leviticus 18:5 in Romans 10:5 to be that the obedience to the law
which results in the enjoyment of the life promised in Leviticus
18:5 is the obedience of faith. Obviously, the way one interprets
Romans 9:31–32a will have to coincide with his interpretation of
Romans 10:5 in relation to verses 6–8. Of that minority of expositors who understand Paul's meaning in these verses to be that
Israel's fall resulted from her failure to respond to the Mosaic law
by an obedience of faith, Flückiger speaks in the clearest and the
most straightforward manner of any that have been discovered
thus far. There are two other commentators who, while having
certain imperfections in their handling of these passages, are really

[18]Felix Flückiger, "Christus, des Gesetzes *telos*," p. 154.

in the Flückiger category in the way they interpret Romans 9:30—
10:10.

John Murray in The New International Commentary on the
New Testament understands the "law of righteousness" after which
Israel pursued (Rom. 9:31) to be not merely the Mosaic commandments, but "that order of institution which was concerned
with justification. But Israel came short of gaining the righteousness to which that institution bore witness . . . ; they did not attain
to what was provided in the institution that was their glory."[19]
Zahn or Godet could easily have written this statement. But
whereas those two commentators said that works-righteousness
was "what the Mosaic law required" (Zahn), or that "the Mosaic
law may be regarded in an aspect . . . according as we lose [its]
elements of grace and fasten on the commandment and turn it to
the satisfaction of human pride" (Godet), Murray affirms that
"[Leviticus 18:5] does not appear in a context that deals with legal
righteousness as opposed to that of faith. . . . The whole passage
[Lev. 18:1–5] is no more 'legalistic' than are the Ten Commandments" in that both are introduced by the words, "I am the Lord
your God."[20] As evidence of how seriously he excludes a legalistic
works-righteousness from his understanding of Leviticus 18:5,
Murray asks how Paul could have used this verse as an example
of what stands in stark contrast with faith (Romans 10:5–8). He
answers that only the wording is "a proper expression *in itself*
[apparently apart from the intended meaning of Leviticus 18:5]
of the principle of works-righteousness in contrast with the righteousness of faith."[21]

Since Murray thus construes the Mosaic commandments as
expressions of grace, he is able to give the *hōs* ("as") in Romans
9:32 its full force and say that Israel's "misapprehension [of the
Mosaic law] was total."[22] At this point, he also parts company
with the majority of Protestant commentators in that he regards
Romans 9:31–32a to teach that Israel failed to attain the righ-

<hr />

[12]John Murray, *The Epistle of Romans*, 2 vols., The New International
Commentary on the New Testament (17 vols.; Grand Rapids: Wm. B. Eerdmans
Publishing Company, 1975), II, 43.
[20]Ibid., II, 249.
[21]Ibid., II, 250.
[22]Ibid., II, 43.

teousness witnessed to by the Pentateuch and, for that matter, the whole Old Testament, because she pursued the right concrete object (the Old Testament Scriptures) in the wrong way.[23]

E. H. Gifford is another commentator whose exposition of this passage basically accords with Flückiger's. Gifford understands the "law of righteousness" which Israel pursued (9:31a) to be the Mosaic law. That law did not hold up an impossible ideal before men. In fact there were a relatively small number of Israelites who did indeed comply with its teachings, and were righteous on that account:

> Such 'a law of righteousness' [Israel] strove to find, and some did find, in God's law revealed to Moses (Luke 1:6 ["They—Zechariah and Elizabeth—were both righteous before God, walking in all the commandments and ordinances of the Lord blameless"]): but the mass of the people 'did not attain unto a law (of righteousness).'[24]

Gifford stresses that this Mosaic law called for an obedience of faith rather than works in which men could boast. Most of Israel did not attain the law because of their preference for the pride of supposedly accomplishing works rather than the humility demanded by the obedience of faith.

Like Murray, Gifford construed *Paul's* use of Leviticus 18:5 in Romans 10:5 as a description of the righteousness of the law, which placed conditions before men that were impossible to keep, in distinction from the righteousness of faith in Romans 10:6–8, in which men could find eternal life through faith. And like Murray, Gifford regarded Paul's usage of Leviticus 18:5 to be contrary to the intended meaning of that verse:

> But in assuming that the condition, "if a man do them," is imprac-

[23]From what has been said earlier in this chapter it is apparent that we regard Murray as wrong in thinking of "the righteousness of the law" (Rom. 10:5) as standing in contrast with the "righteousness of faith" (Rom. 10:6ff.). In drawing such a contrast, Murray reveals the deep impression that covenant theology has made on him. Yet he believes that it is due for a major overhaul. "It appears to me," he says, "that the covenant theology, notwithstanding the finesse of analysis with which it was worked out and the grandeur of its articulated systematization, needs recasting." John Murray, *The Covenant of Grace* (London: The Tyndale Press, 1954), p. 5.

[24]E. H. Gifford, *The Epistle of St. Paul to the Romans* (London: John Murray, 1886), p. 177.

ticable, St. Paul seems exactly to reverse the natural meaning of the words of Moses. *Either* those words really mean that God's law given to Israel consisted of statutes and judgments *which* might be kept and by keeping which they should enter into life; *or else* they are nothing better than an ironical promise based upon an impossible condition. The latter thought cannot be for a moment entertained: for it is God Himself who speaks through Moses, repeating the commandment and the promise twice [Lev. 18:1, 5], and affirming them by the most solemn form of Divine attestation, "I am the Lord."[25]

But more clearly than Murray, Gifford affirms that the meaning which Paul gave Leviticus 18:5 in Romans 10:5 was not Paul's own conviction of what it meant, but rather the Pharisees' misrepresentation of it:

> Did then St. Paul misinterpret or misunderstand the passage [Leviticus 18:5]? Not St. Paul himself, but those unbelieving Jews, whose error he was exposing. To one who sincerely desired "to do justly, and to love mercy, and to walk humbly with his God" (Mic. 6:8), "the law," taken in its fulness and in its spirit was undoubtedly a path of righteousness and life. It was a revelation of God Himself and of His holy will, accompanied by a dispensation full of the means of grace, of pardon, and reconciliation for every humble and contrite soul. ... But the Pharisees, and under their guidance the mass of the people, did not thus regard "*the Law*": to them it was "*law*" and nothing more, a covenant of works as opposed to a covenant of grace, its promise of life depending on the merit of strict and scrupulous obedience.[26]

These three expositors[27] contend that the Mosaic commandments do not enjoin works in which men can boast, but enjoin a conduct that stems from faith, or confidence in God, so that God rather than men receives all the praise. Each believes that Paul in Romans 10:5–8 quoted the two passages from Moses in

[25]Ibid., pp. 183–184.

[26]Ibid., p. 184.

[27]When C. E. B. Cranfield completes the chapters 9 through 16 of the sixth edition of the *International Critical Commentary* series on Romans (Volume I, chapters 1–8 appeared in 1975), it may well be evident that he joins with those interpreting Romans 9:31–32a as do these three expositors just discussed. In commenting on the phrase in Romans 3:27, "the law of faith," he denies that it refers to the abstract principle of justification by faith, and affirms instead that it refers to the concrete Old Testament Scriptures (p. 220). He cites Romans 9:31–32 as a confirmation of this.

order to repudiate the Pharisaic misunderstanding of Moses. Gifford and Murray differ from Flückiger in that they do not regard the quotation of Leviticus 18:5 in Romans 10:5 (introduced by the expression, "the righteousness of the law") to be Moses' expression, but rather an expression of the Pharisees. The true teaching of Moses, as expressed in Deuteronomy 30:11–14, is then set against this Pharisaism in Romans 10:6–8, where it is called "the righteousness of faith." Flückiger, however, argues that it is impossible to understand Paul as meaning that the Deuteronomy quotation is set in contrast with the Leviticus quotation, because whenever Paul alludes to Moses elsewhere (and even in so immediate a context as Romans 10:19), he regards him as an authority to be honored, and not as an adversary to be superseded. Therefore it would be strange for Paul to cite Moses as the proponent of "the righteousness of the law" in Romans 10:5 if he were intending to set him aside in preference for "the righteousness of faith." Also because *Moses* is paraphrased in 10:6–8, it is nonsensical to construe Paul as setting Moses against Moses. Consequently Flückiger concludes that the righteousness of the law, set forth by the intended meaning of the law itself, consists precisely in its being the righteousness of faith which Moses sets forth so clearly in Deuteronomy 30:11–14. So it is from the vantage point of the obedience of faith and not works in which men can boast that Leviticus 18:5 and the rest of the Mosaic law are to be understood.

Each of these three expositors would agree that this was Paul's understanding of the Mosaic law, even though two would construe 10:5 as stating the Pharisaic misinterpretation of it. In contrast to the majority of commentators, they do not have to regard Paul's use of Deuteronomy 30:11–14 as a complete violation of its intended meaning. Furthermore they supply the direct object of the ellipsis in Romans 9:32a in the natural way and also allow the *hōs* ("as it were") to point up the fact that Israel's preference for the boasting of works instead of faith stemmed only from their benighted imagination and had no basis in any canonical passage. So we do not agree with Calvin that Romans 10:5–8 "most clearly" (Inst. III, 11, 17) taught that the *Bible itself* sets forth both a "law righteousness" and a "faith righteousness." We have considered some evidence of another interpretation, which lends no support to the idea that the Bible sets forth two separate messages and that we must therefore "rightly divide" between the two to avoid the grievous error of Galatianism.

But before proceeding to the exegesis of Galatians 3:12, the second of the two Pauline messages which Calvin thought "most clearly" taught the existence of conditional as over against unconditional promises in Scripture, we should complete our consideration of Romans 9:30—10:10 by examining the most crucial verse, Romans 10:4: "Christ is the end (*telos*) of the law for righteousness to everyone that believes." Should *telos* be represented with the rare but possible meaning of "termination" or with the more usual meaning of "goal" or "completion?" Evidence for the answer comes from the immediate context of Romans 10:4.

In Romans 10:2 Paul repeats the theme of 9:31a of Israel's great zeal for God. "I bear them witness," he says, "that they have a zeal for God." Then in 10:2b–3 he reverts to the theme of how misguided this zeal is. "But [their zeal] is not enlightened [lit., not according to knowledge]. For, being ignorant of the righteousness that comes from God, and seeking to establish their own, they did not submit to God's righteousness." If our interpretation of 9:31–32a was correct, the righteousness of God to which Israel would not submit was the very righteousness of faith[27a] which the whole of Mosaism sought to inculcate. Israel was ignorant of this righteousness, but not because so many portions of the Old Testament taught its opposite, or because it was so obscure in Moses and the prophets. Instead, as the *hōs* ("as") in 9:32a made clear, her ignorance was voluntary. She hated the surrender of pride understood in the Mosaic law as a "law of faith" (cf. Rom. 3:27), and following the pure subjectivism of preferring to live so as to boast before God and man, Israel completely distorted

---

[27a]See below, pp. 105–126 et passim, for this book's understanding of the righteousness of faith.

the law. Instead, she taught a boasting in the law that made it a "law of works" (cf. Rom. 3:27).[28]

The Pentateuch itself understood that Israel's ignorance of God's righteousness was caused, not by deprivation of teaching, but rather by a rebellious heart which refused the teaching she had received and substituted another in its place. In Deuteronomy 5:29, Moses recalled that Israel's promise to keep the law was short-lived. Indeed, the people had asked Moses to "speak to us all that the Lord our God will speak to you, and we will hear and do it" (v. 27). But Moses recounted how God himself had said, "Oh that [Israel] had such a mind as this always, to fear me and to keep all my commandments. ..." Later on in Deuteronomy 29:4 Moses said, "To this day the Lord has not given you a mind to understand or eyes to see or ears to hear," and Paul regarded this same hardness of heart to persist down to his own time and on until the second coming of Christ (Rom. 11:7, 25).

[28]Gerhard Friedrich, in his article on Romans 3:27, "Das Gesetz des Glaubens Röm. 3, 27," *Theologische Zeitschrift*, 10 (November 1954), 401–417, challenges the usual Protestant interpretation (e.g., Charles Hodge) of the "law of faith" in Romans 3:27 as representing the abstract principle of justification by faith. Friedrich argues that the "law of faith" represents one very definite side, or inclination, in the concrete Old Testament Scriptures. Paul indicated these two sides of the Old Testament in Romans 3:21, where he said that the righteousness of God that was now revealed in Christ was "apart from the law" (the legalistic side of the Old Testament), and yet was witnessed to by the law and the prophets, including the Mosaic contribution found in Exodus through Deuteronomy. Since the prophets as a whole bear a positive witness to justification by faith, the second use of "law" in Romans 3:21 must include the whole Pentateuch, which included such parts as the patriarchal narratives, where gracious promises are found; the cultic worship which foreshadowed Christ's atonement; the witness to the one God in the Shema of Deuteronomy 6:4, which clashes with the idea that the Jews have better access to God than the Gentiles; and Deuteronomy 30:11–14, from which Paul (Rom. 10:6–8) uses Moses to testify to justification by faith (pp. 411–417).

So Friedrich concludes, "After Paul had spoken of the double nature of the law in verse 21, he must now in [3:27] indicate which side or inclination of the law he means [when he says that we are now under a law of faith and not under a law of works]. ... It is that side of the law which proclaims faith" (p. 415).

Understanding the Old Testament to be a mixture of such contrary ideas as righteousness by faith versus righteousness by works in which men could boast raises what, for us, constitutes the grave difficulty of understanding God as speaking out of both sides of his mouth in canonical Scripture. But Friedrich's affirmation that "the law of faith" (Rom. 3:27) represents, instead of a mere principle, concrete parts of the Old Testament, provides added encouragement for our exegesis of Romans 9:31–32a.

This hardness of heart which caused Israel to reject the law also caused her to reject Christ (9:32b–33). These two rejections of God's righteousness were so closely tied together in Paul's thinking that no conjunction at the middle of 9:32 is required to represent the shift from one to the other. This is a strong argument for understanding the statement "Christ is the *telos* of the law" in 10:4 as meaning that Christ is the "completion" or "goal" of the law in a way that would rule out any thought of his being the "termination" of it.[29] If the reason Israel rejected the law is the same as that by which she rejected Christ, then Christ and the Mosaic law must be of a piece, and there can be no thought of their being antithetical to each other.[30] Israel rejected Christ for the same reason that she rejected the law: both enjoined an obedience of faith. But her pride made her pervert the law's meaning so that she thought it taught that God's blessings to people were contingent on their service to him. Consequently when the Messiah came, Israel rejected him because his purpose to suffer, rather than be glorified, clashed so with her pride.

We note that Romans 10:4 commences with a "for," which signifies that what follows provides an argument in support of what precedes. Understanding the *telos* in Romans 10:4 as "goal"

---

[29]Arndt and Gingrich list only three places in the New Testament where *telos* connotes the meaning of "termination, cessation": "Of Christ's kingdom there shall be no end [*telos*]"—Luke 1:33; Melchizedek had "neither beginning of days nor end [*telos*] of life"—Hebrews 7:3; and Moses put a veil on his face so Israel would not see the end [*telos*] of the glory of the law that was fading away—II Corinthians 3:13. In every other instance *telos* signifies a "goal," or "completion," albeit sometimes with the idea that a process leading toward that goal ends when the goal is reached, e.g., "Then comes the end [*telos*] when Christ shall hand over the kingdom to God and the Father"—I Corinthians 15:24. Indeed, in one of the aforementioned places (II Cor. 3:13) where *telos* means "termination," the subject under consideration has to do with Moses and the law. But here Paul was thinking of the era, or dispensation, of the law which was surely superseded in his thinking by an era with greater glory. The necessary implication of this passage to the greater, however, no more requires a negation of the Mosaic law that characterized the former era than God's having now spoken through his Son in Hebrews 1:1–2 requires a negation of those "many and various ways God spoke" in the Old Testament.

[30]C. E. B. Cranfield, "Some Notes on Romans 9:30–33," *Jesus und Paulus,* Festschrift für W. G. Kümmel zum 70, Geburtstag (2nd ed.; Göttingen: Vandenhoeck & Ruprecht, 1978), p. 41, asks the rhetorical question, "... how could [Israel] believe in Him [Christ], if [Israel] was determined to rely on their own works?"

or "completion" makes it easier for this verse to argue for the one preceding than if *telos* were construed as meaning "termination" or "cessation." Romans 10:3 says that the Jews repudiated God's righteousness both in their rejection of the Mosaic law and of Christ, *because* (10:4) Christ and the Mosaic law, which is "holy and just and good" (Rom. 7:12), are in such a continuum that to repudiate one is to repudiate the other.[31] In other words, Christ is the completion of the law in that, as himself a revelation from God, he embodied in all his teaching and work a pure expression of the righteous standard of God found in the law. Just as the law became the righteousness of God only for those who responded to it in faith rather than works (cf. Rom. 9:31–32a), so Christ becomes the righteousness of God for all who, rather than stumbling at him (cf. Rom. 9:32b–33), submit to him in faith and thus are not ashamed.

How then does Romans 10:5–8, which is also introduced by a "for," extend this line of thought? How does the affirmation of 10:5 that sums up the "righteousness of the law" in quoting Leviticus 18:5 argue for what precedes? And how does 10:6–8 add to the argument which began at verse 5? In order for Paul to support the statement of 10:4 that Christ is such a continuation of the law that both convey the righteousness of God to those who respond to them in faith, he must be able to show that the law calls for a response, not of works in which a man can boast, but of faith in which God receives the credit. So Paul introduces Leviticus 18:5 as a summary expression of what was involved in the "righteousness of the law" with a "for" which signified that 10:5 supported what had just been said in 10:4. But in order to set aside the Pharisaic misinterpretation of Leviticus 18:5 in particular, he paraphrased the Mosaic law in Deuteronomy 30:11–14 by replacing the word "commandment" with "Christ" and calling this paraphrase an expression of "the righteousness of faith." Fur-

---

[31]This is the conclusion to which C. E. B. Cranfield has come in a recent article (supra, n. 30). In commenting on how Israel's rejection of Christ, spoken of in vv. 32b–33, is of a piece with their refusal to submit to the law by faith and their attempt instead to receive a blessing from God by obligating him by good works, Cranfield says, "That [what I have said] tells strongly in favour of the view—unpopular though it may be—that 10:4 *telos ... nomou Christos* means 'Christ is the goal of the law' seems to the present writer very clear."

thermore, in setting forth this paraphrase in terms of commands which forbid attempts to produce great feats of strength and courage in fulfilling the law, Paul was clashing squarely with the Pharisaic misinterpretation which made the law so hard to fulfill that, to use the words of Peter, it was a "yoke upon the neck . . . which neither our fathers nor we have been able to bear" (Acts 15:10). (Jesus himself had spoken of how the Pharisees, in misinterpreting the law, "bind heavy burdens hard to bear, and lay them on men's shoulders"—Matt. 23:4.)

By paraphrasing Deuteronomy 30:11–14 right after a verse spotlighting the righteousness of the law which Moses taught, and by affirming this paraphrase of Moses which inserts the word "Christ" at crucial points, Paul was showing that the righteousness set forth by the law was the righteousness of faith. Since the wording of the law can be replaced by the word "Christ" with no loss of meaning, Paul has demonstrated that Moses himself taught that Christ and the law are all of a piece. Either one or both will impart righteousness to all who believe, and thus the affirmation of Romans 10:4 is supported by Paul's reference to Moses in verses 5–8.

We observed, however, at the beginning of this section that the antithetical use of the terms "righteousness of the law" and "righteousness of faith" in Philippians 3:9 makes it seem that these same terms are likewise antithetical in Romans 10:5–8. Philippians 3:9 reads, ". . . and be found in him, not having a righteousness of my own, based on law, but that which is through faith in Christ, the righteousness from God that depends on faith." While acknowledging the great similarity between Philippians 3:9 and Romans 10:5–8, one must also keep in mind that Romans 10:3 has language which is very similar to Philippians 3:9. Both of these passages refer to the establishing of one's own righteousness in distinction from that which comes from God. Everyone would agree that "their own righteousness" (Rom. 10:3) and "a righteousness of my own" (Phil. 3:9) represent the opposite of "the righteousness of faith" in both Philippians 3:9 and Romans 10:5–8. But whereas Paul uses the word "law" as a synonym for "own righteousness" in Philippians 3:9, the use of "law" has no such meaning in the Romans 9:30—10:10 passage. In the Romans passage, "law" represents only what Moses intended to say in his writings, whereas "law" in Philippians 3:9 (and in many other places in Paul) is used to represent the common misinterpretation of Moses by the Jews in their rebellion against God. In the Romans passage Paul resorted to other words and phrases besides "law" to represent the Jewish rebellion against God, because his purpose here is to show that this consisted in a rebellion against the intended meaning of the Mosaic law. To have used the same word for the rebellion *and* for that which the Jews rebelled against would have produced great confusion in understanding Romans 9:30—10:10.

This consideration of Philippians 3:9 and Romans 10:5-8 demonstrates a conclusion generally held among contemporary biblical theologians that Paul, in his writings, used "law" (*nomos*) in at least two very distinct senses. C. F. D. Moule has said:

> The many shades of meaning attached to *nomos* have to be deduced from the ways in which the word is used: it is clear that *nomos* is used by Paul in (among others) the two quite distinct connections which may be called respectively "revelatory" and "legalistic." [Moule then cites Romans 7:12 as an example of a "revelatory" usage, and Romans 3:28, with its phrase "the works of the law," as a "legalistic" usage of *nomos*.] . . . This contrast between the two contexts in which *nomos* is used is perfectly familiar to all students of Paul.[32]

C. E. B. Cranfield has made the same point:

> it will be well to bear in mind the fact (which, so far as I know, has not received attention) that the Greek language used by Paul had no word-group to denote "legalism," "legalist," and "legalistic". . . . In view of this, we should, I think, be ready to reckon with the possibility that sometimes, when [Paul] seems to be disparaging the law, what he really has in mind may not be the law itself, but the misunderstanding and misuse for which we have no convenient term.[33]

[32]C. F. D. Moule, "Obligation in the Ethics of Paul," *Christian History and Interpretation:* Studies Presented to John Knox, W. R. Farmer, et al., eds. (Cambridge: at the University Press, 1967), pp. 392–393.

[33]C. E. B. Cranfield, "St. Paul and the Law," *Scottish Journal of Theology,* 17, 1 (March 1964), p. 55. But in the next section of this chapter the argument will be presented that Paul used the Greek of the rabbinical phrase for "the works of the law" to represent the legalistic misuse and misunderstanding of it. But since this phrase was rather cumbersome, on a number of occasions he, as in Philippians 3:9, simply used the word "law" to represent not the revelation given by Moses, but the legalistic misunderstanding of the law which the majority of the Jews have espoused since the time of Moses.

Therefore when Paul names *Moses* as the source for his quotation of Leviticus 18:5 in Romans 10:5, he is not using the word "law" to represent the legalistic misunderstanding of this passage but rather the intended meaning which the word had in its original context. When Paul refers to "law" in Philippians 3:9, however, where the flow of thought stresses how he, in his pre-Christian days, had sinned against God chiefly in the pride he felt over the blameless but Pharisaic way in which he thought he was fulfilling the law, the word "law" obviously represents the legalistic misunderstanding of it, and not what the Pentateuch itself intended to teach. Consequently, the contrast which the words "righteousness of the law" and "righteousness of faith" represent in Philippians 3:9 is not indicated by the very similar wording in Romans 10:5 and 6–8.

But there is another objection to this interpretation of Romans 10:5–8 in Galatians 3:12, where Paul used the wording of Leviticus 18:5 to provide an unmistakable contrast between the faith which the gospel enjoins and "law." Galatians 3:12 reads, "But the law does not rest on faith, for 'He who does them shall live in them' [Lev. 18:5]." We must now consider the exegesis of Galatians 3:12 and the verses preceding it to see if Calvin was right in regarding verse 12 as a place where Paul "most clearly" (*Inst.* III, 11, 17) taught that the revelatory law is antithetical to faith and the gospel.

Galatians 3:10–12

In this passage Paul said:

> [10a]For all who rely on works of the law are under a curse; for it is written, [10b]"Cursed be every one who does not abide by all things written in the book of the law, and do them [Deut. 27:26]." [11]Now it is evident that no man is justified before God by the law; for "He who through faith is righteous shall live" [Hab. 2:4]; [12]but the law does not rest upon faith; for "He who does them shall live by them [Lev. 18:5]."

In verse 12 Paul certainly sets up an antithesis between faith on the one hand, and what he meant by "law" on the other. As we peruse the verses leading up to Galatians 3:12 in the immediate context, we find a continuous theme in which Paul contrasts faith with law. (Actually the antithesis begins back at Galatians 2:15, but we will begin at Galatians 3:10.)

It is safe to assume that Paul, in writing Galatians, regarded himself as locked in a life and death struggle with the Judaizers, whose teaching was heavily influencing Paul's converts at Galatia. Paul's agony was so great that he likened his state of mind to the pangs that a mother has in giving birth to a child (Gal. 4:20). Under such conditions he would argue for his point of view from the Old Testament, that common ground which he, like the Judaizers, regarded as the final authority for what was taught. In the six verses leading up to Galatians 3:12, Paul cited the following references from the Old Testament in order to prove various points in his line of thought: Genesis 15:6 (v. 6); Genesis 12:3 (v. 8); Deuteronomy 27:26 (v. 10); Habakkuk 2:4 (v. 11); and Leviticus 18:5 (v. 12). It is possible to construct a rather complete outline of the Judaizers' teachings from the Apocrypha and Pseudepigrapha, from the Talmud and the midrashim of the early centuries of the Christian era, and from allusions in the New Testament. But it is difficult to understand how Paul's use of these Old Testament quotations in the verses immediately preceding Galatians 3:12 would invalidate the influence of the Judaizers and win back his converts.

We single out Deuteronomy 27:26, quoted in verse 10, as a prime example of how apparently ill-suited this quotation is to refute what the Judaizers were teaching. In the Septuagint, which Paul seems to have been quoting, Deuteronomy 27:26 reads, "Cursed is everyone who does not abide by all the commands of this law to do them." Paul used this verse as an argument to support the first half of Galatians 3:10, "For all who rely on the works of the law are under a curse." In the ordinary parlance of Judaism, the term "works of law" represented doing what the law commanded. A very similar expression is found in II Baruch 57:2: "At that time the unwritten law was named amongst [the Patriarchs], and *the works of the commandments* [italics added] were then fulfilled...." From this and other examples, commentators Strack and Billerbeck, among many others, affirm that

Were an individual, according to his duty, to have been led by the Torah, so would his deeds be regarded as *opera praeceptorum,* that

is, works to which the Torah had given direction, and which arise
from obedience to the Torah. The apostle [Paul] has attached the same
meaning [?] with his words *erga nomou* ["works of the law"]: they
are works which are the result of the observance or performance of
the law.[34]

But if this is the meaning that Paul attached to these words,
then his quotation of Deuteronomy 27:26 at the end of Galatians
3:10 is not suitable to argue for the first statement in this verse
that "all who rely on the works of the law are under a curse." As
long as we think of the "works of the law" as compliance with its
precepts, the statement of Deuteronomy 27:26, "Cursed is everyone who does not abide by all the things written in the book of
the law to do them," could only prove that a curse rests on those
who do *not* comply with the law's commands. The Swedish ex-
egete Ragnar Bring points up the difficulty as follows:

> We should note that in vs. 10 Paul quotes a word of scripture
> (Deut. 27:26) which seems to say the opposite of what he wants to
> prove. This verse pronounces a curse on the one who does *not* abide
> by the words of the law. It does not seem to say that he who is "of
> the works of the law" should be cursed. On the contrary, [in Deuter-
> onomy, chs. 27 and 28] blessing seems to be promised to those who
> keep the commandments of the law, which according to a reasonable
> interpretation of Deut. 28:1 ff. is obviously possible. But Paul asserts
> that *Scripture* proclaims that man to be under a curse who is "of the
> works of the law."[35]

Only if Paul used the term "works of law" as representing something sinful and deserving of a curse, would his use of Deuteronomy 27:26 be a proof that the two halves of Galatians 3:10
constitute a coherent argument. Most commentators are convinced that Paul did not give a meaning to this term so opposite
from that of his Judaizing opponents. With the exception of Bring,
all of the commentators render Galatians 3:10 coherent by inserting between its two propositions a third which says something

---

[34]Strack-Billerbeck, *Kommentar zum Neuen Testament*, 6 vols. (Munich:
C. H. Beck, 1961³), III, 160–161 on Romans 3:20.

[35]Ragnar Bring, *Commentary on Galatians*, trans. E. Wahlstrom (Philadelphia: Muhlenberg Press, 1961), p. 120.

like "no one can keep the law perfectly." For example, Randall in the *Expositor's Greek Testament* says, "Paul urges that [resting on the law] entails on [the Jews] a curse of a broken Law. ..." Lange says, "[The citation of Deut. 27:26 in the second half of Gal. 3:10] proves ... that 'as many as are of the law are under a curse,' provided [!] a non-continuance [in obeying the law] can be established." Oepke states, "Paul tacitly presupposes that no human is righteous through a perfect fulfillment of the law." Schlier declares that "to show that a curse is over all those who live by the law, the decisive thought must *be added* [italics mine]: there is no man who can fulfill the law." But he concedes that Deuteronomy 27:26, as it stands in its immediate context, "absolutely presupposes that the law can be fulfilled and is fulfilled." To Galatians 3:10 Lietzmann adds the idea that "no man can keep the law," and then explains that "this necessary thought, although not made explicit, is nevertheless perfectly obvious."

But it is unlikely that Paul intended his readers to insert such a proposition into the middle of Galatians 3:10. Furthermore, the Judaizers at Galatia would have denied the validity of inserting such an idea into this verse. None of them would have agreed that failure for one moment to keep one part of the law consigned one to a curse from which he could not be exonerated so long as he tried to live by the law. The Judaism of Paul's day regarded everyone as having failed to live up to the law. For example, in the midrash on Psalm 143:2 ("Enter not into judgment with thy servant; for no man living is righteous before thee") the following statements appear:

> who can say, I have purified my heart, Proverbs 20:9? No man, by himself, can regard himself as righteous at the day of judgment. Why? ... There is no man who has not sinned, I Kings 8:46. ... Therefore Psalm 143:2 says that before God there is no person living who is righteous.[36]

Judaism, however, also taught that God would forgive a man who repented of his sins. For example, Rabbi Eleazar (c. 150 A.D.), citing Exodus 34:7, which states that God forgives "iniquity and transgression and sin," affirmed that "God forgives the repentant."

[36]Strack-Billerbeck, *Kommentar,* III, 157, on Romans 3:9.

George Foote Moore, one of the great authorities on Judaism, lamented the propensity of Protestants to forget that forgiveness, on the basis of repentance, is central to Jewish thought.[37] So we can almost hear the reply of a Galatian Judaizer to the customary Protestant interpretation of Galatians 3:10: "Yes, we have all sinned, but Moses himself wrote in Exodus 34:7 that God forgives the repentant. Therefore Paul is absolutely out of his mind to say that as long as a man tries to keep the law, he is irrevocably under a curse from God."

The Galatian Judaizers would also have objected to interpreting Deuteronomy 27:26 ("Cursed be he who does not confirm the words of this law by doing them") to mean that the curse comes simply from disobeying the law. In the Jewish understanding of this passage, emphasis was on the causative form of the verb "to stand" (*yaqim*), which the Revised Standard Version translates as "confirm." So the rabbis taught that for a man to avoid the curse threatened in this verse, he must engage in some concrete way of supporting the law, or "causing it to stand." For example, Rabbi Huna (c. 350 A.D.) said:

> When one stumbles into sin and thus becomes worthy of death from God's hand, what should he do in order to live? If he had been accustomed to read one page in the scriptures, now he should read two. . . . But if he had not been accustomed to read the scriptures . . . what should he then do, in order to remain alive? He should go and become a leader in the synagogue, or become a collector of alms. . . . For if [Deut. 27:26] said, "Cursed be he who does not learn," then there would be no hope for him.* But this passage says, "Cursed be he who does not uphold (*yaqim*). . . ."[38]

From this Hebrew rendering of Deuteronomy it is clear that a curse does not fall so much on the one who disobeys a precept of the law as on one whose conduct and attitude undermines the integrity of the law. It is noteworthy that Deuteronomy 27:26 comes at the conclusion of the curses that befall those who com-

---

[37]G. F. Moore, *Judaism*, 3 vols. (Cambridge: Harvard University Press, 1927), I, 507, 521.

[38]Strack-Billerbeck, *Kommentar*, III, 541, on Galatians 3:10. *Note how this statement implies the idea that everyone has failed to live up to all the law's demands. The only exceptions to this in Rabbinism would be the patriarchs, Abraham, Isaac, and Jacob (Prayer of Manasseh 8).

mit such blatant sins as moving land boundaries, incest, bestiality, murder, or hiring someone to commit murder. What is characteristic of the eleven crimes listed in Deuteronomy 27:15–25 is that each implied an open and flagrant renunciation of the law which God had given. Thus if by "works of the law" Paul meant a revolt against God rather than mere compliance with all the commands of the law, then however much the Judaizers might have disagreed that their legalistic attitude was in a class with the eleven crimes in Deuteronomy 27:15–25, they could find no fault with Paul's logical structure in Galatians 3:10.

Therefore in order to achieve coherency in interpreting Galatians 3:10 we have the option either (1) to insert a whole proposition between its two explicit statements, or (2) to regard Paul as using "works of law" to signify what is evil. We have already noted the difficulty with the first option. The problem with the second option is that it understands Paul as giving to "works of law" a meaning precisely opposite from what the Judaizers would give to it. We argue, however, that the second option, though it does present a difficulty, nevertheless has enough evidence to support its plausibility.

Paul regarded the law to be "holy and just and good" (Rom. 7:12), as well as "spiritual" (Rom. 7:14). But unless a person was indwelt by the regenerating power of the Holy Spirit, sin would take command of his life and use the good law to bring sin to full fruition. In Romans 7:5 Paul speaks of how "our sinful passions, aroused by the law, were at work in our members to bring forth fruit unto death," and in Romans 7:13 Paul says, "It was sin [that brought death to me], working death in me through what is good [i.e., through the law], in order that sin might be shown to be sin, and through the commandment might become sinful beyond measure." A few verses earlier Paul had also said that "sin, finding opportunity in the commandment, wrought in me all kinds of covetousness" (Rom. 7:8). The Greek for the word rendered "opportunity" in this verse is *aphormēn*, which represents an essential place for reaching an objective. The Greek language often used it to represent the place from which a military attack could be launched most successfully.

We begin to understand how the "holy and just and good" law provides sin with the most suitable stepping-stone for achieving

its full sinfulness when we understand that the prime objective
of our sinful inclination is to accomplish goals in which we can
take great pride and which others will also applaud. We very
conveniently forget how Paul stressed in I Corinthians 4:7 that
everything a man has or achieves comes to him as a *gift,* so that
he has no reason to boast in anything he is or does. In his description of man's sinfulness in Romans 1:21–22, Paul emphasized
how man refused to credit God for any of his blessings and fool-
ishly credited himself for all his accomplishments. Paul implies
this same point in stressing that a prime objective in God's work
of saving a man is to countermand all the delusions by which
people suppose they can boast in themselves. So, according to
Paul, people are "saved through faith ... not because of works,
lest any man should boast" (Eph. 2:8–9). He also declared, "Not
many of you were wise according to worldly standards, not many
were powerful, not many were of noble birth, but God chose
what is foolish ... weak ... low and despised in the world ... to
bring to nothing the things that are, so that no human being might
boast in the presence of God" (I Cor. 1:26–31). God's priority in
dealing with Christians is to purge them of pride and trust in
themselves. Paul relates how he and his friends had suffered so
greatly as to lose all hope, but "that was to make us rely not on
ourselves but on God who raises the dead" (II Cor. 1:9; cf. II Cor.
12:7–10; Phil. 3:3).

Paul's statements help us understand the sinful aim of unregenerate men (using the words of Isaiah 14:14) to be "like the
Most High." Consequently, when people who are dominated by
such an aim encounter the commands of the Mosaic law, they
conveniently bracket out all that is said about humbly trusting
God (Deut. 6:5;[39] Lev. 26:41; Deut. 8:2–3, 16; and Deut. 10:21),
and twist the meaning of the other commands so that their supposed compliance with them makes them think they have done
something so great that it calls forth the applause of the Almighty
himself. When one is convinced that the Mosaic law, as well as
the other commands in the Bible, comes from God, then all these

[39]The command to love God with all the heart must necessarily entail
trusting him. It is inconceivable that we could distrust and love (in the sense
of delighting in) the same being at the same time.

commands provide the ego with the greatest opportunity (*aphormēn!*) for satisfying its cravings. From this vantage point it is not difficult to see why Paul affirmed that "the power of sin is the law" (I Cor. 15:56).

As Paul looked back on his own life, he saw how his supposedly blameless keeping of the law (cf. Phil. 3:6) had only succeeded in making him "the foremost of sinners" (I Tim. 1:15). Paul recalled that before being confronted with Jesus on the Damascus Road, he was "advanced in Judaism beyond many of my own age among my people, so zealous was I for the traditions of the fathers" (Gal. 1:14). In Philippians 3:4–7 (esp. v. 7) he confessed that it was pride which had fired his zeal to be a blameless keeper of the law. In order to maintain this pride he persecuted Christians because they taught that, despite Jewish distinctives, a person would not be saved unless he believed in Jesus. Such teaching effectively dissipated one's pride in having and adhering to such distinctives. So Paul tried to eradicate Christianity because he believed that in so doing, he was serving God. Before his Damascus Road experience he was convinced that God himself was loudly applauding him because he most zealously worked to uphold the law. After his confrontation with the living Jesus, however, he came to realize that all his zealous efforts had succeeded only in persecuting God. Since he was the most ardent persecutor, he was not overstating things when he labeled himself as having been "the foremost of sinners."

Thus when Paul saw how the Mosaic law had played such an active role in making him "the foremost of sinners," and when he saw how the great majority of Jews prided themselves in supposedly keeping the law, then it was perfectly natural for him to speak of the works produced by the law in those under sin's dominion as *evil* works. As Paul's outlook had become totally opposite from the Judaism around him, so also his meaning of "works of law" had become opposite from the meaning it had in Judaism.

Further support that "works of the law" represented a gross rebellion against the law, instead of compliance with it, comes from a handful of statements in which Paul uses a compound of the verb "work" to express what the law does in promoting sin. In Romans 7:8 (cf. also v. 13) he said that "sin, finding opportunity in the law, wrought in me all kinds of covetousness." The word for "wrought" is *kàteirgasato,* which without the *kata-* would be the simple verb for "work." Likewise in Romans 7:5 he said that "our sinful passions, aroused by the law, were *at work* in our members to bear fruit unto death." Here the word for "at work" is *enērgeito,* which without the *en-* would also be the simple verb for "work."

Furthermore the flow of thought in Galatians 3:21–25 and 4:1–11 reveals that in Paul's thinking the law was a slavemaster and its subjects were its slaves. So the work which these slaves had to do was sinful, as the parallelism between Galatians 3:22 and vv. 23–24, and between 4:1 and 4:8–11, makes clear. Finally we take note of such statements as Romans 6:14, "Sin will have no dominion over you, since you are not under law but under grace," and Galatians 5:16, 18, "Walk by the Spirit and do not gratify the desires of the flesh.... If you are led by the Spirit you are not under the law." Here law in the service of sin causes a man to sin and gratify his ego. Because of statements like these, it is reasonable to regard Paul's "works" of the law to be sinful, evil works.

Another line of evidence that supports the conclusion that Paul's term, "the works of the law," represents an all-out rebellion against God is the unmistakable meaning of the word "law" in Philippians 3:8–9. There Paul said, "For [Jesus'] sake I have suffered the loss of all things and count them as refuse, in order that I may gain Christ [9]and be found in him, not having a righteousness of my own, based on law, but ... the righteousness from God that depends on faith." We recall from the discussion of Romans 9:30—10:10 earlier in this chapter[40] that the phrase "own righteousness" used in Romans 10:3 also represented the way Israel had rebelled against the righteousness of God. In the Jewish parlance of that day, the phrase "own works," which closely resembles "own righteousness," was used to represent rebellion against God. According to II Baruch 48:38, "It shall come to pass at the self-same time, that a change of times shall manifestly appear to every man, because in all those times they polluted themselves and they practiced oppression, and walked every man in *his own works* [italics

---

[40]Supra, pp. 86–88.

added] and remembered not the law of the Mighty One."[41] But no Jew made the "law" a synonym for the term "own righteousness/works," so as to implicate the law somehow in aiding and abetting rebellion against God. Paul, however, in Philippians 3:8–9 did speak of the law as having an active role in man's rebellion against God, and this is not difficult to understand from his concept of how the law provides sin with the best opportunity to become utterly sinful. We conclude, therefore, that Paul used not only the term "works of the law" but also, on occasion, simply the term "law" to describe how it played a vital role in bringing sin to full fruition. There is no rule-of-thumb method for knowing when *nomos* ("law") has this meaning in Paul.[42] Instead we allow contextual considerations such as how Galatians 3:10b could argue for v. 10a, and the parallelism in Philippians 3:9 between "own righteousness" and "law," to conclude that Paul meant *nomos* in the bad sense in Galatians 3:10a.

How then shall we understand "law" in Galatians 3:11, "Now it is evident that no man is justified before God by the law; for 'He who through faith is righteous shall live' [Hab. 2:4]?" We observe that this verse is a negative way of stating the positive proposition of the preceding verse, "All who rely on works of the law are under a curse." Since we have seen several instances so far in this chapter where "law" is used in an evil sense, the natural

---

[41]R. H. Charles, ed., *The Apocrypha and Pseudepigrapha*, 2 vols. (Oxford: at the Clarendon Press, 1913), II, 507.

[42]Earlier in this century, a number of expositors (e.g., J. B. Lightfoot, G. Volkmar, A. H. Gifford, and E. W. Burton) argued that *nomos* without the article carried a stress not on the objective Mosaic law but on law as having the qualities of law, which involved (for them) legalism. But one problem (among others) which this theory cannot adequately explain is the interchange between *ho nomos* and *nomos* without the article in Romans 7:7–12. Since both of these forms are used in parallel with *entolē* ("commandment") in this passage, and since *entolē* refers to a concrete, historical utterance by Moses, it is impossible to think of the anarthrous *nomos* as not also referring to the objective Mosaic law, and not to some abstract quality it might possess. So W. G. Kümmel, *Römer 7 und die Bekehrung des Paulus*, Untersuchung zum N. T. Hrsg. von Hans Windisch, Heft 17 (Leipzig: J. C. Hinrichs'sche Buchhandlung, 1929), p. 55, concludes that "the constantly interchanging use of *nomos* and *ho nomos* in the closely knit line of thought in Romans 7:7–12 provides a coherent meaning only when these two forms signify the same sense, namely, the Mosaic law." Then Kümmel, like Moule (supra, pp. 86–87), recommends letting the immediate context, rather than any rule-of-thumb like the use or non-use of the article with *nomos*, determine the meaning it has in any particular Pauline statement.

way to construe it in Galatians 3:11 is to give it the same meaning that "works of the law" had in 3:10. The meaning of verse 11, then, is that no one is justified before God who boasts in his legalistic way of seemingly (to his way of thinking) living up to the law, for Habakkuk 2:4 makes it clear that not the proud legalist[43] but rather the one who depends on God's faithfulness shall live.[44]

What then is the meaning of "law" in Galatians 3:12, "And the law is not of faith, but he that does these things shall live in them"? There is no reason to suppose that Paul now shifts the meaning of "law" from the legalistic misunderstandings of it to the revelatory law. We note that in verse 12 he continues the contrast begun in verse 11 between faith and its opposite. Since verse 11 contrasts faith, the proper attitude toward God, with its opposite, the improper attitude of legalism, it would be hard not to understand verse 12 as continuing this contrast of attitudes. So the statement in verse 12 that "the law is not of faith" means that "legalism is an attitude of heart which cannot coexist with the attitude of faith."

But it may be objected that "law" in 3:12 must mean the objective law itself, since Paul cites words from Leviticus 18:5 which are in that objective law. But the legalists who gloried so in their supposed loyalty to Moses were constantly quoting the wording of Leviticus 18:5 in support of their life-style. The Psalms of Solomon are generally regarded as an expression of the Pharisaic point of view, and they use the wording of Leviticus 18:5,

---

[43]See the immediate context of Habakkuk 2:4. In the Hebrew the opposite of the person who trusts in God's faithfulness has a soul which is puffed up and is therefore not right. In the LXX, the person who is antithetical to the believer is one who "draws back." The editors of the RSV believe the text of Habakkuk 2:4 should read, "Behold, he whose soul is not upright in him is puffed up, but the righteous shall live by his faith." Both of these verbs—"draw back" and "be puffed up"—represent the opposite of humble, believing trust.

[44]A confirmation of this way of interpreting Paul's meaning in Galatians 3:11 comes from Romans 3:28, a passage which has almost the same wording: "We hold that a man is justified by faith apart from works of the law." In the Romans passage Paul uses the more cumbersome "works of the law" because that verse sums up what he has been saying since Romans 3:21. Thus it is fitting for him to use the term "works of law," which for him always signified the legalistic misunderstanding of the law. But Galatians 3:11 did not function as a summary statement, and so Paul could simply use the word "law" as an abbreviated way of representing the legalistic frame of mind.

"Faithful is the Lord ... to them that walk ... in the law which He commanded that we might live" (Psa. of Sol. 14:1–2). It likewise would be perfectly natural for Paul, in summing up the legalistic affirmation in a single motto, to use this wording. But he does not cite *Moses* as an authority for Leviticus 18:5 here, as he does in Romans 10:5, because the meaning which he intends to convey in Galatians 3:12 is not the meaning that Moses intended.

We recall how Calvin said that Galatians 3:12 showed "most clearly" that much of the revelatory law in Scripture was anti-thetical to faith. But in his commentary on Galatians, he had to maintain coherence between Galatians 3:10 and this verse by inserting a proposition into the middle of verse 10 which does not render this passage "most clear." After examining Paul's think-ing on the link-up between sin and the law, we believe we have found a more plausible explanation to Galatians 3:10 by under-standing "works of the law" to be sinful works. Then "law" in verse 12 would represent the sinful way men understood the law, and would remove all need for making a contrast between gospel and faith on the one hand, and the *revelatory* law of Moses on the other.[45]

The two verses which immediately precede Galatians 3:10 pro-vide additional evidence for the interpretation we have given to "works of the law." Verse 9 states the conclusion, supported both by the verses preceding and following it, that "those who are the men of faith are blessed with Abraham who had faith." In the preceding verse Paul intended that his quotation of Genesis 12:3, "In you shall all the nations be blessed," should prove the con-clusion set forth in verse 9, that only men of faith share in the blessing of Abraham, who was also a man of faith. Verse 10—"all who rely on the works of the law are under a curse"—supports the conclusion of verse 9 by showing that the opposite of faith, namely, works of the law, brought people to a curse, the opposite of the blessing spoken of in verse 9. If faith brings a blessing, then something which is truly the opposite of faith would be expected to bring a curse, the opposite of blessing.

[45]Further evidence for understanding Galatians 3:10 in this manner comes from an exegesis of the first occurrences (three times) of "works of the law" in Galatians 2:16. See Daniel P. Fuller, "Paul and 'The Works of the Law,' " *Westminster Theological Journal,* 38 (1975–76), pp. 37–40. See also Addendum on p. 120.

But how verse 8 supports verse 9 is not so easy to understand. How did Paul expect his readers to conclude from his quotation of Genesis 12:3 in the last half of verse 8 (henceforth designated as 8b) that the blessing of God, such as Abraham enjoyed, came to men exclusively by faith? It is helpful to realize that this conclusion was already stated (albeit in other words) in the first half of verse 8 (hereafter 8a) in the affirmation that "the scripture [i.e., God] would justify the Gentiles by faith." But why does it necessarily follow that because God said that in Abraham all nations will be blessed (8b), therefore all the Gentiles (or nations) would be justified by faith (8a; cf. v. 9)?

A promising lead for grasping the intended argument in Galatians 3:8 comes from a very similar statement in Romans 3:29–30. There Paul, after making the summary statement in verse 28 that a man is justified by faith and not by the works of the law, argues for this conclusion by the rhetorical questions, "Or is God the God of the Jews only? Is he not the God of the Gentiles also?" He then answers, "Yes, [he is the God] of the Gentiles also, [30]since God is one; and he will justify the circumcised on the ground of their faith and the uncircumcised through their faith."

Paul deals with virtually the same subject matter in Galatians as in Romans. The great difference in style between the two epistles is due to the fact that Galatians was written quickly, while Paul was filled with anger over the inroads the Judaizing heresy was making in the Galatian churches, and Romans was written more slowly and deliberately, since he was not trying to rid the Roman church of any heresy (cf. Rom. 15:14). Instead, Paul was summarizing the major elements of his thinking so that church would be motivated to provide him with a base for missionary operations in the western Mediterranean area. Consequently matters that are merely touched upon in Galatians sometimes receive additional explanation in Romans. Like Galatians 3:8–9, Romans 3:29–30 affirms that God is the God of all the nations, and that he will justify all peoples, including the Jews, on the basis of their trusting in him. But unlike Galatians 3:8–9, this Romans passage supports the conclusion that God stands ready to justify all peoples who believe in him by alluding to the oft-repeated Jewish creed of Deuteronomy 6:4, "Hear, O Israel: The Lord our God is one Lord." The name for this confession is the Shema, which is

the Hebrew for the imperative *"Hear,* O Israel. . . ." It is significant that Paul uses the Greek conjunction *eiper* to introduce the
Shema as an argument that God is also the God of the Gentiles.
In addition to meaning "since" or "because," *eiper* conveys the
idea that what is about to be said is a commonly accepted truth.[46]
Certainly the Shema would be something that every Jewish reader
would accept as unquestionably true.

The allusion to the Shema in Romans 3:29 provides the basis
from which Paul draws two corollary conclusions. One line of
argument is that on the basis of the Shema, God is just as much
the God of the Gentiles as he is of the Jews. A Jewish objector,
however, would say, Why must the one true God be a God for all
men? Why can't he devote all or at least the greater part of his
concern just to the Jews? This is precisely how the early rabbis
understood things. God was the Supreme Being who had all things
under his control. Nevertheless he was only the God of the Jews.
In commenting on Exodus 20:2, "I am the Lord your God, who
brought you out of the land of Egypt . . . ," Rabbi Simeon ben
Johai (c. 150 A.D.) said, "God spoke to the Israelites, 'A God I
am over all who come into the world, but my name I have as-
sociated only with you; I have not called myself the God of the
nations of the world, but the God of Israel'."[47] The use of Genesis
12:3 in Galatians 3:8 indicates how Paul might well have replied
to such a statement as he carried on his continuous argument
with the Jews. In using this verse, he could prove that *all* the
ethnic entities of earth were to enjoy the blessings that Abraham
and his posterity enjoyed because God was equally the God of all
men. Paul could also have found support for his statement from
Isaiah 54:5, "The God of the whole earth he is called," and from
Isaiah 45:22, "Turn to me and be saved, all the ends of the earth!
For I am God, and there is no other." So the Shema, read in
conjunction with Genesis 12:3 and other Old Testament passages,
would prove the conclusion that the one God was the God of
both the Jews and the Gentiles who desired to bless each equally.

The second conclusion that Paul drew from the Shema in Ro-

---

[46]F. Blass and A. Debrunner, *A Greek Grammar of the New Testament,* trans.
R. W. Funk (9–10th ed., Chicago: The University of Chicago Press, 1961), Art.
454(2).

[47]Strack-Billerbeck, *Kommentar,* III, 185.

mans 3:29–30 was that faith was the basis on which God would justify both Jew and Gentile.[48] This was the same conclusion which he drew in Galatians 3:8a from the quotation of Genesis 12:3. The two arguments which support this conclusion share the idea that God wants all the ethnic entities of earth to have equal access to his blessings. The great diversity in cultural distinctives and behavioral characteristics between various peoples due to heredity and past history does not incline God to bless one group more than another. Hence the condition for receiving God's blessing must consist in an action that all people are equally capable of fulfilling. The only such action for which all peoples, despite their great diversities, have an equal aptitude, is ceasing to place any value on some particular distinctive they possess, in contrast to that of some other ethnic entity, and to trust instead in the God who holds before all men the merciful promise to be their God.[49] If God favored one nation because of some distinctive like circumcision, then it would not be true that he was equally the God of other nations who did not practice circumcision.

Gerhard Friedrich argues that the Shema, which the Jew repeats more often than any other statement in the Pentateuch, demonstrates that "even the law itself contains the teaching of justification by faith alone, as Deuteronomy 6:4 ['Hear, O Israel: The Lord our God is one Lord'] shows."[50] For the Judaizers to insist that the Gentile Galatians must be circumcised in order to be in line for God's full blessings entailed nothing less than a denial of the Shema, the basic creed of Israel. Their sinful disposition caused them to take the "good and just and holy" law (Rom. 7:12), including the Shema, and twist it around so that their teachings were contrary to the law and reinforced their own sinful tendencies. What the Judaizers at Galatia were insisting on, then,

---

[48]Commentators generally agree that the change of preposition from "of their faith" for the Jews to "through their faith" for the Gentiles in Romans 3:30 was not intended to point up any difference between the way a Jew or a Gentile was saved, but rather was used for the rhetorical purpose of avoiding monotony.

[49]Romans 10:12 is another passage where Paul expresses this concept: "There is no distinction between Jew or Greek; the same Lord is Lord of all and bestows his riches upon all who call upon him." Despite the great differences between the Jews on the one hand and the Gentiles on the other, all are equally capable of calling upon God to avail themselves of his blessings.

[50]G. Friedrich, "Das Gesetz des Glaubens Röm. 3, 27," p. 416.

was not merely a disobedience of the law but an undermining of its basic foundation found in the confession that God alone is God. Hence their works, stemming from the law under the dominion of sin, transgressed the law, and worse, undermined and destroyed its basic credal underpinnings. As Deuteronomy 27:26 says in the Hebrew, they were accursed for not upholding, or causing the law to stand.

By the same token Paul argues that in emphasizing faith, as he does in Romans 3:21–30, he is fulfilling Deuteronomy 27:26 in that he is causing the law to stand. In Romans 3:31 he says, "Do we then overthrow the law by this faith? By no means! On the contrary, we uphold the law." Paul uses language here that is strikingly similar to Deuteronomy 27:26, which Paul uses in Galatians 3:10 to prove that those relying on "works of the law" are under a curse, and not in line for the blessings of God, which are dispensed only to those who believe. Along this line of interpretation, the "law of faith" in Romans 3:27 would refer to the Mosaic law as it was intended to be understood.

Consequently, data from before Galatians 3:10, as well as from that verse itself, provide a strong basis for the conclusion that by "works of the law" Paul meant a usage of the law that destroyed its very foundations, and that all those guilty of such works were under the curse of Deuteronomy 27:15–26. In light of this conclusion, Calvin can no longer say that Galatians 3:10–12 is, along with Romans 10:5–8, a passage which "most clearly" affirms an antithesis between the conditional promises of the law and the supposedly unconditional ones of the gospel. To the contrary, Galatians 3:10–12 affirms that the law and the gospel are one and the same, and the antithesis stated in Galatians 3:12 represents the Jewish *mis*interpretation of the law. We also conclude that the two passages (Galatians 3:10–12 and Romans 10:5–8) indicate that all God's soteric promises are fulfilled on the basis of satisfying the condition which the Scripture calls "the obedience of faith" (Rom. 1:5; 16:26).[50a] Therefore all talk of distinguishing between conditional "law" promises and unconditional "gospel" promises will have to cease. We will have to modify Calvin's most fundamental statement of this in *Institutes* III, 2, 29:

[50a]See below, pp. 113 to 120, for a detailed exposition of the nature of this obedience.

faith properly begins with the promises, rests in it, and ends in it. For in God faith seeks life: a life that is not found in commandments or declarations of penalties, but in the promise of mercy, and only in a freely given promise. For a conditional promise that sends us back to our own works does not promise life unless we discern its presence in ourselves. Therefore, if we would not have our faith tremble and waver, we must buttress it with the promise of salvation, which is willingly and freely offered to us by the Lord in consideration of our misery rather than our deserts.

A radical revision will also have to be made of the statement by the early Lutheran theologian, Johann Gerhard (1582–1637):

> We hold that the Law differs from the Gospel ... as regards the promises. Those of the Law are conditioned, for they stipulate perfect obedience and demand perfect obedience as the condition of their realization. ... Lev. 18:5: "Ye shall therefore keep My statutes and My judgments; which if a man do, he shall live in them." But the promises of the Gospel are gratuitous and are offered as gifts. ... Accordingly the Gospel is called the word of God's grace. ...[51]

We would also have to disagree seriously with the *New Scofield Bible*'s note on Exodus 19:5, where Israel promises to keep the law (p. 95):

> To Abraham the promise preceded the requirement; at Sinai the requirement preceded the promise. In the New Covenant the Abrahamic order is followed. ... The Christian is not under the conditional Mosaic Covenant of works, the law, but under the unconditional New Covenant of grace.

Neither could the note on Romans 10:4 remain in the *Ryrie Study Bible* if our exegesis of the immediate context of this verse and of Galatians 3:10–12 is correct. In the note on Romans 10:4 Ryrie says, "Christ is the termination of the law. It could not provide righteousness based on merit, but Christ provides righteousness based on God's grace in response to faith" (RSB 1716). But would the holy God, who is not "served by human hands, as

---

[51]Quoted by C. F. W. Walther, *The Proper Distinction between Law and Gospel,* translated from the German edition of 1897 by W. H. T. Dau (St. Louis: Concordia Publishing House, 1928), p. 271. He cites this quotation as coming from Johann Gerhard's *Locus de Evangelio*, Art. 26.

though he needed anything" (Acts 17:25), ever teach in *his* Word how men could *merit* his blessing?

The conclusion, then, is that instead of two sets of promises in the Bible—conditional and unconditional—there is only one kind of promise throughout Scripture, and the realization of its promises[52] is dependent upon compliance with conditions which are well characterized as "the obedience of faith" (Rom. 1:5; 16:26). But three questions arise in response to this conclusion: (1) If God's blessings come only through the obedience of faith, how is it possible to maintain the scriptural assertion (e.g., Eph. 2:8–9) that men are saved by grace alone (*sola gratia*)? (2) If men must do certain things in order to carry out the obedience of faith, how can the scriptural emphasis that man is saved by faith, apart from works, be maintained (*sola fide*)? (3) How is it possible for God to receive all the glory and credit for man's salvation (*sola gloria*) (I Cor. 1:29, 31), if men must comply with the conditions of the obedience of faith to be saved? In concluding this chapter we shall attempt to answer each of these questions.

II. The Obedience of Faith

Romans 4:3–5 is perhaps the best passage to help us understand how the obedience of faith does not compromise but supports *sola gratia, sola fide,* and *sola gloria.* Romans 4:3 reiterates Genesis 15:6, which says "Abraham believed God, and it was reckoned to him for righteousness." The next two verses constitute Paul's interpretation of that Genesis passage. Romans 4:4—"to one who works, his wages are not reckoned as a gift but as his due"—echoes the Jewish interpretation that Abraham, by believing God and doing many other righteous works, had earned God's blessing in much the same way as a workman obligates an em-

---

[52]We acknowledge that the Noahic Covenant of Genesis 8:15—9:17 and the Davidic Covenant of II Samuel 7:11–16 consist of promises of what God will do with no condition attached to them. It would seem that one reason no conditions are stipulated for the Noahic Covenant is that this is the only nonredemptive covenant in Scripture. It merely insures, as it were, the stability of the stage on which the drama of redemption is to be played out. No conditions are attached to the Davidic Covenant since it is so tied up with the work of redemption effected by David's greater Son, the Lord Jesus Christ.

ployer to pay him for services he has rendered.[53] Paul, however, did not conceive of Abraham in this way. This becomes clear from verse 5 whose wording, "And to him who works not ... ," places it in contrast to verse 4. We then note that verse 5 also refers to Abraham in that it speaks of one who, although a sinner, trusts God's promises and is consequently counted as righteous.

But if verse 5 is intended as a contrast to verse 4, what role do Abraham and others like him play if they are antithetical to the workman of verse 4? An obvious answer is that those like Abraham are the ones for whom work is done, such as clients, employers, customers, and patients, and *God* is the Workman who provides Abraham with some much needed service. To be sure, this is a surprising conclusion since we often think of the workman as inferior to the employer. But when we recall how an employer, a client, a customer, or a patient can be very dependent upon someone who provides him with an essential service, we begin to understand that the workman is, in fact, superior. Thus, regarding God as the Workman whose clients depend upon his mercy does not belittle him.

In order to understand how the obedience of faith regards salvation as all of grace, does not mix works with grace, and gives all glory to God, it is necessary to analyze the workman's motivation for providing a service to a client or customer, as well as the customer's motivation for receiving the full benefit from the workman.

One obvious reason why workmen ply their trade is to earn a livelihood. In a book entitled *Working,* fifty people in various vocations reported on what they liked and/or disliked about their jobs. Wages were very important. A supermarket checker said:

> the pay is terrific. I automatically get a raise because of the union. Retail Clerks. Right now I'm ready for retirement as far as the union goes. I have enough years. I'm as high up as I can go. I make $189 gross pay. When I retire I'll make close to five hundred dollars a month. This is because of the union ... full benefits. ... The young kids don't stop and think what good the union's done. (p. 377)[54]

[53]See Strack-Billerbeck, *Kommentar,* III, 186–202, which sets forth all the basic Jewish affirmations regarding Abraham in the early centuries of the Christian era.

[54]Studs Terkel, *Working* (New York: Avon Books, 1972). Copyright by Pantheon Books, a division of Random House, Inc. Permission to use this quotation and the five more that follow kindly granted by the publisher.

But this checker did not want to stop working and live off her pension, because the satisfaction in doing her job transcended the satisfaction of earning money. "When I'm on vacation, I can't wait to go, but two or three days away, I start to get fidgety. I can't stand around and do nothin'. I have to be busy at all times. I look forward to comin' to work. It's a great feelin'. I enjoy it somethin' terrible" (p. 380).

The expertise with which she could do her job helped this supermarket checker to enjoy her work. "I know the price of every [item]. ... On the register is a list of prices, that's for the part-time girls. I never look at it" (p. 375). She also enjoyed being regarded as trustworthy: "I catch [mistakes] right then and there. I tell my customers, 'I overcharged you two pennies on this. I will take it off your next item.' So my customers don't watch me when I ring up. They *trust* me [italics added]" (p. 378). Giving each customer the fullest service also gave her satisfaction:

> What irritates me is when customers get very cocky with me. "Hurry up," or "Cash my check quick." I don't think this is right. You wait your time and I'll give you *my full and undivided attention* [italics added]. You rush [me] and you're gonna get nothin'. (p. 378)

From the tape recordings of people in many vocations, the author concluded that "satisfaction" from work involved "a meaning ... well over and beyond the reward of a paycheck" (p. xiv). The workman's ultimate satisfaction is in the joy of using a skill which meets some need in other people's lives and in being trusted and honored for meeting that need. In other words, *grace* is the basic impulse for all that a workman does. In the Greek the word for "grace" (*charis*) is closely allied with the verb for "joy" (*chairō*).[55]

The Bible clearly teaches (e.g., Eph. 2:8–9; Tit. 2:11) that grace is what motivates God to work for the salvation of men. In theological circles grace is customarily defined as doing someone a favor he does not deserve. Ryrie, for example, declares that grace is "the unmerited favor of God and is the basis of our salvation, justification, election, faith, and spiritual gifts ..." (RSB 1600).

---

[55]In TDNT the Greek words for "joy" and "grace" are discussed in the same article.

The problem with such a definition, however, is that it speaks only of the unworthiness of the recipient, and says nothing about the distinct nature of the motive that impels the gracious act. In Webster's *Dictionary of Synonyms* (1942) grace is defined, as it should be, by focusing attention on the motive of the doer and showing what is distinctive about a gracious motive in distinction from other motives. It says, "Grace ... implies a benignant attitude toward those who are dependent on one and a disposition to bestow favors or to make concessions to them."

We argue that grace motivated the supermarket checker to stay with her job and serve her customers as she did, and that her example provides an analogy for why God seeks to bring salvation to men. As the checker continued her job because of the joy it gave her to be appreciated for the skill with which she could meet a certain need in people's lives, so God wants the joy of being appreciated by human beings as he works to fulfill their deepest needs.

If we remain with the theological definition of grace which says nothing about God's motive for showing grace and stresses only that grace is the recipient's enjoyment of unmerited favor, then it is virtually impossible to understand the several passages in Scripture which clearly indicate that the enjoyment of God's gracious benefits depends on meeting certain conditions. But when the definition of grace focuses primarily on a motive that impels God to act, then one can make sense out of the passages which imply that grace is conditional. II Corinthians 6:1 then becomes understandable: "We entreat you not to accept the grace of God in vain." So do James 4:6 and I Peter 5:5, which declare that "God opposes the proud but gives grace to the humble." According to Acts 13:43, "Paul and Barnabas ... urged [certain people] to continue in the grace of God," and in Galatians 5:4 Paul warned the Galatian churches that if they continued to follow the false teaching of the Judaizers, "you have fallen away from grace." All these verses imply the possibility of missing the blessings of God's grace if the would-be beneficiary has the improper attitude.[56]

Certainly the customers whom the checker served could act

---

[56]In his comment on Galatians 5:4, even Ryrie concurs that if people choose legalism as their way of life, they will no longer enjoy the grace of God.

in such a manner that she would not feel like adding up their bills or cashing their checks. She declared, "You rush [me] and you're gonna get nothin'." Likewise, unless people come to God with an attitude of humility in which they believe that he will do his best for them as they patiently yield to his way of conducting their lives, they will not experience his grace in bringing them many blessings.

From this it becomes evident how the emphasis that salvation is by grace alone (*sola gratia*) is easily compatible with the promises of the Bible, which, with the exception of the Noahic and Davidic covenants, are conditional. Nevertheless, in stressing that salvation is by grace alone, we want to honor the negation implied in Ephesians 2:8–9, "For by grace you have been saved by faith; and this is not your own doing, it is the gift of God—⁹not because of works, lest any man should boast." People have sometimes concluded from the clause, "and *this* is not your doing," that the antecedent of the pronoun "this" is the preceding word "faith." They then argue that salvation is so exclusively a work of grace that we are not even responsible for exercising the faith by which we are saved but must rather wait for God to work in us. But such an understanding of Ephesians 2:8–9 clashes with the fact that the pronoun "this" is neuter, whereas the preceding "faith" is feminine in the Greek. It is better to understand "this" as defined by "gift of God" found in the next clause of verse 8. Thus, Ephesians 2:8–9 affirms that people must ever remain customers, the beneficiaries of the Workman who supplies them with needs which they cannot meet by their own efforts. In the concept of *sola gratia* ("by grace alone"), neither in justification nor in working out their salvation (sanctification) do people ever reverse roles with God and regard themselves as workmen who are supplying God with some need. In our emphasis on *sola gratia,* it is imperative that we stress the need for men to have the proper attitude toward the Workman so that they can fully benefit from his desire (grace!) to impart blessings.

In what sense, then, are works to be excluded from that attitude which is indispensable for receiving God's grace? Depending on the context, the word "works" in Paul's vocabulary means either (1) those actions such as a workman like the supermarket checker would perform, or (2) the things done by a client, cus-

tomer, patient, or employer in order to benefit fully from the
expertise of a workman. According to Paul, men should never
think of themselves as doing the first kind of works for God.
Neither in his decision to become a Christian nor in his subsequent walk as a follower of Christ should a man think of himself
as working for God in the sense of supplying God with some
need, so that God should be obligated and grateful to man. Ephesians 2:8–9, Romans 3:27, Romans 9:32, and Galatians 3:5 are
examples of this first use of works. An examination of these passages makes it clear that Paul forbids a man to perform such
works for God, for he is not "served by men's hands as though he
needed anything" (Acts 17:25).

But in other contexts Paul uses the word "works" in an entirely
different sense. Twice in his epistles he speaks of a "work of faith"
(I Thess. 1:3; II Thess. 1:11). He also speaks of how "faith expresses itself in love" (Gal. 5:6—a literal rendering), and of how
people need "to walk in the steps of the faith of Abraham" (Rom.
4:12—again a literal rendering). Paul opened and closed his epistle to the Romans by summing up his apostolic task as that of
bringing about "the obedience of faith ... among all nations"
(Rom. 1:5; 16:26). This is the sort of work in which the beneficiary of a workman engages in order to realize the greatest possible benefits from that workman. For those being served by the
supermarket checker, it means being patient and honoring her as
doing her best to service her customers. For those being served
by a physician it means being confident and adhering to the cure
and the health regimen prescribed by the physician.

For those who would be served by God (who unlike all the
other "gods" "works for those who wait for him"—Isa. 64:4), the
works of faith involve doing all that is commanded in Scripture.
That is why the Mosaic law is a "law of faith" (Rom. 3:27; cf. 9:31f.).[57]
The rest of God's scriptural commands are of the same sort, for it is
unthinkable that he would command men in his own verbally-
inspired book to commit the greatest sin, which in his eyes consists
of trying to merit his favor.

It is a terrible thing, then, when Calvin says, "So ought we to
recognize that God's benevolence has been set forth for us in the

[57]Supra, pp. 76–80.

law, if we could merit [*demereo* in the Latin, meaning "earn thoroughly"] it by works ..." (*Inst.* III, 17, 2). It is inconceivable that God would ever speak, in his Word, with the irony necessary to command men to produce works having enough worth to merit his applause. If this were so, then not only in Exodus through Deuteronomy but throughout Scripture whenever there is a condition attached to a promise, God would be speaking as though he condoned that action in which men's sin reaches its apex, namely, to think that they, as workmen, are rendering valuable service for God, who is regarded as a client.

In every other religion of the world, people are urged to be like the Pharisee in the temple, who recounts a great list of accomplishments which, in his perception, constitute service rendered to a needy god. It is no wonder that God says that a proliferation of such works makes him "weary" (Isa. 1:14). See also Psalm 50:7–13, where God declares his displeasure with the works in which men boast, and then compare verses 14–15, where he, regarded as the Workman who stands ready to serve, asks only that men (1) be thankful, (2) honor him by keeping their promises, and (3) call upon him for deliverance in the day of trouble.

Indeed, it is only fitting for a workman to take pride in the expertise by which he does his work. But the "work" that a person does to gain optimal benefit from what a workman is doing for him—this "work of faith" entails no pride, but only an acknowledgement of how greatly the client needs the services administered to him and how grateful he is for them. The work done by a client is a work *of faith* because it entails a confidence that the workman has the resources and the expertise to meet the need of the client.

Throughout the Bible God has given men the superlative promise that he will be their God. This promise appears as early as Genesis 17:8 and as late as Revelation 21:7. In the promise, "I will be your God," language conventions are used which signify that in some real way God becomes man's possession. Such a promise means that just as all there is about a car is for the benefit of its owner—its wheels, tires, accelerator, and so on—so likewise all that God is as God, he is for the benefit of those who trust him for what he is able to do for them. In Jeremiah 32:38 God promises, "I will be their God," and then explaining what this means in verses 40–41, he declares, "I will not turn away from doing good to them. . . . I will rejoice in doing them good . . . with all my heart and all my soul." This means that God wants so much to do good to those who trust him that he will use all his power and wisdom for their benefit.

Every command in the Bible should be understood as specifying an obedience which is inspired from knowing that God has promised to be one's God. Surely one would not use God's name in a flippant manner (commandment #3, Exod. 20:7) when in his own heart he is convinced that the happiness of his whole future depends on God's being the God that is signified by his name. A man whose hope is banked on God's promise that all that he is as God, he will be for that man, will not feel he must resort to theft (commandment #8, Exod. 20:15) in order to attain a happy future, for surely such a God will supply all his needs. Neither will such a man be covetous or jealous of what others have (commandment #10, Exod. 20:17), for if all that God is, as God, he will be to him, then that person will be content with God's promise, "I will never fail you nor forsake you" (Heb. 13:5).

Faith, then, is basically a confidence directed toward a future in which God will do and be all that he has promised in the Bible. To be sure, such faith is impossible without the confidence that God has forgiven our sins (Rom. 3:24) and will not withhold his promises from us because of them. Nothing gives us more assurance in the forgiveness of sins than our knowledge that Christ's death and shed blood assuaged God's wrath against us for refusing to believe his promises. One of God's promises is that he will give everyone his just deserts at the proper time. He has promised, "Vengeance is mine, I will repay" (Rom. 12:19). On the basis of such a promise God therefore commands, "You shall not take vengeance or bear any grudge against the sons of your own people, but you shall love your neighbor as yourself" (Lev. 19:18). Harboring a grudge against another person and hoping for vengeance is the same as saying that God's promise in Romans 12:19 to avenge all evil is a lie. It is no wonder, then, that Jesus said in Matthew 18:35, "So also my heavenly Father will do to every one of you if you do not forgive your brother from your heart." The reason God will not forgive such people is that an unforgiving heart is an unbelieving heart. Far from being works in which men boast, forgiving another is, in the Scriptural framework, a "work of faith."

When one understands what a "work of faith" is, he ceases to be troubled by those Bible passages which stress the works one must do in order to be saved, or more fully blessed, while others speak only of believing. Matthew 18:35 makes God's forgiveness dependent on a person's willingness to forgive his neighbor, while the gospel of John often speaks of the need to "believe" on Jesus in order to be saved (e.g., John 3:16; 5:24, etc.). Nevertheless John also says that a man will be saved or lost depending on whether or not he has done good or bad (John 5:28–29). But what is an apparent contradiction between Matthew and John and even between passages in John itself vanishes when one understands that a "work of faith" or the "obedience of faith" presupposes an inseparable connection between faith and resulting works. Since the connection is *inseparable*, and genuine faith cannot but produce works, the Bible sometimes speaks of faith and sometimes of works when it speaks of the condition to be met in receiving the forgiveness of sins or subsequent blessings from God. So there is no need for establishing an elaborate division in Scripture as is done in covenant theology and dispensationalism.

Legalism, then, is no longer defined, as it has been in these two systems, as doing things "in order to . . ." gain a blessing from God. We have seen how present-day dispensationalism and covenant theology urge forgiveness of one's neighbor on the basis of blessings already received from Christ, rather than "in order to" be saved or blessed.[58] But we propose that a legalist, or one caught up in a modern form of the Galatian heresy, is a person who presumes that because of some distinctive he has acquired, he is able to render needful service to God and his fellow man. We avoid legalism and Galatianism by renouncing any claim to have resources which would be useful for others or for God. Instead of resting in what we are or have, our whole energy is directed toward discerning what we must do *in order to* "continue in God's kindness" (Rom. 11:22) and "keep ourselves in the love of God" (Jude 21). According to Galatians 2:20 we are to

[58]Supra, pp. 55–58.

live out our Christian lives *only* by a confidence in the Son of God that is strengthened by recalling how he loved us and gave himself up for us. By remembering what Jesus did for us in going to the cross, we can be confident that he will daily provide the necessary resources and guidance for our hearts to be ruled with his peace, and for us to be a blessing to others.

This is what it means to live by faith, and such confidence in God's all-sufficiency is the only thing we can ever do that pleases him. "Without faith it is impossible to please God" (Heb. 11:6). "[God's] delight is not in the strength of the horse, nor his pleasure in the legs of a man; but the Lord takes pleasure in those who fear him, in those who hope in his steadfast love" (Psa. 147:10–11). But as we have pointed out, true faith must soon do certain concrete things, so in the course of trusting God and in order to remain in his kindness, we must do all the works of love and obey the commandments of the Bible (cf. I Cor. 7:19–20 and Gal. 5:6).

In Galatians 2:20, Paul is talking about how the Christian life is continued, that is, about the process of sanctification. Thus this verse would have only an incidental implication for justification, that is, for how a person initially becomes converted. When Paul goes on to say in Galatians 2:21, "I do not nullify the grace of God; for if justification [literally, "righteousness"] were through the law, then Christ died to no purpose," he means that the righteousness about which he speaks is an actual living out of good deeds and is not the imputed righteousness received in justification. An investigation of the word "law" in the immediately preceding context of verse 21 shows that the law to which Paul died in verse 19 represented "legalism" rather than the "Mosaic law." So from Galatians 2:20 we learn that sanctification is by faith alone and not other sources. We scorn the cross of Christ if we make living the Christian life a matter of works that are not impelled simply by faith. The basic problem Paul was addressing in Galatians was sanctification and not justification or how to be saved.

Galatians 3:2–3 also supports this interpretation. Paul argues, "Let me ask you only this: Did you receive the Spirit by works of the law, or by hearing with faith? Are you so foolish? Having begun with the Spirit [and faith], are you now ending [i.e., improving your Christian life] by the flesh [in taking up the Jewish distinctives]?" This passage leaves no doubt that the problem at Galatia was sanctification, rather than justification. Galatianism, therefore, is a faulty view of sanctification.

The Judaizers at Galatia were telling the Christians that they must submit to certain Jewish distinctives such as circumcision and dietary regulations. There was no dispute about whether or not the Galatians had commenced the Christian life properly; the whole issue had to do with sanctification, as to how one progresses in the Christian life. Paul's emphasis is that one makes progress in the Christian life simply by the faith with which he commenced it. In Galatians 3:5 he says, "Does he who supplies the Spirit to you and works miracles among you do so by the works of the law, or by the hearing of faith?" The obvious answer to this question is that faith alone is the way by which the Christian life is to proceed. As one became a Christian by submitting himself to the care of the Workman, so one learns to live like Jesus and receive a continuous stream of blessings from him simply by faith, that is, by an obedience which keeps him in the place where he can always benefit from the Workman's skill. Any thought that the ongoing Christian life consists of doing things for God is Galatianism—the error in the early Church that made Paul angrier than any other, including the incest at Corinth.

Galatians 5:6 provides another argument to support the conclusion that sanctification, like justification, is by faith alone. There Paul says, "For in Christ Jesus neither circumcision nor uncircumcision is of any avail, but faith working through love [avails everything]." According to Paul, a faith which banks its hope on the promises of God can never be devoid of the works of love, and therefore faith is all that is needed for carrying on the Christian life.

Any teaching that implies that good works are done alongside of and coordinately with faith, instead of as the result of faith, is Galatianism.

NOTE. In its understanding of sanctification, present-day dispensationalism has made statements that open it to the charge of being a modern form of the Galatian heresy. I Corinthians 3:14 says, "If the work which any man has built on the foundation survives, he will receive a reward." In commenting on this basic scriptural affirmation concerning the rewards Christians will receive at the future judgment, the *New Scofield Reference Bible* says, "God, in the N.T. Scriptures, offers to the lost, salvation; and for the faithful service of the saved, He offers rewards. The passages [some teaching salvation and others rewards] are easily distinguished by remembering that salvation is invariably spoken of as a free gift ... whereas rewards are earned [!] by works" (NSB 1235). Commenting on this same passage, the *Ryrie Study Bible* says, "Salvation is a free gift, but rewards, for those who are saved, are earned" (RSB 1730).

Such statements unmistakably place sanctification on a different basis from justification. Whereas salvation, that is, justification, is for the dispensationalist by faith alone, the process of sanctification, in which good works are produced, cannot be by faith alone, since the good works which bring rewards at the judgment seat of Christ are earned. Therefore in dispensationalism, *sola fide* cannot apply for sanctification as it does for justification. Apparently, those who supplement their faith with human initiative and thus produce good works are those who will receive a reward, in distinction from those who are content simply to live justified by faith. But Galatians 2:20; 3:2–3, 5; and 5:6 make it clear that all the good that one does during his Christian sojourn on earth comes through faith alone. Paul would be as angry with modern dispensationalism (and also covenant theology) as he was with the Galatian churches, who were at fault for wanting to add works to their faith. The verses we have cited in Galatians prove that faith alone produces good works.[59]

Calvin is liable to the same charge as modern dispensationalism. He taught that

> even though [believers] have ... been so moved and quickened through the directing of the Spirit that they long to obey God, they still profit by the law. ... However eagerly they may in accordance with the Spirit strive toward God's righteousness, the listless flesh always so burdens them that they do not proceed with due readiness. The law is to the flesh like a whip to an idle and balky ass, to arouse it to work. (*Inst.* II, 7, 12)

---

[59]The Scriptures clearly teach that God rewards the good works of believers. But the Scriptures are equally clear that God *alone* will receive all the glory in the world to come. In Psalm 46:10 God commands, "Be still, and know that I am God. I am exalted among the nations, I am exalted in the earth!" Likewise according to Isaiah 2:11 and 17, "The Lord alone will be exalted in that day." How can Christians receive varying degrees of rewards at the judgment without getting any glory, so that the Lord *alone* will be exalted in that day? There

We remember that for Calvin the law, in distinction from the gospel, has conditional promises which are conducive to works but not at all to faith (*Inst.* III, 2, 29).

Therefore to the extent that one uses the law—understood as what a workman does for an employer—to aid in sanctification, he is submitting to that which is contrary to faith. Consequently Calvin could never predicate *sola fide* to sanctification as well as to justification, and thus he is guilty of the Galatian heresy.

END OF NOTE

An analogy for understanding how to live the Christian life without being a legalist is to think of ourselves as being sick and needing a doctor's help in order to get well. Men begin life with a disposition so inclined to evil that Jesus called them "children of hell" (Matt. 23:15). Isaiah 1:5–6 also used strong language in describing the sinfulness of men. "The whole head is sick, and the whole heart faint. From the sole of the foot even to the head there is no soundness in it, but bruises and sores and bleeding wounds; they are not pressed out, or bound up, or softened with oil." In Mark 2:17 and elsewhere Jesus likened himself to a doctor with the task of healing man's sins; he received the name "Jesus" because it was his mission to "save his people from their sins" (Matt. 1:21). The moment we turn from loving things in this world to bank our hope on God and his promises summed up in Jesus Christ, Jesus takes us, as it were, into his clinic to heal us of our hellish dispositions. This first act of faith certainly involves confidence that Christ's death and shed blood (Rom. 3:24) is more than adequate for placating God's wrath against us for all our sins. True faith means not only being confident that one's sins are

---

would be no way to reconcile this apparent contradiction if Christians "earn" greater rewards by working more diligently or wisely for God. But if we follow the teaching of Galatians 2:20; 3:2–3, 5; and 5:6, *all* our works will result simply from trusting in God's promises and keeping ourselves in the center of his will where we can continue to enjoy the fullness of his blessings. Confidence in the faithfulness of God to keep his promises will then be the mainspring that will initiate all our actions. But actions originating in this way can only give glory to God. So the rewards that he gives in heaven will show the precise value of each of our works in the extent to which they gave glory to him. Nowhere in the Bible is there any mention of *earning* a reward.

forgiven but also means believing God's promises that we will
have a happy future through eternity. Or, to revert to the meta-
phor of medicine and the clinic, we must entrust our sick selves
to Christ as the Great Physician, with confidence that he will work
until our hellishness is transformed into godliness. We avoid legalism to the extent that we acknowledge how truly sick we are
and look away from ourselves and, with complete confidence in
the Doctor's expertise and desire to heal us, follow his instructions (the obedience of faith!) *in order to* get well. We should
understand that the entire business of our lives is the convalescence involved in becoming like Christ. Even though progress is
made we must still keep our whole attention focused on the task
of following the guidance of the Great Physician *in order to*
become completely healed. Although Paul had made some progress in becoming godly, nevertheless his policy was that of "for-
getting what lies behind and straining forward to what lies ahead;
I press forward toward the goal for the prize of the upward call
of God in Christ Jesus" (Phil. 3:13–14). The moment one begins
to glory in some advance that he has made and believes that he
possesses some resource which makes him useful to man and
even God, then he is involved in legalism and the Galatian error.

Several implications should be drawn from this "Doctor" analogy. First, it helps to point up the futuristic aspect of faith. We
remain in the Doctor's clinic and carefully follow his instructions
because we are confident of the good that will come to us in the
future. Faith is virtually the same as hope, when hope is defined
as firm confidence that what has been promised will come to
pass. We have already seen how faith, understood as certain hope,
impels people to live in a godly manner.

Another implication that arises from the doctor analogy is that
lapses of faith do not prove disastrous so long as there is a reaf-
firmation of confidence in the Doctor within a reasonable (but
not precisely-defined) time. Everyone knows that an ordinary
doctor will forgive a certain amount of failure by the patient to
follow his health regimen. But it is also common knowledge that
a patient who persistently fails to follow his doctor's instructions
will finally be told that because he lacks confidence in the doctor,
he had better go somewhere else. That is why the Bible emphasizes persevering faith. Paul told the Colossians that God had now

reconciled them through Christ "provided that you continue in the faith, stable and steadfast, not shifting from the hope of the gospel which you heard ..." (Col. 1:23; cf. I Cor. 15:2). Likewise the writer of Hebrews stressed that "we share in Christ, if only we hold our first confidence firm unto the end" (Heb. 3:14). Consequently Paul exhorted his readers to "work out your own salvation with fear and trembling ..." (Phil. 2:12). In Romans 11:19–24 he makes it clear that unbelief is the one thing we are to fear. But it is interesting to consider that as we fear unbelief, we will resort to the Word of God in order to remind ourselves of his many promises. Thus as we take these to heart, we will be filled "with all joy and peace in believing" (Rom. 15:13). So long as we believe, we experience joy rather than fear.

A further implication to be drawn from the doctor analogy is that while he will prescribe certain general instructions for all his patients to follow, he will also make up individual health regimens for the particular needs of each patient. For example, he may direct some to leave their homeland to go to proclaim the gospel in a foreign land. There is great temptation in such circumstances for people to revert to the legalism of thinking that they are being heroes for God because they are leaving their homeland to endure the rigors of living in a foreign land. Those who are directed to do hard jobs for God must remind themselves that these rigors are simply for their health. As these difficulties help them become more like Christ, they will sing a song of praise unto God, and as a result "many will see it and fear and put their trust in the Lord" (Psa. 40:3). People who regard themselves as invalids rather than heroes will make excellent missionaries.

It should now be clear why the necessity for obedience in no way clashes with *sola gratia* ("by grace alone"), for the Doctor is administering his cure just from the sheer joy he has in extending a blessing to others and in being appreciated for what he does. The Doctor does not bless people because they are the workmen who have rendered some necessary service to him which obligates him to reimburse them with medical care.

It should also be clear why the obedience of faith is *sola fide* ("by faith alone"), for obedience is impelled wholly by faith and is not something added on to faith as though it were coordinate with it. Depending on how one construes the "and" in "Trust and

Obey," he will avoid or become ensnared in the Galatian heresy.

Finally, there should be no difficulty in understanding how the Doctor receives all the glory (*sola gloria*), the credit for the cures that are performed, and for the additional patients that flock to his clinic because of the glowing testimonies of those who have already experienced partial healing. Just as the greatest insult we can say to another is, "I don't trust you," so the greatest compliment we can give to another is, "I trust you." That is why Romans 4:20 ties Abraham's faith so closely to the way in which he glorified God. The "obedience of faith" surely upholds the biblical teaching that God should receive all the credit.

Addendum to footnote 45 on p. 99:

Another plausible way of construing Galatians 3:12 (suggested by two former students, Douglas Knighton and Donald Westblade) is to regard Galatians 3:12's use of the wording of Leviticus 18:5 as declaring what the obedience of faith would consist of, in contrast to the "law" (legalism) of the Pharisees, which as the first half of the verse affirms, "does not rest on faith." The paraphrase of Galatians 3:12 would then be, "The law, understood in the legalistic sense it had in verses 10 and 11, does not rest on faith. But, on the other hand, Leviticus 18:5's declaration that 'He who does these things shall live in them' expresses compliance with the obedience of faith taught in all the Mosaic law." An advantage this construction would have over the one set forth above is that Paul's use of Leviticus 18:5 would, like the other quotes from the Old Testament, be taken at face value and, in particular, would be a positive statement of the negative affirmation of Deuteronomy 27:26 quoted in verse 10.

For an exegetical consideration of the crucial passages regarding Paul's use of the word "law" in Galatians 3:18, see the Appendix (pp. 199ff.).

CHAPTER FIVE
The Abrahamic Covenant

In the preceding chapter we have demonstrated that dispensationalism's basic concern of separating law and grace finds no support in the two Pauline passages which Calvin regarded as proving that there are unconditional promises (in the gospel) in distinction from conditional ones (in the law). Our purpose in the remainder of this book is to consider the cardinal affirmations dispensationalism makes in expounding its system from the Abrahamic Covenant through to the any-moment rapture of the Church from the earth and into the millennial age. We will attempt to show how these affirmations lead dispensationalism into difficulties which, it will be argued, could be avoided if its advocates were willing to acknowledge that all biblical promises (except those in the Noahic and Davidic Covenants) are conditional.

From the name "dispensationalism" one might expect that the starting point for an analysis of this system would be the early dispensations in the first few chapters of Genesis, which record creation, the fall, the Noahic Covenant, and so on. We would surely be justified in expecting this, since dispensationalists claim that *all* the passages in the Bible have an equal right to speak.

Yet dispensationalism barely mentions these chapters. In Chafer's eight-volume *Systematic Theology,* only one-third of one page is devoted to them (ST I, 40–41). J. N. Darby scarcely has more than a dozen lines in his entire writings about God's dispensational dealings with man before Abraham.[1] The only importance that Ryrie finds in his *Dispensationalism Today* for the dispensations prior to Abraham is the rather hypothetical argument that if God

---

[1] J. N. Darby, "The Apostasy of Successive Dispensations," *Collected Writings*, I, 194, and "The Hopes of the Church of God," I, 568–569.

did a new thing in the call of Abraham, after already saving people during at least two millennia and three dispensations, then God would not be acting inconsistently to do a new thing again in calling out the heavenly people, the Church (DT 142–143).

Dispensationalists begin their exposition with Abraham. In a series of articles appearing in 1951–52 which defended dispensationalism against the claims of amillennialism, President Walvoord of Dallas Seminary affirmed that the Abrahamic Covenant "furnishes the key to the entire Old Testament and reaches for its fulfillment in the New. . . . The analysis of its provisions and the character of their fulfillment set the mold for the entire body of Scripture truth."[2] The obvious explanation for why dispensationalism says scarcely anything about the times before Abraham is that its overriding concern is not to set forth the whole of redemptive history as it is, but to keep the Church separate from Israel and from the Galatian error into which the supposedly legal statements of Scripture relating to Israel would lead it.

While writing my thesis on dispensationalism twenty-two years ago, the question rose in my mind that if Israel, beginning with Abraham, were the earthly people, and the Church that came into being two millennia later were the heavenly people, what kind of people were the pre-Abrahamic saints who, according to Hebrews 11:4–7, believed God as did Abraham and the rest of the Old Testament saints (Heb. 11:8–39), and the Christians after Pentecost (Heb. 12:1–2)? Were Abel, Enoch, and Noah God's earthly or heavenly people? Because I was unable to find any answer to this question in dispensational literature, I wrote to President Walvoord of Dallas Seminary requesting his view on this subject. He replied:

> [The question of the place of Gentile saints in the Old Testament] is a point which is usually not discussed, and you are correct that there is very little literature on the subject. I do not recall any place where Dr. Chafer discusses the matter in detail, but I believe it would be fair to state that his point of view is that the church is the heavenly people and that all other saints are earthly people. Scripture revelation

---

[2]John F. Walvoord, "The Abrahamic Covenant and Premillennialism," *Bibliotheca Sacra*, 108 (1951), 414. This essay appears serially as follows: 108 (1951), 414–22; 109 (1951), 37–46; 136–50; 217–25; 293–303. Henceforth citations from this essay will be designated as ACP with the page number.

concerns itself primarily with the place of Israel and the church, and therefore does not deal in detail with the place of Gentile saints in the Old Testament.[3]

A dispensationalist begins a detailed exposition of his system with the promises made to Abraham because that is when the Jewish nation commenced. He pays special attention to the beginning of Israel and makes certain emphases regarding the Abrahamic Covenant which help him to show, later on, that the Church is separate from Israel. The dispensationalist believes that these emphases are nothing more or less than what necessarily results from a strict adherence to a literal, non-analogy-of-faith hermeneutic. Ryrie affirms that "since literal interpretation results in taking the Scriptures at face value, it also results in recognizing distinctions in the Scriptures. ... The extent to which [the interpreter] recognizes distinctions is the evidence of his consistent use of the literal principle of interpretation" (DT 97).

The distinctions which a dispensationalist claims to find through this literal hermeneutic are related to the particular blessings for the two groups in the Abrahamic Covenant and also with the question of whether or not the Abrahamic Covenant is conditional.

I. The Beneficiaries of the Abrahamic Covenant

The dispensationalist argues that a literal interpretation of Genesis 12:1–3 makes it unmistakably clear that in addition to the blessings destined for Abraham and his physical descendants, there are also blessings that will be mediated through Abraham to people from the various Gentile nations of earth. Genesis 12:1–3 says:

[1]Now the Lord said to Abram, "Go from your country and your kindred and your father's house to the land that I will show you. [2]And

[3]Letter from Dr. John F. Walvoord, President, Dallas Theological Seminary, November 5, 1956. His book on *The Millennial Kingdom* (supra, p. 48), published in 1959, concurs with this answer. About the phrase in Hebrews 12:22–23, "We are come to ... the heavenly Jerusalem ... to the spirits of just men made perfect," Walvoord says (p. 326) that this designation "seemingly [refers] to all Old Testament saints." Then he continues, "... while the saints of all ages are included in the New Jerusalem, their separate identity [from the Church] is maintained, that is, Old Testament saints are still classified as such [i.e., the earthly people]." Future citations from this volume will be denoted by MK with the page number.

I will make of you a great nation, and I will bless you, and make your name great, so that you will be a blessing. ³I will bless those who bless you, and him who curses you I will curse; and by you all the families of the earth shall bless themselves."

Concerning this passage Walvoord says:

> the premillennial [i.e., dispensational] interpretation of the Abrahamic Covenant takes its provisions literally. In other words, the promises given to Abraham will be fulfilled by Abraham; the promises to Abraham's seed will be fulfilled by his physical seed; the promises to "all families of the earth," will be fulfilled by Gentiles, or those not of the physical seed. While possession of the land forever is the promise to the physical seed, the promise of blessing is to "all the families of earth." Both are to be fulfilled exactly as promised. (ACP 419)

Farther on in this series of articles Walvoord argues that "nothing should be plainer than that Abraham, Isaac, and Jacob understood the term *seed* as referring to their physical lineage" (ACP 138). All would be well if dispensationalism let a "face value" hermeneutic control the conclusions reached about the "seed of Abraham" and other cardinal matters discussed in the next two chapters. But there is evidence that the theological concern to keep the Church separate from Israel often predominates in reaching the conclusions that are drawn from the crucial passages.

Difficulties in the dispensational understanding of the "seed of Abraham"

The dispensationalist finds nothing in Genesis 12:3 itself or elsewhere in the Old Testament which indicates that the people from all nations who bless themselves in Abraham enjoy a status which would justify their designation as the "seed of Abraham." In fact at one point Walvoord goes so far as to say that the "blessing [of Gen. 12:3] is promised to those *outside* the seed of Abraham" (MK 161; italics added). But Paul forthrightly calls these people the "sons" or the "seed" of Abraham in Galatians 3:7 and 29. After quoting Genesis 15:6, "Abraham believed God, and it was reckoned to him as righteousness" (Gal. 3:6), Paul continues, "You see that it is men of faith who are sons of Abraham. And the scripture, foreseeing that God would justify the Gentiles by faith, preached the gospel beforehand to Abraham, saying, 'In you shall

all the nations be blessed' [Gen. 12:3]" (Gal. 3:7–8). Later on in Galatians, chapter 3, Paul declares that since Christ was a physical descendant of Abraham, therefore all those who are united to him by faith are also "Abraham's offspring" (Gal. 3:29; cf. 3:16). Paul's language in Galatians 3 forces Walvoord to conclude that "there is a spiritual as well as a natural seed of Abraham" (ACP 419). But these people do "not [fulfill] the promises pertaining to Israel. . . . They are Abraham's seed in the spiritual sense only and heirs of the promise given to 'all the families of the earth' " (ACP 421).

In other words the essential concern of dispensationalism is to keep the seed of Abraham, which consists of his physical descendants, separate from the "spiritual" seed which consists of those who are somehow blessed through him. There is nothing, however, in Galatians 3 to indicate that Paul thought of these as sons of Abraham only in a figurative, "spiritual" sense. He called those who were united to Christ through faith the "seed of Abraham" (*tou Abraam sperma*). Because Christ was a physical descendant of Abraham, there would then be every reason to regard those united to him as the seed of Abraham in a physical sense. So if a "face value" hermeneutic were the only concern in interpreting Galatians 3:6–29, there would be no need to designate the people mentioned in Galatians 3:7 and 29 a "spiritual" seed in distinction from a "physical" seed of Abraham. In fact the very language conventions of Galatians 3 require the idea of an ontological or physical relationship to Abraham. But the dispensationalist has the great theological concern of keeping Israel separate from the Church, and *this* requires understanding those mentioned in Genesis 12:3 and Galatians 3:6–29 as the "seed" of Abraham only in such a spiritual, figurative sense that language conventions are all but violated.

Another difficulty in the dispensational understanding of the seed of Abraham arises from the way they interpret Genesis 17:4–8. This passage is parallel to Genesis 12:2–3 in that it also apprises Abraham of how he is going to relate to a multitude of nations. Whereas Genesis 12:3 says that "all the families of the earth shall bless themselves" in Abraham, Genesis 17:4–8 states that Abraham himself will father a *multitude* of nations. Speaking to Abraham God says:

⁴Behold, my covenant is with you, and you shall be the father of
a multitude of nations. ⁵No longer shall your name be Abram, but
your name shall be Abraham; for I have made you the father of a
multitude of nations. ⁶I will make you exceedingly fruitful; and I will
make nations of you, and kings shall come forth from you. ⁷And I will
establish my covenant between me and you and your descendants
[seed] after you throughout their generations for an everlasting covenant, to be God to you and to your descendants [seed] after you.

Dispensationalists do not honor the language convention involved in the word "multitude" and its Hebrew equivalent. According to Walvoord, Abraham's fathering of a multitude of nations
"had a most literal fulfillment in the descendants of Ishmael, Esau,
and the children of Keturah, Abraham's second wife" (MK 147).
And the editors of the *New Scofield Bible* say, "Abraham was ...
promised that he would father other [sic] nations (cf. Gen. 17:6,
20), principally fulfilled through Ishmael and Esau" (NSB 19).
According to Genesis 17:20, Ishmael would found one nation, and
we know that Esau founded the Edomites (Gen. 36:8–9). But
nothing is known about the five sons of Keturah founding five
nations, let alone a "multitude of nations." So the interpreter is
surely on the wrong track in trying to find in Abraham's mere
physical posterity that *multitude* of nations that Abraham was to
sire.

A further difficulty for those adhering to this way of handling
Genesis 17:4–8 comes from what is said immediately after the
promise that Abraham would sire a multitude of nations. In Genesis 17:7–8 God says:

⁷And I will establish my covenant between me and you and your
descendants after you throughout your generations for an everlasting
covenant, to be God to you and to your descendants after you. ⁸And
I will give to you, and to your descendants after you, the land of your
sojournings, all the land of Canaan, for an everlasting possession; and
I will be their God.

Again, a "face value" interpretation of this passage would have to
include the nations that Abraham would sire as part of the descendants who would receive the promise of the land of Canaan
and that God will be their God. To be consistent, the dispensationalist would have to grant that the Arabs and the Edomites are

just as much the beneficiaries of the Abrahamic Covenant as are the Jews. But they could never agree to this.

An additional problem which emerges from the dispensational understanding of the seed of Abraham is that a strict adherence to all that might plausibly be gleaned from the "face value" statements concerning a certain subject matter at one point may clash with further statements about that subject matter in the text. Taken at its face value, the promise to Abraham in Genesis 12:2–3, 7; 13:14–17; and 15:5 applies to all of Abraham's physical descendants. If these were the only passages to be taken into account, then Walvoord's hermeneutical principle that "the promises to the 'seed' must be limited in their application according to the context" (ACP 416) does open the way for him to say that "nothing should be plainer than that Abraham, Isaac, and Jacob understood the term *seed* as referring to their physical lineage" (ACP 138). He then would also have every right to say that "the promises given to Abraham's seed will be fulfilled by his physical seed; [and] the promises to 'all the families of the earth' will be fulfilled by . . . those not of the physical seed" (ACP 419).

But of course Walvoord is aware that in the passage of time God expressly excluded some of Abraham's physical descendants from receiving the promises. Ishmael and the five sons by Keturah did not receive the promise, even though they were of Abraham's physical lineage. Much to his distress, God told him that the covenantal promise would apply only to Isaac (Gen. 17:18–19). Concerning Isaac God said, "I will establish my covenant with him as an everlasting covenant for his descendants after him" (Gen. 17:19). In this context, the "face value" meaning of this statement is that all Isaac's children will be heirs. But when his wife was about to give birth to twins, God expressly took the covenantal blessings from Esau the first-born and gave them to Jacob, the second-born (Gen. 25:23). So Walvoord concedes that "God is not undertaking to fulfill the promise to *all* the physical seed of Abraham, but through *some* of them, chosen as the line of the seed" (ACP 138). Walvoord thinks, however, that with the exclusion of Esau from the blessing, the narrowing-down process is ended, for he affirms that "it is clear that all the twelve tribes [from Jacob], not only Judah, were considered the seed of Abraham and in particular the seed of Israel" (ACP 138). He stresses this same point in *The Millennial Kingdom* on page 161.

But according to Paul and other New Testament spokesmen, this narrowing-down process does not stop with Jacob but continues until the second coming of Christ, when it will in fact cease and "all [ethnic] Israel shall be saved," because at that time the Messiah will "banish ungodliness from Jacob and . . . take away their sins" (Rom. 11:26–27). Then all the ethnic descendants of Jacob alive at that time will enjoy the fulfillment of the promise of the land made to Abraham. But as for the time between Jacob and the second coming, Paul argues from the narrowing-down process in Isaac and Jacob (Rom. 9:7b–13) to the conclusion that until the second coming "not all who are descended from Israel belong to Israel" (Rom. 9:6). According to Romans 11:1–6, only the small remnant who had repented of their sins and put their trust in the Lord enjoyed the blessing of having God as their God (Gen. 17:8). It was for this reason that both John the Baptist (Matt. 3:8–9) and Jesus (John 8:39–44) taunted the Israelites for presuming that they enjoyed God's favor simply because they were descendants of Abraham through Jacob.

Both Ryrie (RSB 1448) and the *New Scofield Bible* (NSB 1137) attempt to explain this denial that the Jews of Jesus' day were the beneficiaries of the Abrahamic Covenant by interpreting the exhortation of John the Baptist and Jesus to consist in a call for all Israelites to become members of what the Old Testament called the "remnant," or what Walvoord calls "spiritual Israel" (ACP 420). But when dispensationalists argue that throughout the Old Testament terms such as "son of Abraham" or "Abraham's seed" refer only to those who are of physical descent from Abraham through Jacob, what justification do they now have for giving an entirely different interpretation to these terms? If the dispensationalist's understanding of the "seed of Abraham" in the Old Testament is correct, then it was nonsensical for John the Baptist and Jesus to exhort Israelites to become Abraham's seed, and they could in no way be held responsible for acceding to such an exhortation.

Despite these difficulties, Walvoord regards all Jews as the physical seed of Abraham, for he is convinced that this is the meaning the term had in the patriarchal narratives and throughout the Old Testament. Dispensationalism could no longer stand if his understanding of the "seed of Abraham" were narrowed down to denote the remnant. For Walvoord, the remnant melted naturally into the Church when the Church came into existence. Along with the believing Gentiles, they became the one body of Christ in which there is neither Jew nor Gentile. Thus if the term "seed of Abraham" in the Old Testament represented only the remnant, it would be impossible for dispensationalism to maintain its all-important distinction between Israel and the Church.

So Walvoord insists that the "seed of Abraham," or similar expressions in the patriarchal narratives, represents Abraham's physical descendants through Jacob. Consequently the content of the promises that were made to this group remains in effect. There is no great difficulty in the idea that from the time of Jacob onward his progeny would become very numerous. And surely there is no problem in understanding that ethnic Israel will some day inhabit the land that God marked out for Abraham's descendants. But in the dispensational understanding of things, this group as a whole also enjoys the promise of Genesis 17:7–8 that God will be their God. While the promise of a numerous seed can be regarded as fulfilled, and the promise of the land can await its fulfillment at some future time, God's promise to be their God has to be fulfilled all along. Thus concerning this promise in Genesis 17:7–8 Walvoord says, "Those in the covenant [the physical descendants of Jacob] are promised that God will be their God in the *general* and *providential* sense" (MK 142; italics added).

This greatest of all promises is found throughout Scripture, from Genesis 17:7–8 to Revelation 21:7. But every appearance of it in the Old Testament, apart from its first mention in Genesis 17, sees its fulfillment as coinciding with Israel's repentance and regeneration. In Jeremiah 24:7, for example, God says, "I will give them [Israel] a heart to know that I am the Lord, and they shall be my people and I will be their God." The same linkage between regeneration and this promise is found in Jeremiah 30:22; 31:33; 32:38; Ezekiel 37:26–27; and Zechariah 8:8. After Genesis 17:7–8, the next appearance of the promise is in Leviticus 26:12. Here too it appears within the context of Israel's regeneration, for Leviticus 26:41 speaks of the promise as being fulfilled when Israel's "uncircumcised heart is humbled and they make amends for their iniquity." Therefore when Walvoord takes the first mention of this promise and regards it as applying only "in the general and providential sense," it is obvious that he does so to keep a system of theology intact, even at the expense of misinterpreting the promise in Genesis 17. We believe there is another way of handling the biblical data on the seed of Abraham which avoids these difficulties without resorting to an analogy-of-faith hermeneutic.

Another approach to the "seed of Abraham"

On the basis of a "face-value" hermeneutic in all of God's statements through Genesis 15, we conclude that Abraham was apprised that his physical descendants would become very numerous and that they would eventually occupy the land which God had marked off for Abraham. But when Abraham heard God's further statement about the covenant in Genesis 17:4–8, he must have realized that what he had been previously told had been only an introduction. After initially informing Abraham (Gen. 12:3) that by him "all the families of the earth shall bless themselves," God was now greatly complicating the picture by changing Abram's name to Abraham because Abraham was going to be "the father of a multitude of nations." How was Abraham to fit this all together? "All the nations of the earth" who would bless themselves through Abraham and the "multitude of nations" whom Abraham fathered, would be virtually the same group. The "multitude of nations" would have to include the vast majority of the world's ethnic entities already in existence. How then was Abraham to father them all?

God then instituted the rite of circumcision, and instead of limiting it to Abraham's offspring, as Abraham might well have expected, God said, "Every male throughout your generations, whether born in your house or bought with your money from any foreigner who is not of your offspring . . . shall be circumcised. So shall my covenant be in your flesh an everlasting covenant" (Gen. 17:12–13). This had to mean that even the lowliest servant in Abraham's household was somehow related to the covenant that God had promised to make with his seed, even though such a servant was no blood relation to Abraham. Such words certainly implied the possibility that being of the seed of Abraham was not simply a matter of blood relationship. This provided a hint as to how Abraham might succeed in fathering a multitude of nations.

Later on in chapter 17 still another message from God forced Abraham to question the precise nature of his descendants. When Ishmael was born Abraham thought that God's promises for his posterity would be fulfilled in Ishmael's progeny. He soon realized, however, that this was not to be. God declared that through Abraham's son born by Sarah, she would become "a mother of nations; kings of peoples shall come from her" (Gen. 17:16). Abraham earnestly requested God to fulfill the promises through Ishmael, but God replied, "No, but Sarah your wife shall bear you a son, and you shall call his name Isaac. I will establish my covenant with him as an everlasting covenant for his descendants after him" (Gen. 17:18–19). Initially, Abraham had thought that all his offspring would receive the promised blessings, and that from their posterity would come the great multitude that he was to sire. Now, however, he realized that his first-born, Ishmael, as well as Ishmael's offspring would no longer figure in the fulfillment of the great promises God had given to him. The numerous posterity would stem only from Isaac and his offspring. Abraham surely thought that all of Isaac's offspring would be included in the promises.

Abraham no doubt went to his grave sharing Isaac's conviction that his offspring would be included in the promises. But God told Isaac's pregnant wife, Rebekah: "Two nations are in your womb, and two peoples, born of you, shall be divided; ... the elder shall serve the younger" (Gen. 25:23). As things turned out Rebekah gave birth to twins, Esau and Jacob. Although he was born after Esau, Jacob received the patriarchal blessing, and the resultant enmity between the two brothers ruled out any thought of both helping to sire a single but very populous nation. So Isaac, like his father Abraham, learned that only one of his children would receive the blessings promised to his father and him.

Jacob had twelve sons, from whom sprang the twelve tribes that comprised the nation of Israel. Dispensationalism believes that at this point the narrowing-down process ended, because each of Jacob's sons sired a tribe, the sum total of which made up the nation of Israel. But Paul drew a different conclusion from the winnowing process that excluded Ishmael and Esau from the promises made to Abraham and Isaac. In Romans 9:6 he affirmed that "not all who are descended from Israel [Jacob] belong to Israel." In support of this statement Paul then proceeded in verses 7–9 to speak of how Ishmael had been excluded in favor of Isaac, and in verses 10–13 of how Esau had been passed over in favor of Jacob. Paul argues that being Abraham's seed depends primarily on being one whom God calls through his word and his promise. Regarding Ishmael's exclusion he said, "This means that it is not the children of the flesh who are the children of God, but the children of promise are reckoned as descendants" (Rom. 9:8). Then with regard to Esau's exclusion he declared that it came to pass "in order that God's purpose of election might continue, not because of works but because of his call" (Rom. 9:11).

In that the establishment of those who first became the seed of Abraham always occurred through a specific intervention from God, Paul was convinced that a precedent was set that was to continue on through redemptive history. Later on in the same chapter he cited statements from Isaiah as proof for this conclusion: "Though the number of the sons of Israel be as the sand of the sea, only a remnant of them shall be saved [Isa. 10:21]" (Rom. 9:27), and also, "If the Lord of hosts had not left us children [literally, "a seed"], we would have fared like Sodom and been made like Gomorrah [Isa. 1:9]" (Rom. 9:29). In between these two statements Paul again emphasized the importance of God's intervention and the fulfillment of his word. According to Isaiah 10:22, "The Lord will execute his sentence [literally, "word"] with rigor and dispatch" (Rom. 9:28).

Such a conclusion would cohere well with the statements of John the Baptist and Jesus which said that the Jews were not the seed of Abraham simply because they could trace their descent back to Jacob. It would also show why both John and Jesus declared that the Jews must respond to the word of God in repentance and faith before they could enjoy the blessings promised to Abraham. Then too, if the response to the word of God was essential for being the seed of Abraham from the time of Isaac onward, there would be no need to regard God as the God of these people only in "the general and providential" sense. As in every other instance in the Old Testament, God would be the God only of a person who was regenerated, and thus the promise of Genesis 17:7–8 would be soteriological as it is elsewhere in the Old Testament.

Paul's emphasis that the word of God must intervene in order for people to become the seed of Abraham becomes most explicit in his stress in Galatians, chapter 3, that people become the physical seed of Abraham by virtue of union with Christ, who was a physical descendant of Abraham. Since union with Christ came by the response of faith to the word of God and by the indwelling of the Holy Spirit, members from any and all nations of earth could become bona fide descendants of Abraham. In talking about the seed of Abraham in Galatians 3:8, Paul appealed to Genesis 12:3, where God promised Abraham that all the families of earth would be blessed in him. Later on in that chapter he affirmed that Christ was the seed of Abraham (v. 16), so that those who are united to Christ by faith are Abraham's seed (v. 29). Then in Romans 4:12–17 Paul appealed to Genesis 17:5 (whose similarity to Genesis 12:3 has already been noted[4]) as part of his proof that the enjoyment of the Abrahamic promise "depends on faith, in order that the promise may rest on grace and be guaranteed to all [Abraham's] descendants—not only to the adherents of the law but also to those who share the faith of Abraham, for he is the father of us all, as it is written, 'I have made you the father of many nations' ..." (Rom. 4:16–17). This makes it clear that Paul understood that Abraham would father a multitude of nations through Christ. These nations would achieve union with him, and thus would be Abraham's veritable seed through faith and the indwelling Holy Spirit. The later revelation of Christ provided the key to what must have remained an enigma to Abraham as he tried to understand both Genesis 12:3 and 17:5. With this later revelation, one does not need to try to determine how Abraham fathered, in a simple physical sense, a *multitude* of nations.

This line of interpretation does not subtract anything from the promises made to Abraham in Genesis, chapters 12 through 15. We have already seen how, according to Romans 11:26–27, all of ethnic Israel will be converted at the second coming of Christ. Then the physical descendants of Abraham through Jacob who are alive at that time will occupy the land and will truly be the

[4]Supra, p. 125.

seed of Abraham, because there will then be an intervention of and response to the word of God in which God banishes ungodliness from Jacob. According to Zechariah 12:10, God promised, "I will pour out on the house of David and the inhabitants of Jerusalem a spirit of compassion and supplication, so that when they look on him whom they have pierced, they shall mourn for him, as one mourns for an only child...."

During the ensuing millennium many nations on earth will say, "Come, let us go up to the mountain of the Lord, to the house of the God of Jacob; that he may teach us his ways and that we may walk in his paths" (Isa. 2:3). As these people repent and turn to the Lord, they will enjoy union with Christ through the indwelling Holy Spirit, and Abraham will indeed become the father of a multitude of nations, and many kings will also be the seed of Abraham. Something similar to this has happened in the missionary outreach during the present dispensation, as whole peoples have turned to Christ because of encouragement from their leaders.

Such an interpretation of the seed of Abraham avoids all the difficulties encountered in the dispensational attempt to postulate that there are at least two seeds of Abraham. Dispensationalism cannot accept a single seed of Abraham, for this places the Church in a continuum with the remnant, or what they regard as "spiritual Israel." This, they feel, would expose the Church to the virus of legalism that Israel carries. Such an interpretation would also raise the question of the role of obedience in enjoying the blessings promised in the Abrahamic Covenant, and it is to this question that we now turn our attention.

II. The Question of Conditionality in the Abrahamic Covenant

Dispensationalism places considerable emphasis on the unconditionality of the Abrahamic Covenant. Walvoord declares:

> As given in the Scriptures, the Abrahamic covenant is hinged upon only one condition. This is given in Genesis 12:1, "Now Jehovah said to Abram, Get thee out of thy country, and from thy kindred, and from thy father's house, unto the land that I will show thee." ... The one condition having been met, no further conditions are laid upon Abraham; the Covenant having been solemnly established is now dependent upon the divine veracity for its fulfillment. (MK 149)

The *New Scofield Bible* makes the same affirmation: "The Abrahamic Covenant reveals the sovereign purpose of God to fulfill through Abraham His program for Israel, and to provide the Saviour for all who believe. The ultimate fulfillment is made to rest upon the divine promise and the power of God, rather than upon human faithfulness" (NSB 20).

Some of the evidences to which the dispensationalist points to support the unconditionality of the Abrahamic Covenant are (1) that it is called an "eternal" covenant in Genesis 17:1, 13, 19; I Chronicles 16:17; and Psalm 105:10; (2) at no time when God repeats the covenant to Abraham, Isaac, or Jacob, or in subsequent times in Israel's history, is a condition attached to the promise; (3) the perpetuity of the Abrahamic Covenant was solemnized by a divinely-ordained ritual in which God passed between the parts of the sacrifice that were cut asunder (Gen. 15:7–21; cf. Jer. 34:18), and this signified God's attaching an oath to the promises he made to Israel's physical seed; and (4) the covenant is repeated even after Abraham, Isaac, and Jacob had sinned, and also after times of apostasy in Israel.

It is helpful to inquire into the reasons why a dispensationalist strongly emphasizes the unconditionality of the Abrahamic Covenant. We have already noted the non-salvific and secular dispensational interpretation of Genesis 17:7–8, where God promises, "I will be a God to your descendants after you."[5] In fact the dispensationalist secularizes this and all other direct promises to Abraham and his allegedly physical seed. The following quotation from Walvoord demonstrates how a dispensationalist wants to view the blessings to Abraham's seed in such a way that no one could ever regard them as being part of the Church's hope for the future:

> While Abraham is personally justified by faith because of his trust in God's promise concerning his seed, it is obvious that the Abrahamic covenant itself is not the gospel of salvation even though the promised blessing anticipated the gospel (cf. Gal. 3:8) [which quotes Genesis 12:3]. Those in the covenant are promised that God will be their God in the general and providential sense. It is true that Christ is the fulfillment of the promise of blessing to all nations. But the covenant

[5]Supra, p. 129.

does not contain the covenant of redemption, a revelation of the
sacrifice of Christ, a promise of forgiveness of sin, a promise of eternal
life, or any [!] of the elements of salvation. ... While the Abrahamic
covenant is essentially gracious and promises blessings, it deals for
the most part with physical blessings and with a physical seed. To
make the covenant a phase or a statement of the covenant of redemption is hardly justified by the study of its precise provisions. (MK
142–143)

In that the dispensationalist emphasizes that the blessings
promised to Abraham's seed through Jacob are physical rather
than spiritual and soteriological, and in that he stresses the certainty that all ethnic Israel will enjoy these physical blessings
someday, he rules out any possibility for the Church, which is
wholly separate from Israel's physical seed and enjoys such rich
spiritual blessings as forgiveness and eternal life, to have any part
or lot in the promises made to this physical seed. To admit even
one spiritual blessing to physical Israel would create a difficulty
for dispensationalism, for then physical Israel would be enjoying
something of what the Church enjoys, and that would be a step
in the direction of merging the two. Likewise it would be harder
to keep Israel and the Church separate if the dispensationalist
were to make the fulfillment of the promises to Abraham's physical seed dependent on Israel's obedience, for if she were to prove
unworthy of these promises, then one might construe the Church
as becoming the beneficiary of these promises in lieu of Israel.
But by insisting on the unconditionality of the Abrahamic Covenant and the non-spiritual nature of its promised blessings, the
dispensationalist separates Israel's future from that of the Church.

We have noted, however, that after God foretold Israel's blessings, he also described the blessings for the Gentiles, who would
make up a considerable portion of the Church. In Genesis 12:3
God said that "by you [Abraham] all the families of the earth shall
bless themselves." The dispensationalist argues that just as the
promises to physical Israel are unconditional, so also are the
promises to the families of earth who will bless themselves in
Abraham. For example, the *New Scofield Bible* says that "the New
Covenant [in which Gentiles participate] ... secures the eternal
blessedness, under the Abrahamic Covenant, of all who believe.
It is absolutely unconditional and, since no responsibility is by it

committed to man, it is final and irreversible" (NSB 1318). Likewise, Walvoord observes:

> A parallel [with the unconditionality of the promises made to Israel] can be found in the doctrine of eternal security for the believer in the present dispensation. Having once accepted Jesus Christ as Savior [which parallels Abraham's initial act of faith in leaving his home land, supra, pp. 134–135], the believer is assured a complete salvation on a gracious principle quite [?] independent of attaining a degree of faithfulness or obedience during this life. (MK 149)

Thus while none of the blessings which were promised to Israel is transferred to the Church by the promise of Genesis 12:3, the unconditionality of the Abrahamic Covenant which was affirmed just before this promise, is transferred to the Church.

Some problems arising from this concept of unconditionality
Among the many statements of dispensationalists which cite evidence from Scripture that the Abrahamic Covenant is unconditional, there is the acknowledgement that Scripture sees obedience as essential if God is finally to fulfill the promises of the Abrahamic Covenant and establish Israel. Walvoord says, "It is anticipated that there would be a godly remnant, as there was [had been all along?], in whom the covenant would have its complete fulfillment (cf. Gen. 18:18–19)" (MK 153). Genesis 18:18 says:

> Abraham shall become a great and mighty nation, and all the nations of the earth shall bless themselves by him. ... I have chosen him, that he may charge his children and his household after him to keep the way of the Lord by doing righteousness and justice; so that the Lord may bring to Abraham what he had promised him.

This passage is especially significant because unlike other passages which talk of the establishment of the Abrahamic Covenant because of Abraham's past obedience (Gen. 22:15–18, 26:3–5), it speaks of how essential it is for Abraham to train his family and household in the way of the Lord, so that after he dies, his posterity may live in the way he lived. This passage definitely teaches that Abraham's posterity must keep the way of the Lord, *so that* "the Lord may bring to Abraham what he has promised him."

It cannot be stated more clearly that in order for the promises of the Abrahamic Covenant to be fulfilled, Abraham's posterity must be living, generally speaking, as godly a life as did Abraham. A "face-value" interpretation of this passage necessarily implies that God's promises to Abraham will not be fulfilled so long as his posterity remains disobedient. Thus this passage, along with Walvoord's affirmation that "there would be a godly remnant ... in whom the covenant would have its complete fulfillment" (MK 153), stands in direct contradiction to his earlier statement that "the Abrahamic covenant is confirmed repeatedly by reiteration and enlargement. [But] in none of these instances are any of the added promises conditioned upon the faithfulness of Abraham's seed or of Abraham himself" (MK 150). To be sure, there are no *added promises* in Genesis 18:18–19, but that passage surely makes the fulfillment of the reiterated promises contingent upon the faithfulness of Abraham's seed.

A much greater problem, however, for the alleged unconditionality of the Abrahamic Covenant arises from God's establishment of the Mosaic Covenant with Israel. According to Ryrie this covenant ends the dispensation of "promise"—the way he characterizes the time from Abraham to Moses—and commences the dispensation of "law." Concerning the change which took place at Sinai Ryrie says:

> What ... determine[s] the distinguishability of [these] two dispensations is simply the *different* [italics added] bases on which [God] dealt with [Israel]. Promise and Law are sharply contrasted by Paul in Galatians 3, even though he maintains that the law did not annul the promise. And the Mosaic law is kept so distinct from the promise to Abraham that it is difficult not to recognize a different dispensation. ... If anything is kept distinct in [Galatians 3] the law is. Therefore, the separate dispensation of Promise or of the Patriarchs [from the Law] is justified. (DT 61)

The *New Scofield Bible* also sharply contrasts the dispensation of Promise and that of Law:

> To Abraham the promise preceded the requirement; at Sinai the requirement preceded the promise. In the New Covenant [partially established for the Christian, but fully for Israel in the millennium, p. 804] the Abrahamic order is followed. ... The Christian is not under

the conditional Mosaic Covenant of works, the law, but under the unconditional New Covenant of grace. (NSB 95)

We saw earlier[6] that Ryrie believed that every dispensation had the revelation of the grace of God in one or more forms, so that men always could be saved by grace. Every dispensation also had at least one condition where "requirement preceded promise," and such tests demonstrated how men failed in every dispensation. Dispensationalists would certainly simplify things if they could decide whether the names they give to the various dispensations denoted one of the "tests" peculiar to that dispensation, or one of the gracious revelations that are supposed to be found everywhere. Ryrie's explanation of today's dispensationalism would have been more easily understood if, after giving the name "promise" to the period between Abraham and Moses, he had characterized the Mosaic era with a term denoting the gracious revelation imparted then. Or if he felt that man's test through the law was such a salient feature of the era from Moses to Christ, it would have clarified things if he had also characterized the Abrahamic era by a word appropriate to the way men were tested then. One gains the impression, however, that grace stands out so clearly in the Abrahamic dispensation that the dispensationalist must characterize it by the gracious idea of "promise," which is the form by which the saving revelation of that era was known. He would, it seems, be as hard pressed to designate the "test" in the Abrahamic period as he was to point out the scarcely perceptible gracious revelations in the Mosaic era.[7]

In any event, dispensationalists draw the strongest possible contrast between the Abrahamic and Mosaic eras. Sometimes they have perceived the difference to be so great that they have charged Israel with making a grave blunder by promising God, through Moses, that "all that the Lord has spoken [in giving the law] we will do" (Exod. 19:8). C. H. Mackintosh said, "Instead of rejoicing in God's holy promise [i.e., the unconditional one made to the patriarchs], they undertook to make the most presumptuous vow

[6]Supra, pp. 41–42.
[7]Supra, pp. 39–41.

that mortal lips could utter."[8] C. I. Scofield, in his *Reference Bible*, declared that the Jews "rashly accepted the law" (p. 20). L. S. Chafer insisted that "[Israel's] choice [of accepting the law] was in no way required by God"; rather, "Israel deliberately forsook their position under grace, which had been their relationship to God until that day, and placed themselves under law" (ST IV, 162). Contemporary dispensationalists, however, go no farther than saying that "the law was not imposed until it had been proposed and voluntarily accepted" (NSB 94). The implication of this statement seems to be that Israel could have rejected the law without displeasing God.

How then is the dispensationalist able to insist that the promises of Abraham to Israel were unconditional if Israel had submitted to a law in which being God's people depended upon fulfilling the condition of obeying his voice and keeping the Mosaic Covenant (Exod. 19:5)? Walvoord's answer seems to be that individuals and certain groups of Israelites, rather than the nation as a whole, enjoyed blessings or suffered curses depending on whether or not they bided by the law. In answer to the objection that the Abrahamic Covenant must have been conditional because the priest, Eli, was severely punished for allowing his sons to sin, Walvoord said, "The covenant with Eli's house was a part of the Mosaic covenant, which all agree is a conditional covenant, which was not intended to be eternal" (MK 154). Thus the Abrahamic Covenant remained in effect only for the nation as a whole. In an earlier treatise Walvoord talked of how "Israel is promised curses as well as blessings under her covenants" (APC 140). By the use of the word "covenants," Walvoord included the conditional Mosaic Covenant along with all the other unconditional covenants (MK 150).

NOTE. That Israel put herself under the Mosaic Covenant with its curses and blessings constitutes another reason why dispensationalists are so anxious to keep the Church separate from Israel. Failure to maintain this complete separation would enable the Church to qualify for the blessings (e.g., Deut. 28:1–14) but it "puts the church in a compromising position of being involved

---

[8]C. H. M[ackintosh], *Notes on the Book of Exodus* (New York: Fleming H. Revell, n.d.), p. 244.

in Israel's curses also" (APC 140). In other words, the doctrine of eternal security would no doubt be compromised.

END OF NOTE

The biggest problem with the inauguration of the conditional Mosaic Covenant for the dispensationalist emerges in the question of what happens to this covenant when God deals with ethnic Israel again, after the rapture of the Church, and inaugurates the unconditional new covenant for Israel. According to Ryrie, during the seven-year period of the great tribulation, before the Lord returns to earth with his Church, there is no reinstitution of the Mosaic law, because according to his interpretation of the *telos* in Romans 10:4,[9] the law was *terminated* at some point between the beginning of Jesus' ministry and the end of the book of Acts. Thus Ryrie says, "It would be a very unusual thing to reinstitute a dispensation after a lapse of two thousand years or more. ... [Therefore] it would seem more natural to consider the Tribulation as a distinct dispensation with similarities to the Mosaic economy" (DT 55). As for the millennial kingdom that is established at the end of this seven-year period, when Christ returns from heaven with his Church, Ryrie says that "man will be responsible for obedience to the King and His laws" (DT 63). The Sermon on the Mount, in Ryrie's view, is at least a sample of the "laws" that will be in force when Christ rules the earth during the millennium. But he stops short of affirming that there is any teaching similar to the gospel in the Sermon on the Mount. "It is usually charged," he says, "that dispensationalists teach that the Sermon [on the Mount] is all law and no gospel. To those who object to this claim, we merely ask, Where can one find a statement of the gospel in the Sermon?" (DT 108). So Ryrie affirms that there will be a great deal of legal, non-gospel revelation to which all must submit during the millennium.

In his *Study Bible*, however, Ryrie declares that the new covenant "will be made in the future with the whole nation of Israel (Jer. 31:31); it will be unlike the Mosaic covenant in that it will be unconditional (Jer. 31:32 [?]) ..." (RSB 1171). Therefore in the millennium people will have to submit to the unconditional new covenant as well as to the Sermon on the Mount, which has

[9]Cf. supra, p. 104.

no gospel, and is at least very similar to the conditional Mosaic law. However, such a conclusion is explicitly contrary to Jeremiah 31:31–34, where God declares that he will "make a new covenant with the house of Israel and the house of Judah, *not like* the [Mosaic] covenant which I made with their fathers. . . ."

The editors of the *New Scofield Bible* entangle themselves in the same difficulty. Concerning the Sermon on the Mount they state, "In this sermon our Lord reaffirms the Mosaic law of the O.T. theocratic kingdom as the governing code of his coming kingdom on earth" (NSB 997). Earlier they say, "As fulfilled after the second coming of Christ, the kingdom of heaven will be re-alized in the future millennial kingdom as predicted by Daniel . . . and covenanted to David . . ." (NSB 994). But concerning the new covenant they declare that it is "unconditional" (NSB 1318) and therefore in stark contrast with the Mosaic Covenant. They further state that "the [new] covenant remains to be realized for Israel according to the explicit statement of [Jer. 31:31]" (NSB 804).

A possible solution to these problems

The requirement that men meet stated conditions in order for God to bless them is perfectly compatible with prophecy. In Genesis 18:18–19, where God makes it absolutely explicit that Abraham's seed must keep the way of the Lord *in order to* enjoy the blessings of the Abrahamic covenant, God also declares that everything that has to do with Abraham and his seed is predes-tined: "I have chosen [Abraham], [in order—the literal Hebrew] that he may charge his children and his household after him to keep the way of the Lord. . . ." In other words, not only was the enjoyment of the blessings of the Abrahamic Covenant made cer-tain by God's electing work, but also the obedience needed by its beneficiaries in order to enjoy the blessings.

Walvoord as much as admits that this is the case when he affirms that "there would be a godly remnant . . . in whom the covenant would have its complete fulfillment" (MK 153). Far from coming to pass as a mere human contingency, the godliness of this remnant (which will be all ethnic Israel alive at the time of the second coming—Rom. 11:26) is the work of the new cove-nant. This becomes abundantly clear when, in describing that future day when the new covenant would be inaugurated for the house of Israel, Ezekiel quotes God as saying:

> [25]I will sprinkle clean water upon you, and you shall be clean from all your uncleannesses, and from all your idols I will cleanse you. [26]A new heart I will give you, and a new spirit I will put within you; and I will take out of your flesh the heart of stone and give you a heart of flesh. [27]And I will put my spirit within you, and *cause you to walk in my statutes* [italics added] and be careful to observe my ordinances. [28]You shall dwell in the land which I gave to your fathers, and you shall be my people and I will be your God. (Ezek. 36:25–28)

Like Genesis 18:18–19, this passage makes certain both the end, that God would unite Israel in the land, and the means necessary for achieving this end, namely, that Israel be godly.

So the door is then wide open for the dispensationalist to affirm the conditionality of the Abrahamic and new covenants without running the slightest danger of jeopardizing the certainty that they will be fulfilled. If Walvoord acknowledged that the Abrahamic and new covenants are as conditional as the Mosaic Covenant, then he would not have to state the exact opposite of Genesis 18:18–19 in his affirmation that in no place is the reiteration of the Abrahamic promises made conditional upon the faithfulness of Abraham's seed.

In all the passages in which God promises that he will inaugurate the new covenant for Israel, he stresses that the conditional elements which were found in the Mosaic Covenant are to remain in place. We have seen this to be the case in Ezekiel 36:25–28, and it is also true in Jeremiah 31:31–33, where the prophet quotes God as saying:

> [31]Behold the days are coming, says the Lord, when I will make a new covenant with the house of Israel and the house of Judah, [32]not like the covenant which I made with their fathers when I took them by the hand to bring them out of the land of Egypt, my covenant which they broke, though I was their husband, says the Lord. [33]But this is the covenant which I will make with the house of Israel after those days, says the Lord: *I will put my law within them* [italics added], and I will write it upon their hearts; and I will be their God, and they shall be my people.

The only difference between the new covenant and the old

Mosaic Covenant which it replaces is that the people under the new covenant are given a new heart which has the inclination, or the predisposition, to want to keep God's laws. We saw how Ryrie interprets the statement "... not like the covenant which I made with their fathers ..." to mean that the new covenant, unlike the old or Mosaic Covenant, will be unconditional.[10] But a face-value interpretation of Jeremiah 31:31–34 should allow the passage itself to tell how the new covenant is unlike the old, rather than submit to the theological concern of maintaining the distinction between a conditional and an unconditional covenant.

If dispensationalists were willing to grant that the Abrahamic and new covenants are as conditional as the Mosaic Covenant, then they would avoid the grave difficulty inherent in their system of having both a conditional and a non-conditional covenant operating side by side in the seven-year tribulation period and in the Messianic kingdom that immediately follows. And they could agree that because people would then be regenerated, the old Mosaic Covenant would become the new covenant.

But the greatest objection that would be raised both by dispensationalists and covenant theologians against interpreting these covenants in this way is that regarding them all as being conditional like the Mosaic Covenant would encourage people to try to earn their salvation by keeping the law and doing good works in which they can boast. But the purpose of the whole of the preceding chapter was to show that Paul understood the Mosaic law to be a law of faith, so that compliance with it would produce the obedience of faith and the works of faith. Since such compliance is of faith, boasting is excluded, for the two cannot exist in the same person at the same time.

If chapter four succeeded in overcoming this objection, then we would be freed from the onerous and problematic task of dividing the Bible between law and gospel, or between conditional and unconditional promises or covenants. The covenant theologian would no longer be a covenant theologian because he would see all the commands and conditions for receiving blessings in the Bible as part of a covenant of grace. The term "covenant of works" would drop out of his vocabulary. Today's

---

[10]Supra, p. 141.

dispensationalists would no longer be faced with the vexing and as yet uncompleted task of listing, for each dispensation, the tests which prove that men fail God, and the gracious revelations by which they can find salvation despite their failure. No longer would they be requested to be consistent in naming their dispensations either by a word designating one of the peculiar tests in each, or by a word designating one of the gracious revelations found in each. They could identify the various eras in redemptive history by names taken from the most salient feature of that era, because the same essential message of the obedience of faith is being proclaimed from Genesis to Revelation.

CHAPTER SIX
The Kingdom of God

According to the writer on *basileia* ("kingdom") in the *Theological Dictionary of the New Testament*, "The kingdom of God implies the whole of the preaching of Jesus Christ and his apostles."[1] An analysis of the biblical texts shows that the fundamental starting point for understanding the New Testament concept of "kingdom" (*basileia*) "is reign [i.e., 'right to rule'] rather than realm."[2]

Dispensationalists, however, do not often begin their expositions of the kingdom of God with the idea of a "right to rule" but with the concrete, specific realm of the glorious Messianic, Davidic kingdom as outlined in the Old Testament prophecies. Thus they construe the announcement of the nearness of the kingdom of God both by John the Baptist and by Jesus in the early portions of the synoptic Gospels to mean that the glorious realm of the Davidic kingdom is about to appear. A prime argument they use to support this conclusion is that neither John nor Jesus identifies or defines this kingdom. Therefore, they argue, it must be the glorious Davidic kingdom which the Jews were expecting. According to Ryrie, "The Jewish people of Christ's day were looking for this Messianic or Davidic kingdom to be established on earth, and this is what John proclaimed as being 'at hand' " (RSB 1448). The editors of the *New Scofield Bible* declare, "The promise of the kingdom to David and his seed, and described in the prophets (2 Sam. 7:8–17 ...; Zech. 12:8) enters into the N.T. absolutely unchanged (Lk. 1:31–33)" (NSB 1248).

---

[1]K. L. Schmidt, "*basileia*," *Theological Dictionary of the New Testament*, 9 vols., ed. G. Kittel, trans. & ed. G. W. Bromiley (Grand Rapids: Wm. B. Eerdmans Publishing Company, 1964), I, 583.

[2]Ibid., I, 582.

This fundamental affirmation of dispensationalism regarding the nature of the kingdom of God proclaimed at the outset of Jesus' ministry raises certain problems. The purpose of this chapter is to show why these problems rise and what dispensationalists do to try to solve them. We will then argue that these solutions fail in their purpose. If dispensationalism were to regard *basileia* ("the kingdom") as primarily a "right to rule" and only derivatively as a "realm," then, it will be argued, all these difficulties would vanish. Such a solution, however, would place the Church in a continuum with Israel, and this would be totally unacceptable to dispensationalism because of its great concern to keep the Church free from the supposed legalism that pervades God's dealings with Israel.

I. What Happens to the Predictions of the Messiah's Sufferings?

Dispensationalists strongly affirm that, according to such Old Testament prophetic scriptures as Psalm 22 and Isaiah 52:13—53:12, the Messiah must be one who both suffers and is glorified. According to the editors of the *New Scofield Bible*,

> as redemption is only through the sacrifice of Christ, so Messianic prophecy of necessity presents Christ in a twofold character: (1) a suffering Messiah (e.g. Isa. 53); and (2) a reigning Messiah (e.g. Isa. 11). This duality—suffering and glory, weakness and power—involved a mystery which perplexed the prophets (Lk. 24:26–27; I Pet. 1:10–12). (NSB 711)

But according to I Peter 1:11, the Old Testament prophets "inquired what person or time was indicated by the Spirit of Christ within them when predicting the sufferings of Christ and the *subsequent* [italics added] glory." Naturally, the prophets had many unanswered questions about the matters they were proclaiming, but that the Messiah would first suffer and later reign in glory was not one of them. According to Zechariah 9:9 the Messiah will first be "afflicted[3] and riding upon an ass," and only afterward

---

[3]The Hebrew word *'ānî* has variously been translated "meek," "humble," "lowly," and "afflicted." Of these, "afflicted" seems best to convey its meaning, which is poor, oppressed, bowed down, full of suffering.

will he "command peace to the nations" and reign "from sea to sea and from the River to the ends of the earth" (Zech. 9:10). Likewise in Isaiah 52:13—53:12, the sufferings of the Messiah are depicted in considerable detail as happening before the glories. To be sure, Isaiah 52:13 tells of his glories, 52:14—53:10 describes his sufferings, and then 53:11–12 repeats the theme of his triumph. But even if the glories are sometimes spoken of before the sufferings, it is clear that since the glories are unending, the sufferings are therefore temporary and must as a result come first. Alva McClain, one of the editors of the *New Scofield Bible*, said, "[The prophets] saw clearly the sufferings and glory of the Messiah. It is fairly certain also that they understood the *sequence* of events: the suffering would come first, and the glory would 'follow'."[4]

According to Luke 2:25–35, Simeon was a Jew who understood perfectly from the prophets that the Messiah must first suffer and then be glorified. So clear were the Old Testament prophets on this point that Jesus rebuked his disciples for refusing to learn that the sufferings of the Messiah must precede the glories: "O foolish men and slow of heart to believe all that the prophets have spoken. Was it not necessary that the Christ should suffer these things and enter into his glory?" (Luke 24:25–26).

The editors of the *New Scofield Bible*, however, omit any reference to this verse and thus stop short of affirming that the Old Testament prophets understood that the sufferings of the Messiah must precede the glory. Ryrie likewise fails to affirm this, for in his note on I Peter 1:11 he says, "The O.T. prophets did predict both the suffering (Isa. 53) and glory (Isa. 11) of the Messiah, without distinguishing that the former would be fulfilled at His first coming and the latter at His second" (RSB 1865).

A dispensationalist cannot agree that the Old Testament prophets predicted that the Messiah must first suffer and then be glorified because then the kingdom that John the Baptist and Jesus announced could not have been the glorious Davidic kingdom, since it had to involve the sufferings of Christ which climaxed at his crucifixion. John the Baptist clearly proclaimed that the Mes-

---

[4]Alva J. McClain, *The Greatness of the Kingdom* (Grand Rapids: Zondervan Publishing House, 1959), p. 168.

siah must first suffer: "Behold, the Lamb of God who takes away
the sin of the world" (John 1:29). Yet in order to maintain the
coherency of its system, dispensationalism insists that when John
the Baptist declared, "The kingdom of God is at hand; repent and
believe in the gospel" (Mark 1:15), the words "at hand" meant
that "no known or predicted event must intervene. When Christ
appeared to the Jewish people, the next thing, in the order of
revelation as it then stood [sic], should have been the setting up
of the Davidic kingdom" (NSB 996). Likewise Dwight Pentecost,
a professor at Dallas Seminary, has stated that "['at hand'] is not
a guarantee that the kingdom will be instituted immediately, but
rather that all impending events have been removed so that [the
Davidic kingdom] is now imminent."[5] Such wording insists that
even the Old Testament prophecies and John the Baptist's testi-
mony (John 1:29) which placed the sufferings of the Messiah first
were set aside by John's statement in the synoptics that "the kingdom of God is at hand," so that the way was cleared to set up the
glorious Davidic kingdom apparently without the predicted sufferings ever coming to pass.

The reason that dispensationalism goes to such extremes in
expounding its system is that if the announcement that the kingdom of God was at hand meant that the suffering of Christ would
occur first, then there would have to be a certain delay between
the time that Jesus would suffer and the time when he would
establish the glorious Messianic kingdom. But the dispensationalist believes that the teachings of both John the Baptist and Jesus
in the early part of the synoptic Gospels conform to the legalism
that pervades God's dealings with Israel, and therefore fit in with
the imminent establishment of the Davidic kingdom. If the sufferings of the Messiah were implied in the pronouncements made
at the outset of Jesus' ministry, then these affirmations would set
forth the message of God's grace and would pertain to the Church,
whose whole existence was based on the substitutionary atonement effected by Christ's death. We have seen, however, that Ryrie
and other dispensationalists deny that there is any gospel teaching
in the Sermon on the Mount, the most detailed teaching Jesus

[5] J. Dwight Pentecost, *Things to Come* (Findlay, Ohio: Dunham Publishing
Company, 1958), pp. 449–450.

gave at the beginning of his ministry.[6] Therefore, in order to keep the Church free from this "legalistic" taint which purportedly characterizes Jesus' early teaching in Matthew, Mark, and Luke (but not John!), the dispensationalist must stop short of conceding that the Old Testament prophets affirmed that the Messiah should first suffer. Then the way is clear to confirm that the announcement of the kingdom of God at the outset of Jesus' public ministry as recorded in the synoptic Gospels concurs only with the glories of the Davidic kingdom.

For Ryrie, the message that Jesus preached to Israel at the outset of his ministry had nothing to do with salvation but only with the "test"[7] which reveals man's failures and condemns him. In his interpretation of the call of John the Baptist and Jesus for men to repent, covenant theologian Oswald Allis declared that in order to be saved, people at all times must heed such a command to repent.[8] But Ryrie's response to Allis was that the message of repentance which Jesus initially preached was so different from what a man today must do to be saved that if Allis really believed men had to comply with that repentance, as well as with the repentance required in the Church age, then "one would be forced to conclude that [Allis] ... teach[es] more than one way of salvation" (DT 167).

According to Ryrie, the repentance Jesus taught early in his ministry is outlined in the Sermon on the Mount, whereas the repentance people are to exercise today is set forth in the book of Acts. The repentance taught in the Sermon on the Mount requires the fulfillment of a number of extremely difficult if not impossible ethical commands, and for this reason serves as a test that exposes man's failure. On the other hand, the required repentance in Acts is really "a synonym for faith":[9]

> Like faith, [repentance] is the human requirement for salvation and yet it is the gift of God. ... The word [repentance] means to change one's mind about Jesus of Nazareth being the Messiah. This involved

[6]Supra, p. 141.
[7]Supra, pp. 41–45.
[8]Oswald T. Allis, *Prophecy and the Church* (Philadelphia: Presbyterian and Reformed Publishing Company, 1945), p. 70.
[9]Charles C. Ryrie, *Biblical Theology of the New Testament* (Chicago: Moody Press, 1959), p. 116.

no longer thinking of Him as merely a carpenter's son of Nazareth, an impostor, but now receiving Him as both Lord and Messiah. Thus, repentance as preached by the apostles . . . was actually the act of faith in Jesus Christ which brought salvation to the one who repented.[10]

The only modification of this that Ryrie has made in his *Study Bible* is that "there is also a repentance needed in the Christian life in relation to specific sins" (RSB 1648). So Ryrie continues to keep the initial act of repentance as the equivalent of faith, in which one changes his mind about Jesus. But he says nothing about the need to change one's ethical attitude in this initial act.

If we note well the great contrast that exists in Ryrie's mind between the repentance of the Sermon on the Mount and the repentance of the book of Acts, we will grasp the basic reason why the dispensationalist feels compelled to regard the kingdom preached by Jesus in his early ministry (according to the record of the synoptic Gospels) to be the glorious Davidic kingdom proclaimed by the prophets, even though these prophets said that the sufferings must come first. The dispensationalist goes to such extremes in the way he defines faith and repentance that in the book of Acts repentance is seen as the expression of the grace of God to sinners, whereas he regards it in the Sermon on the Mount as an expression of a legalistic test to show men their failure.

Is the repentance and faith of the book of Acts so different from that in the Sermon on the Mount that they represent two mutually exclusive ways of responding to God? In defining repentance in Acts, Ryrie says that a person must receive Jesus as both Lord and Messiah. The gospel of Luke reports Jesus as saying, "Why do you call me 'Lord, Lord,' and not do what I tell you?" (Luke 6:46), and the preceding verses include the shorter version of the Sermon on the Mount—often called the Sermon on the Plain (Luke 6:17–49). Since Luke also wrote Acts, which clearly teaches that people must accept Jesus as Lord to be saved (e.g., Acts 16:31), and since Luke 6:46 declares that regarding Jesus as Lord implies obeying his words (and in the immediate context of this verse there are many statements which appear in the Matthean account of the Sermon on the Mount), we therefore con-

---

[10]Ibid., pp. 116–117.

clude that Luke believed that during what the dispensationalists call "this present church age," men must bank their hope on Jesus as Lord and render to him that "obedience of faith" or the "works of faith" (explained in chapter four of this book) in order to be saved.

But Ryrie's definition of repentance and faith in Acts seems to deliberately avoid any explicit allusion to an ethical change of behavior. Perhaps he fears that defining repentance in this way would mislead someone into thinking that his salvation depended, in part, on his good works. But Luke had no such qualms about regarding repentance as involving a radical change in ethical behavior. His report of Peter's dealings with Simon the sorcerer at Samaria is instructive on this point: "Even Simon himself believed, and after being baptized he continued with Philip" (Acts 8:13). Simon had certainly changed his mind about Jesus and now regarded him as having powers to accomplish the greatest works. As far as Ryrie's definition of repentance/faith would go, Simon would pass muster. But in Luke's view, Simon's repentance/faith was woefully deficient, for when Peter came to Samaria and the Holy Spirit fell upon the believers, Simon demonstrated his lack of repentance by asking Peter if he could buy from him the power to impart the Holy Spirit to people. Peter replied:

> Your silver and gold perish with you, because you thought you could obtain the gift of God with money! You have neither part nor lot in this matter, for your heart is not right with God. Repent therefore of this wickedness of yours, and pray to the Lord that, if possible, the intent of your heart may be forgiven you, for I see that you are in the gall of bitterness and in the bond of iniquity. (Acts 8:20–23)

Another place in Acts where repentance and faith explicitly involve a radical ethical change of behavior is Paul's exhortation to the Athenians. In concluding his sermon on the Areopagus he said, "... now [God] commands all men everywhere to repent, because he has appointed a day in which he will judge the world in righteousness ..." (Acts 17:30–31). From this it is clear that the repentance which God commanded of men involved an ethical change represented by the word "righteousness." The word "righteousness" obviously stands for compliance with many specific duties, and not a few of these are explicitly stated in the

Sermon on the Mount. Since "righteousness" in Acts is so at one with righteousness in the Sermon on the Mount, Ryrie is attempting the impossible to draw a contrast between the two.

The dispensationalist not only wants to keep the Church free from the sort of repentance implied by the Sermon on the Mount but also free from the repentance preached by John the Baptist: "Bear fruits worthy of repentance. . . . Even now the axe is laid at the root of the trees; every tree therefore that does not bear good fruit is cut down and thrown into the fire" (Luke 3:8–9). We saw how Ryrie's critique of Oswald Allis[11] declared that if such teaching represented how a man could be saved, then it represented a totally different salvation from the salvation found in Acts. But according to Luke, Paul used very similar language in Acts when, standing before Agrippa II, he summarized the way he had always preached since Christ appeared to him on the Damascus road: "Wherefore, O King Agrippa, I was not disobedient to the heavenly vision, but declared first to those at Damascus, then at Jerusalem and throughout all the country of Judea, and also to the Gentiles, that they should repent and turn to God and perform deeds worthy of repentance" (Acts 26:19).

From this comparison between what Luke reported in his Gospel and what he reported in Acts, we conclude that the message of John the Baptist and Jesus was essentially the same message that Peter and Paul preached during the first decades of the Church's existence. Luke obviously did not regard any difference to exist, and so he saw no need to postulate that John the Baptist and Jesus, in the early days of their ministries, were preaching a message suited for the establishment of the glorious Davidic kingdom but not at all suited for the Church that would soon be established, for the time being, instead of that kingdom.

We have seen that according to Luke 24:26, Jesus must first suffer and then enter into his glory. Luke regarded the kingdom proclaimed by John the Baptist and Jesus to mean precisely this. Such an idea, of course, would be nonsensical if the term "kingdom" had, as its basic concept, an empirical realm, for one who ruled over such a realm would surely have the power to protect himself from suffering and dying on a cross. But the Jew of Jesus'

---

[11]Supra, p. 150.

day had more than adequate evidence from the Old Testament that the fundamental concept of the Davidic kingdom was the God-given authority, or right, to rule over a realm which would belong forever to some descendant of David. This was all spelled out in the Davidic Covenant, whose basic statement appears in II Samuel 7:10–16, and is referred to again in II Samuel 23:5; Psalms 89 and 132:11; and Jeremiah 33:20–21. In analyzing the terms of this covenant, Walvoord makes the highly significant observation that

> By the term "throne" it is clear that no reference is made to a material throne, but rather to the dignity and power which was sovereign and supreme in David as king. The right to rule [!] always belonged to David's seed. By the term "kingdom" there is reference to David's political kingdom over Israel. By the expression "for ever" it is signified that the Davidic authority and Davidic kingdom or rule over Israel shall never be taken away from David's posterity. The right to rule will never be transferred to another family.... (MK 196)

After David died a succession of his posterity ruled over an empirical realm until 586 B.C. After that Judah was led off in captivity into Babylon, and Jeremiah's prophecy that no kings would sit on David's throne (Jer. 13:13–14) was fulfilled. Of David's realm Ezekiel had also said, "A ruin, ruin, ruin I will make it [the kingdom of Judah]; there shall not even be a trace of it until he comes whose right [!] it is, and to him will I give it" (Ezek. 21:27). Jeremiah said that while the realm itself would vanish, nevertheless the Davidic Covenant, in which God had promised that someone would always have the right to reign on David's throne, could no more be nullified than the terms of the Noahic Covenant, by which there is promised a succession of night and day (Jer. 33:19–22).

Walvoord understands that the right to rule is the foundational promise in the Davidic Covenant, which declared that David would never lack an heir to reign. But if "right to rule" rather than "realm" is foundational for the Davidic Covenant, then it is plausible that when John the Baptist and Jesus announced the imminent coming of the kingdom of God, the God-given authority that would rule and save people from their sins was on the verge of revealing its powers. This authority of the kingdom of God became present upon earth in the person of Jesus Christ. He proved that he even had authority to forgive sins by healing a lame man after assuring him that his sins were forgiven (Matt. 9:1–8 et par.).

But in order for Jesus to have the right or authority to forgive sins, God had to devise a way whereby he could forgive sins and regard men as righteous without impairing his own righteousness (cf. Rom. 3:25–26). God accomplished this by having Jesus atone for men's sins through his incarnation, during which he suffered the most terrible humiliation at the hands of men and finally was put to death on the cross. While Jesus was on the cross God poured out upon him the wrath that men deserved for their sins. Only through the cross did Jesus guarantee the perpetual right for salvation to proceed from a scion of David. Because of Jesus' death on the cross God could exercise the most miraculous powers for the benefit of *sinful* men during Jesus' earthly ministry (and during the eras before and after the cross) without impairing his righteousness.

But because he had to *suffer* and die to provide God with a way to maintain his righteousness while blessing sinners to the extent of becoming *their* God,[12] Jesus was often limited in the powers of the kingdom. He said, "I have a baptism to be baptized with; and how I am constrained until it is accomplished!" (Luke 12:50). The Messiah who had to suffer and die in order to procure the right to occupy David's throne and exercise power in saving people from their sins, had to submit often to suffering instead of exercising those powers which his suffering would make possible. Thus it is no wonder that the prophets declared, as Jesus put it, that "the Christ should suffer these things and enter into his glory" (Luke 24:26).

If dispensationalists would stop insisting that Christ made a sincere offer to Israel to establish the glorious Davidic kingdom during the earlier part of his ministry, they would no longer be embarrassed by the seemingly inescapable corollary that suffering and dying on the cross for men's sins was not Jesus' basic aim during his early ministry but came in as an afterthought when it became apparent that the Jews would not conform to the con-

[12] Cf. supra, p. 129.

ditions necessary for the establishment of the glorious Davidic kingdom. J. N. Darby once remarked, "Suppose for a moment that Christ had not been rejected, [then] the kingdom would have been set up on earth."[13] This can only mean that if Jesus' sincere offer had been accepted by the Jews, he would not have been crucified. But how, then, could God have blessed sinful men with the glories of the Davidic kingdom without impairing his own righteousness?

Every leading dispensationalist has tried to argue that such a conclusion is not necessarily implied by Jesus' sincere offer of the glorious Davidic kingdom. It is beyond the scope of our inquiry, however, to catalogue the various ways in which they try to extricate themselves from this difficulty. We simply say that if dispensationalists acknowledged the fact that the Old Testament prophets predicted that the Messiah must *first* suffer and *then* be glorified, and if they acknowledged that Jesus' sole purpose in his first advent was to suffer and die for the sins of the world, then they would not have to explain why the crucifixion was not an afterthought. Their fears that the Church would be tainted by the legalism which allegedly pervades God's dealings with Israel would vanish if they would understand (as was emphasized in chapter four) that a holy God would never require anything from sinful men except the obedience and works of faith, which bring all glory to him. It is unthinkable that a holy God would ever propose to men, even hypothetically, that they try to earn his favor by works in which they could boast. Boasting only arouses God's wrath; it never elicits his favor.[14]

NOTE. There is evidence that Jesus' teachings at the outset of his ministry, namely, in the Sermon on the Mount, were not given for people under the dominion of a glorious king but to a very small minority suffering from all sorts of persecution from the great majority of people. If the Sermon on the Mount had been composed for those about to enjoy the Messiah's rule, Jesus surely would not have talked about the persecution of his followers (Matt. 5:10–12). Neither would there have been only a "few" who would find the strait and narrow gate that led to life (Matt.

---

[13]J. N. Darby, "Lectures on the Second Coming of Christ," *Collected Writings*, XI, 431.

[14]This last criticism applies to covenant theology as well as dispensationalism.

7:14), for Isaiah 2:3 speaks of how the nations of earth would go to Jerusalem in great numbers to learn how to walk in the paths of the Lord. Furthermore, if Jesus' empirical kingdom had been on the verge of being established on the earth it would have been unnecessary for him to exhort his hearers to carry the burden of a Roman soldier two miles instead of just one (Matt. 5:41). Likewise, Jesus' warning against false prophets would have been meaningless (Matt. 7:15–23) if the Messiah himself was about to take complete charge of the world.

In fact, as one views the Sermon on the Mount as a whole, one can see that it was written for a small, godly remnant to tell them how to relate to a world that was almost totally evil. Thus it fits far better with the sufferings of the Messiah than with his establishment of a glorious Davidic kingdom.   END OF NOTE

II. When Was the Offer of the Glorious Davidic Kingdom Withdrawn from Israel?

If the dispensationalist affirms that the Davidic kingdom was offered at the beginning of Jesus' ministry, there must have been some point where the offer was withdrawn, because Christ was crucified at the end of his ministry. According to Dwight Pentecost, "the establishment of the theocratic kingdom depended upon the repentance of the nation, the recognition of John the Baptist as the promised fore-runner, and the reception of Jesus Christ as the theocratic king."[15]

But Israel did not fulfill these conditions; thus somewhere in the midst of Jesus' ministry there came a "turning point of immense significance" (NSB 1021). According to the editors of the *New Scofield Bible* this "turning point" came when Jesus began to predict that he must go to Jerusalem to "suffer many things from the elders and chief priests and scribes and be killed and on the third day be raised" (Matt. 16:21). They contrast this announcement with Jesus' statement in Matthew 4:17, where he said, "Repent, for the kingdom of heaven is at hand," and conclude that these are "two sharply contrasted phases of our Lord's teaching ministry" (NSB 996).

A problem arises, however, in that as dispensationalists read the last half of Matthew and the book of Acts they find additional statements either by Jesus or his apostles which again offer the Davidic kingdom to Israel. Then too, there are Scriptural pas-

[15]Pentecost, *Things to Come*, p. 453.

sages prior to Matthew 16:21 which seem to indicate that Jesus has ceased his supposedly legalistic preaching and is graciously offering salvation to the Church he is about to build on the basis of his death and resurrection. In the view of the editors of the *New Scofield Bible*, there had been a "moral rejection" (NSB 1010) of the Davidic kingdom as early as Matthew 11:20, when Jesus upbraided the cities of Chorazin and Bethsaida because they did not repent, and when he shortly afterward uttered the exceedingly gracious and non-legalistic invitation, "Come to me, all who labor and are heavy-laden . . ." (Matt. 11:28–30). The "official rejection" of this kingdom, however, did not come until Matthew 27:21–23 when Israel cried out, "[Jesus'] blood be upon us and on our children" (NSB 1010). They confuse things, however, by declaring that there is another "official rejection" (NSB 1248) in Matthew 21:42–43, where Jesus said that the kingdom would be given to another nation bringing forth appropriate fruits of repentance.[16]

Some dispensationalists do acknowledge that there are additional offerings of the glorious Davidic kingdom to Israel. Alva McClain, one of the editors of the *New Scofield Bible*, regards Peter's entreaty to Israel to repent and thus receive the "times of refreshing" from the presence of the Lord (Acts 3:19) as a bona fide offer of the kingdom. He says, "It is hard to imagine how words could have made any plainer the historical reality of this reoffer of the King and his Kingdom to the nation of Israel."[17] Arno C. Gaebelein, a member of the older generation of dispensationalists, affirms that Paul made another offer of the Messianic kingdom to Israel when he spoke from morning to evening to the non-Christian Jews at Rome, "testifying to the kingdom of God and trying to convince them about Jesus both from the law of Moses and the prophets" (Acts 28:23).[18] And William Kelly, one of the early Plymouth Brethren writers, argued that the Messianic kingdom was offered to the Jews until the destruction of Jerusalem in 70 A.D.[19]

---

[16]Scofield had distinguished between this rejection and the one at Matthew 27:21 by calling the former "the official rejection" (SB 1226) and the latter "the final official rejection" (SB 1011).

[17]McClain, *Greatness of the Kingdom*, p. 405.

[18]Arno C. Gaebelein, *The Acts of the Apostles* (New York: Publication Office of "Our Hope," 1912), p. 62.

[19]William Kelly, *Lectures on the Gospel of Matthew* (new ed.; New York: Loizeaux Brothers, 1943), p. 226.

Dispensationalists explain this phenomenon by saying that the synoptic Gospels and Acts are a record of the gradual transition made from the presentation of the Davidic kingdom to the Jews to the point where the newly-established Church alone prevailed. Since there are repeated offerings of the Davidic kingdom to Israel after Matthew 11:20, it follows that "a strong legal and Jewish coloring is to be expected up to the cross" (NSB 987). And, we might add, if there are continued offerings of the glorious Davidic kingdom to the Jews in Acts and beyond, then that "legal coloring" could well emerge in certain sayings of the apostles in the book of Acts and in their epistles after the founding of the Church at Pentecost.

But the mixture of law and grace which is purportedly found in Jesus' sayings in the synoptic Gospels (and possibly on into the book of Acts) does not occur in the writings of Paul. According to the editors of the *New Scofield Bible*:

> The doctrines of grace are developed in the [Pauline] Epistles
> ...; but they are implicit in the Gospels, because they rest on the
> death and resurrection of Christ and upon the great germinal truths
> He taught, truths of which the Epistles are the unfolding. The Christ
> of the Gospels is the perfect manifestation of grace. (NSB 987)

In another note they say:

> [The Pauline epistles] develop the doctrine of the Church. ... The
> doctrine of grace found in the teaching of Christ is also given further
> revelation through Paul. ... Immediately after his conversion he
> preached Jesus as the Messiah; but the relation of the Gospel to the
> law ... needed clear explanation. In Arabia this explanation was given
> Paul "by the revelation of Jesus Christ" (Gal. 1:11–12). The result was
> that he taught salvation by grace through faith wholly apart from the
> works of the law. (NSB 1209)

But whereas the synoptic Gospels (Matthew, Mark, and Luke) have that "strong legal and Jewish coloring" (NSB 987), the Gospel of John is different in that it draws so heavily upon Paul who "chronologically and theologically ... was antecedent to John."[20] Ryrie says that "some of the principal features of Paulinism are taken up by John not in the sense of borrowing but in the sense

---

[20]Ryrie, *Biblical Theology*, p. 312.

of building upon them as the historical antecedents that they were."[21]

Consequently dispensationalism and covenant theology have always drawn a strong distinction between John and the other three Gospels. For example, Lewis Sperry Chafer said:

> Under the condition laid down in the kingdom teachings, life is entered into by a personal faithfulness (Matt. 5:28–29; 18:8–9). . . . [Luke 13:24] opens with the words, "Strive to enter in at the strait gate." The word *strive* is a translation of *agonidzomai*, which means "agonize." It suggests the uttermost expenditure of the athlete's strength in the contest. Such is the human condition that characterizes all the kingdom passages which offer entrance into life. [But] an abrupt change is met after turning to the Gospel of John, which Gospel was written to announce the new message of grace, which is, that eternal life may be had through *believing*. No two words of Scripture more vividly express the great characterizing relationship in law and grace than *agonize* and *believe*. Grace is the unfolding of the fact that One has agonized in our stead, and life is "through his name," not by any degree of human faithfulness and merit. (ST IV, 224)

Martin Luther made a similar distinction between the synoptic Gospels and the Gospel of John in the preface to his translation of the New Testament (1522): "John's Gospel is the only Gospel which is delicately sensitive to what is the essence of the Gospel, and is to be widely preferred to the other three and placed on a higher level."

John Calvin made the same distinction in the foreword to his commentary on John:

> The doctrine, which points out to us the power and the benefit of the coming Christ, is far more clearly exhibited by [John] than by the [Synoptists]. . . . The three former [synoptic Gospels] exhibit [Christ's body], if we may be permitted to use the expression, but John exhibits his soul. On this account I am accustomed to say that this Gospel is a key to open the door for understanding the rest. . . . In reading [the four Gospels], a different order would be more advantageous, which is, that when we wish to read in Matthew and others that Christ was given to us by the Father, we should first learn from John the purpose for which he was manifested.

[21]Ibid., p. 313.

These quotations confirm a major thesis of this book: today's dispensationalism is a special form of covenant theology in that it wants to draw the sharpest distinction between the legal teachings, which supposedly preponderate in the synoptic Gospels, and the gracious teachings, which are supposedly found largely in John's Gospel and in Paul. If dispensationalists and covenant theologians could understand that the promises conditioned upon the fulfillment of specific works, and found in the synoptic Gospels, are nothing but the works of faith, and that John's Gospel is about faith itself with occasional mention of the works it produces (e.g., John 5:28–29), then they could understand that our Lord taught but one message when he was upon earth. They would not have to attempt this "rightly dividing" of the Word which requires such subtle theological understanding that even the most eminent theologians fail to agree on how all the divisions should be made.

Dispensationalists and covenant theologians make such subtle and yet important distinctions because they (rightly) want to discourage all works in which men boast. But if they realized that the works which are the condition for promised blessings are the works of faith in which it is impossible to boast, they would no longer view God as constantly switching back and forth between two very opposite messages.[22] They would not have to affirm that Jesus taught the works in which men can boast in the greater part of Matthew, Mark, and Luke, and then the faith which saves without boasting in the Gospel of John.

The dispensational problem of exactly when Jesus withdrew the offer to establish the glorious Davidic kingdom for the Jews would also vanish, along with the attempt to distinguish between the "moral rejection," the "official rejection," and the "final official rejection." If dispensationalists conceded that from the outset of his public ministry Jesus proclaimed a kingdom understood not as a specific kind of realm, as was the glorious Davidic kingdom, but as a kingdom basically understood (as Walvoord clearly concedes it to be)[23] as "the right to rule" made possible by his death on the cross, then this right to rule could be manifested in several different kinds of realms; one of these could entail the sufferings

[22]Supra, p. 63, n. 30.
[23]Supra, p. 154.

of God's people alluded to in the Sermon on the Mount,[24] and another would be the glorious Davidic kingdom foretold by the Old Testament prophets. Understanding the kingdom as primarily a right to reign would also solve the next problem confronting dispensationalism, namely, that according to Matthew 21:43, Jesus took the *same* kingdom from the Jews who had rejected it, and gave it to other peoples who accepted it.

III. How Could Jesus Offer the Same Kingdom to the Gentiles Which He Had Offered to the Jews?

In Matthew 21:33–40 Jesus related to the Pharisees the parable of the wicked husbandmen who were given the job of tending a vineyard. These husbandmen were so rebellious that they not only repeatedly rejected the various overseers sent by the owner to collect profits, but finally killed the owner's son. In concluding the parable Jesus quoted from Psalm 118:22–23 that "the very stone which the builders rejected has become the head of the corner; this was the Lord's doing and it is marvelous in our eyes." Then Jesus said, "Therefore I tell you, the kingdom of God will be taken away from you and given to a nation producing the fruits of it" (Matt. 21:43).

It would seem that the dispensationalists would have to regard the kingdom that is taken from the Jews to be the Messianic kingdom which Jesus had been offering them since the inception of his ministry. The editors of the *New Scofield Bible* consider Matthew 21:43 to be "an official rejection" (NSB 1248) of this Davidic kingdom, but disclaim that this "kingdom" has anything to do with the Messianic kingdom:

> Matthew here uses the expression "kingdom of God," referring to a sphere of genuine faith in God. . . . The Kingdom of God is declared to be "taken from you," i.e., taken from the scribes and Pharisees represented in the parable as the wicked farmers, and given to a nation, i.e., any people who will bring forth the fruits of salvation. This passage teaches that unbelieving scribes and Pharisees would not be saved, because of their rejection of the Son. Others who will manifest the fruits of salvation will take their place. . . . (NSB 1029)

The problem with this interpretation, however, is that it con-

---

[24]Supra, pp. 156–157.

cerns a verse which follows a parable that climaxes in the rejection of Jesus by the Jewish nation as a whole. Therefore a face value interpretation of Matthew 21:43 would have to mean that the kingdom which Jesus had offered to the Jews was now being withdrawn from them as a nation and was going to be offered to other groups of people. The dispensationalist cannot say that the kingdom of God spoken of here is simply that sphere inhabited by all those who at any time in redemptive history truly believe and are saved. As do all of today's dispensationalists, Ryrie argues that "in some places the word *kingdom* is used of a universal, timeless, and eternal kingdom (Matt. 6:33)."[25] This is the sort of kingdom which the editors of the *New Scofield Bible* see in Matthew 21:43, but the immediate context of this passage rules out the possibility of seeing it as something "timeless" which has nothing to do with specific things that had just been happening in redemptive history. In speaking about Jesus' presentation of the kingdom earlier in his ministry, Ryrie made a special point of ruling out the possibility that this kingdom could be the "spiritual reign [of God] in individual lives" (DT 173). He then goes on to say, "If it were a spiritual kingdom Christ was offering, then 'such an announcement would have had no special significance whatever to Israel, for such a rule of God has *always* been recognized among the people of God' " (DT 173).[26]

But there is virtually no difference between what Jesus is saying in Matthew 21:43 and what he said in Matthew 4:17, when he announced that the kingdom of heaven is at hand, for in both passages, on Ryrie's presuppositions, Jesus has been talking about a specific, concrete kingdom that God had been offering to a certain people at a certain point in redemptive history. Therefore if Matthew 4:17 could not refer to something "timeless," then neither can the kingdom spoken of in Matthew 21:43 be timeless. The dispensationalist, however, renders it timeless, for otherwise the Church, which now becomes the recipient of this kingdom, would become involved in a kingdom pervaded by legalism.[27]

The dispensationalist's problem in Matthew 21:43 could be

---

[25]Ryrie, *Biblical Theology*, p. 74.

[26]Ryrie was quoting here from Alva McClain, *The Greatness of the Kingdom*, p. 303.

[27]Supra, pp. 149–153.

easily solved if he accepted Walvoord's conclusion that the Davidic kingdom is primarily a "right to reign."[28] When the right to reign is the foundational idea of the kingdom, then the precise configurations in which this realm manifests itself can change without changing any essential aspect of the kingdom itself. We, of course, do not believe that the kingdom offered in Matthew 4:17 was the Messianic kingdom, but even if it were, this kingdom could now be offered in another form to a different people without its essential nature being changed in the least, because the basic feature of the Davidic kingdom is the "right to rule," and not a particular realm. That the Church, who receives this kingdom, would not therefore become adulterated with legalism and Galatianism is simply because Jesus' call to repentance and his teachings in the Sermon on the Mount consist only of the call to the obedience of faith and the works of faith. Jesus is surely not calling men to do works in which they can boast.

Dispensationalists, nevertheless, believe that at some point (they indicate several possibilities)[29] Jesus withdrew his offer from Israel to establish the glorious Messianic Davidic kingdom. This offer will not be repeated until after an interregnum during which the kingdom of God exists in the so-called "mystery form" set forth in the parables of Matthew 13. During this time Jesus founds his Church, and several features of the "mystery form" of the kingdom will be well-suited to coexist with the Church. But when the Church is raptured from the earth, a Jewish remnant will again proclaim the nearness of the Davidic kingdom. After going through a period of terrible tribulation this remnant will be rewarded for their efforts when Jesus returns from heaven to establish his kingdom with its seat of government at Jerusalem. Then the "new covenant" predicted in Jeremiah 31:31–34 will be established with Israel. But this presents the dispensationalist with a difficult problem because Jesus said during his Last Supper, "This cup is the new covenant in my blood" (I Cor. 11:25; cf. Luke 22:20). The Davidic kingdom and the new covenant are inseparably linked in dispensationalist thinking. This leads us, then, to the statement of the last problem.

[28]Supra, p. 154.
[29]Supra, pp. 157–158.

IV. How Can Jesus Institute the New Covenant without the Establishment of the Davidic Kingdom?

Although the exact wording "new covenant" appears in the Old Testament only in Jeremiah 31:31–34, there are at least half a dozen passages where God, as in the passage in Jeremiah, promises to regenerate Israel, cause her to walk in his statutes, forgive her sins, and be her God (Lev. 26:40–46; Deut. 30:1–10; Jer. 32:37–41; Ezek. 11:17–21; 36:24–31; and 37:24–27). In Ezekiel 37:24–27, the establishment of David as king is predicted in the same breath as the promises that God will make an "everlasting covenant" with Israel. Dispensationalists insist that it is impossible to have the new covenant without the inauguration of the Davidic kingdom. Walvoord declares, "The premillennial [dispensational] position is that the new covenant is with Israel and the fulfillment [of it is] in the millennial kingdom after the second coming of Christ" (MK 209).

We have referred to Jesus' words at the Last Supper about inaugurating the new covenant. Furthermore the writer of Hebrews speaks several times about how Christ in his death and resurrection inaugurated a "new covenant" (Heb. 9:15; 12:24), a "better covenant" (Heb. 7:22; 8:6), and an everlasting covenant (Heb. 13:20). He clearly contrasts this "new covenant" with the old Mosaic Covenant in Hebrews 7:22–23; 9:15; 12:18–24, and cites Jeremiah 31:31–34 in support of this contrast in Hebrews 8:8–13 and 10:16–17. Such passages offer considerable evidence for concluding that this inspired writer regarded Jesus' work as a fulfillment of the new covenant promised in Jeremiah 31:31–34. But then a promise for Israel would find some fulfillment in the Church, and this would refute dispensationalism's basic premise that God's dealings with Israel remain separate from his dealings with the Church. C. I. Scofield felt this evidence was strong enough for him to make the statement, inconsistent with his dispensationalism, that "the New Covenant secures the personal revelation of the Lord to every believer ... and secures the perpetuity, future conversion, and blessing of Israel" (SB 1297).

But both L. S. Chafer and John F. Walvoord demur from Scofield's statement and argue that in addition to the new covenant which will be inaugurated for Israel in the millennium, there is another covenant for the Church that somehow, in their thinking, is "new." Walvoord affirms that "*a* new covenant has been provided for the church, but not *the* new covenant for Israel" (MK 214). Walvoord understands that the writer of Hebrews cites Jeremiah 31:31–34 in Hebrews 8:8–12 in order to establish the thesis of Hebrews 8:6 that Christ is mediator of a better covenant than the Mosaic Covenant. He declares, however, that "nowhere in [Hebrews 8:6–13] is the new covenant with Israel declared to be in force. The only argument is that . . . the prediction of a new covenant automatically declares the Mosaic covenant as a temporary . . . covenant" (MK 216).

But if the writer of Hebrews regarded this new covenant, which is predicted in Jeremiah, as referring only to what God will do for Israel (as Walvoord would insist), and not at all to the new covenant which Christ has mediated to the Church, then that inspired writer could not view Jesus' covenant with the Church as "new" in comparison with the old Mosaic Covenant, and he could not argue from the transitoriness of that covenant to the perfection of Christ's covenant with the Church. There must be a continuity between the subjects with whom God has worked and will work in order to respect the language conventions of the words "old" and "new." Only the future covenant that God will make with Israel can properly be called "new," for there is already an "old" covenant for Israel. Naturally dispensationalists affirm that only Israel, and not the Church, has an old, imperfect covenant to which a later, new covenant is contrasted. But since in dispensationalist terms there is no continuity between Israel and the Church, it is breaking language conventions to talk of a "new" covenant for the Church that is in contrast to an old covenant for Israel.

It may be that Walvoord senses this difficulty, for he stresses that in Hebrews 12:24 the writer uses a Greek word for "new" that can also have the meaning of "recent": "Jesus is declared to be the Mediator of the new covenant in the sense of a *recent* covenant. The time element is in contrast to the old covenant, i.e., the Mosaic, which has been in force for many centuries" (MK 218). But the word "recent" is so close to the idea represented by the word "new" that the dispensationalist is still violating language conventions. In short, he cannot allow a face value interpretation of Hebrews, because he would then get the Church intermeshed with Israel and her purported legalism.[30]

As stated earlier, dispensationalism could easily extricate itself from this problem if it viewed the kingdom promised to David as the "right to reign" rather than a realm. We have seen how Jesus, in Matthew 21:43, explicitly states that the kingdom is to be taken from Israel and given to another people. Instead of bringing the blessings of salvation to Israel by ruling over her, he brings them to the Church over whom he rules from the Davidic throne in heaven (Acts 2:30–33). Indeed, the sort of realm in which Jesus' right to rule now manifests itself in the Church is considerably different from the Messianic kingdom which he will establish at his second coming. But it is the Davidic kingdom nonetheless, and it is this kingdom that is now established. To understand that Jesus has inaugurated the new covenant of Jeremiah 31:31–34 with the Church is simply honoring the express statements of Scripture, both in the Old Testament prophets and in various places in the New Testament. Indeed, the particular configurations of the realm that Jeremiah foresaw have not yet been established, but the "right to rule" has certainly been established for the Church by Jesus' death and resurrection. On a number of occasions Paul writes about Christians who are enjoying the benefits of the kingdom of God. In Romans 14:17 he says, "The kingdom of God is not meat and drink but righteousness and peace and joy in the Holy Spirit." In I Corinthians 4:20 he reprimands those trusting in their eloquent rhetoric by saying that "the kingdom of God does not consist in talk but in power." Then in Colossians 1:13 he speaks of how God "has delivered us from the dominion (lit. kingdom) of darkness and transferred us to the kingdom of his beloved son. . . ."

Other such verses could be cited, but these are sufficient to show that Jesus' kingdom is well established in his rule over the Church, and as a necessary corollary of the establishment of his kingdom there must be the establishment and application of the new covenant. If the dispensationalist were willing to view the

---

[30]It should also be noted that Paul in II Cor. 3:6 does the same thing as the writer of Hebrews and contrasts the new covenant for the Church (Paul claims to be a minister of this new covenant!) with the old Mosaic Covenant.

kingdom of God as a "right to rule," he would not have to struggle so to explain the passages in Hebrews which refer to the inauguration of the new covenant. Knowing that this new covenant inclines people to the obedience of faith, that is, to living lives characterized by the works of faith, he would be free from the fear that the Church, by being in a continuum with Israel, would become adulterated with legalism and Galatianism.

CHAPTER SEVEN
The Parenthesis Church

According to dispensationalism, when Israel rejected the Messianic kingdom proffered her by John the Baptist and Jesus, God withdrew the offer for the time being and established another realm of the kingdom whose parameters constituted the way he would deal with the world until the time came once again to establish the Davidic kingdom for Israel. These parameters are set forth in the "mysteries" of Matthew 13. "Mysteries" is a biblical term often understood as meaning a truth now revealed for the first time. The Parable of the Sower and the Soils (Matt. 13:1–9, 18–23), the Parable of the Tares and the Wheat (13:24–30, 36–43); and the Parables of the Hidden Treasure and the Pearl of Great Price (13:44–47) sketch out the most basic features of Jesus' mode of working during this intervening period between the rejection of the Davidic kingdom and its future establishment. The editors of the *New Scofield Bible* summarize this new revelation in the mysteries of the parables about the kingdom of heaven:

> [These parables] taken together describe the result of the presence of the Gospel in the world during the present age, that is, the time of seed-sowing which began with our Lord's personal ministry and will end with the harvest (vv. 40–43). The result is the mingled tares and wheat, good fish and bad, in the sphere of Christian profession. It is Christendom. (NSB 1013)

All of this marks a "new beginning" (NSB 1013). Instead of laboring exclusively in Israel—God's vineyard (Isa. 5:1–7)—the Lord is now beginning to sow the seed of the word of God throughout the world. But only a minority responds to it. Others make a half-hearted response, which means that a sphere of mere professors of Christianity now closely exists with those who have genuine faith. So the kingdom that is now revealed is "entirely distinct from the Messianic kingdom which Jesus had been offering."[1]

But it is within these parameters that God brings to pass a number of other "mysteries," or new revelations, which supposedly set forth the unique features of the Church—that group of people totally separate from Israel as a nation. God will work with the Church on earth until he resumes his work with Israel after rapturing the genuine believers out of "Christendom" into heaven. Some of the more notable mysteries regarding the Church are (1) the Church as one body composed of Jews and Gentiles; (2) the mystery of the indwelling Christ; and (3) the translation (rapture) of the living saints at the end of this age (NSB 1014).

I. The Uniqueness of the Church

The passages in which the word "mystery" (*mystērion*) occurs in Paul constitute the basic argument for dispensationalism's affirmation that the Church is unique and separate from any purpose God has for Israel. A crucial presupposition for its argument is that "mystery" always conveys the idea of a truth "once hidden ... but now revealed" (MK 232). Indeed, this is its meaning in some Pauline contexts. Bornkamm acknowledges that one of the antitheses implied by *mystērion* is "the antithesis between then and now."[2] An example of such a usage would be Romans 16:25–26, which speaks of the mystery "which was kept secret for long ages but is now disclosed and through the prophetic writing is made known to all nations, according to the command of the eternal God." But another antithesis implied by this word is between "now and the one day."[3] In Colossians 2:2–3 Paul speaks of how he labors in order to help believers eventually to "have all the riches of the assured understanding and the knowledge of God's mystery, of Christ, in whom are hid all the treasures of wisdom and knowledge."

---

[1]Pentecost, *Things to Come*, p. 142.
[2]G. Bornkamm, "*mystērion*," *Theological Dictionary of the New Testament*, 9 vols.; ed. G. Kittel; trans. G. W. Bromiley (Grand Rapids: Wm. B. Eerdmans Publishing Company, 1967), IV, 822.
[3]Ibid.

In Paul's thinking this knowledge, which inheres in Christ, will someday become fully manifest in the world as God completes his plan for redemptive history. In Ephesians 1:9–10, Paul uses the term "mystery" to represent the eschatological purposes God has for the world and its history; purposes which will become completely manifest in the fulness of time, when he will unite in Christ all things in heaven and earth. Believers now have this knowledge in part and are enjoined to increase their knowledge and understanding of the riches of the glory of this mystery (Col. 1:27; cf. Eph. 1:18). In Ephesians 3:8–10 Paul represents "the unsearchable riches of Christ" by the term "mystery," and declares that it is through the Church that all the many facets of God's wisdom in Christ will be revealed.

Such knowledge becomes known as God takes the initiative at certain points in history to reveal what is in Christ to certain people. Consequently there is the contrast between what is now made known and what has hitherto been hidden, as in I Corinthians 2:6–7:

> We speak the wisdom of God in a mystery, which God decreed before the ages for our glorification, a wisdom [lit. mystery] which none of the rulers of this age understood, for if they had, they would not have crucified the Lord of glory. But, as it is written, "What no eye has seen, nor ear heard, nor the heart of men conceived, what God has prepared for those who love him," [these things] God has revealed to us through the Spirit.

The idea of hiddenness, which is such a primary aspect of this word, arises partially from the hardness of men's hearts in their refusal to believe God. Thus it does not always arise (as dispensationalists are wont to emphasize) from the fact that there was a time when God had not yet taken the initiative to reveal it in some way. Their failure to understand what Paul means by "mystery" constitutes one problem with their argument from several of Paul's references to this word to their conclusion that the Church itself is a mystery in the sense of being totally unforeseen in the earlier prophetic revelation of the Old Testament.

The mystery "which is Christ in you, the hope of glory"
(Col. 1:27)

That Christ would indwell believers and that his presence in them would be the guarantee and the hope of the blessings and glory that Christians would enjoy for eternity is "the mystery hidden for ages and generations, but now made manifest to his saints" (Col. 1:26). According to Walvoord this mystery "is Christ indwelling" (MK 240). Earlier revelations of Scripture never set forth that Christ (or deity) would indwell believers.

Other passages in Paul, and the Upper Room discourse of the Gospel of John, spell out some crucial elements of this mystery. That Christ should dwell in the believer indicates a closer and more vital relationship to Christ (and God) than had been envisioned in the Old Testament. According to Colossians 2:19 Christ is "the Head from whom the whole body, nourished and knit together through its joints and ligaments, grows with a growth that is from God." I Corinthians 12:13 declares that all believers were baptized by the Holy Spirit into this organism of which Christ is the Head. Since Acts makes it clear that this baptizing by the Holy Spirit occurred from Pentecost onward, therefore God began building his Church only from that time.

Something of this mystery was at least hinted at during the Upper Room discourse (John, chs. 14 to 17) that Christ gave to his disciples prior to his crucifixion. Here he promised that upon returning to the Father he would send the Holy Spirit who "dwells with you, but shall be in you" (John 14:17). According to the usual dispensational interpretation this means that "the Spirit thus given is promised to abide with believers in this present age forever, in contrast to the ministry of the Spirit in the Old Testament in which He would come only in a temporary way as in the case of King Saul."[4] Whereas Israel is regarded as a people or nation "among whom" God dwelt, "the Church is regarded as a living organism *in whom* Christ dwells, united by vital life and growing by inner spiritual supply" (MK 239; italics added). In the Upper Room discourse Jesus also described the relationship with his disciples that the Holy Spirit would make possible: "You in

[4]John F. Walvoord, *The Church in Prophecy* (Grand Rapids: Wm. B. Eerdmans Publishing Company, 1964), p. 37; henceforth designated as CP with page number.

me, and I in you" (John 14:20). He spoke too of believers' being related to him as a branch is to the main stem of a vine (John 15:1–6).

All of this is an elaboration on the mystery of Colossians 1:27, which is "Christ indwelling." Of the mysteries relating to the Church, Walvoord says, this "revelation in Colossians of the church as an organism is most important" (MK 237). From such a mystery Walvoord argues that "if the qualities observed here which are the very essence of the church in the present age are described as mysteries, it is not too much to regard the church itself as unheralded in the Old Testament" (MK 239). Here Walvoord basically concludes that the Church is not represented in the Old Testament prophecies and plays no part in God's purposes for Israel.

But the problem with this understanding of the "mystery" of Colossians 1:27 is that the indwelling of the Holy Spirit in people was certainly not unknown in Old Testament revelation. Joshua was "a man *in* whom was the Holy Spirit" (Num. 27:18). The preposition in Hebrew is *be-*, "in, inside." The Holy Spirit came "upon" Saul (I Sam. 10:6, 10; 11:6) and later departed from him (I Sam. 16:14), but there is every indication that the Holy Spirit remained *in* Joshua throughout his life, for he persevered in serving the Lord until his death (Josh. 24:15).

Paul's statement in Romans 8:8 that those who are in the flesh cannot please God and his statement in Romans 8:9, "You are not in the flesh, you are in the Spirit, if the Spirit of God really dwells in you," are also noteworthy. These are general statements which must apply to human beings at whatever time they lived in history. Hebrews 11:6 also says that "without faith it is impossible to please God," and Hebrews 11 recounts the notable examples of people in the Old Testament who pleased God by believing him. But if Romans 8:8–9 is true, then these who succeeded in pleasing God in the Old Testament did so, not only because they believed God, but because they were indwelt by the Holy Spirit, for those not *in*dwelt by the Holy Spirit (regenerated) were in the flesh, and could do nothing to please God. So deity indwelling man through the Holy Spirit was not known for the first time at Pentecost. Because it followed so closely after Christ's death, resurrection, and ascension, Pentecost marked the occasion when God *officially* gave the Holy Spirit to indwell men, in order to show that it was only through the work of Christ that it was possible to give the Holy Spirit to sinful men who, by themselves, deserved nothing. But it is a great mistake to regard the official giving of the Spirit at Pentecost as the first time God ever regenerated men by causing the Holy Spirit to indwell them.

Then too, the prophecies regarding the new covenant with Israel expressly state that God will cause the Holy Spirit to dwell *in* his people. "A new spirit will I put within you" is affirmed twice in Ezekiel 36:26–27. Since prior revelation shows that the Holy Spirit permanently indwelt at least one man in the Old Testament and he will *in*dwell all of Israel in the future, it is impossible to say that the mystery of Colossians 1:27 "is Christ indwelling," if mystery always has to mean a revelational truth hitherto unknown.

In what sense, then, was "Christ in you, the hope of glory" a mystery in Paul's thinking? We argue that when Paul used the word "mystery" in this context he had reference to all the facets of revelation which are summed up in Christ and which will be openly manifest in creation in "the fulness of time" (Eph. 1:10). "Mystery" here represents the "riches of the glory." Paul's prayer in Ephesians 1:19 that his readers might know "what is the hope to which he has called you and what are the riches of his glorious inheritance in the saints" is obviously a parallel passage to Colossians 1:27. Hence the mystery in Colossians 1:27 of "Christ in you, the hope of glory" does not consist in "Christ indwelling" so much as in a lively knowledge of the glory of what God has prepared for those who love him (cf. I Cor. 2:7–10).

Indeed, this mystery had been "hidden for ages and generations, but is now made manifest to the saints" (Col. 1:26). But the previous hiddenness of this mystery does not mean that it had never been revealed to anyone, for we have seen that the deity dwelling in men through the Holy Spirit had already been made known and experienced in the Old Testament. The hiddenness refers instead to its having been generally hidden from the Gentiles. Between Abraham and Pentecost God took virtually no initiative to send his revelation to the Gentiles but "allowed all the nations to walk in their own ways" (Acts 14:16). So Paul emphasizes in Colossians 1:26–27 how "God *chose* to make known how great *among the Gentiles* are the riches of the glory of this mystery, which is Christ in you, the hope of glory." So if much of this mystery had already been revealed to Israel in Old Testament times, then it would be impossible for the dispensationalist to argue from the mystery in Colossians 1:26–27 to the conclusion that the Church itself is a mystery totally outside the purview of Old Testament prophecy for Israel.

The mystery that "the Gentiles are fellow heirs" (Eph. 3:5–6)

In Ephesians 3:5–6 Paul speaks of the mystery of Christ "which was not made known to the sons of men in other generations as it has now been revealed to his holy apostles and prophets by the Spirit; that is, how the Gentiles are fellow heirs, members of the same body, and partakers of the promise in Christ Jesus through the gospel." In verse 3 Paul remarks that he had already been speaking about this mystery just a few sentences before, and this indicates that Ephesians 2:11–22 is an elaboration upon the summary statement of the mystery found in Ephesians 3:6. Some of the salient propositions of the Ephesians 2:11–22 passage are: (1) the Gentiles who were once separated from Christ, aliens from Israel, and strangers to its covenants of promise, have now been brought nigh by Christ's death on the cross (vv. 11–13); (2) by death Christ created "in himself one new man in place of two," and this "one new man" is also "one body" through the cross (vv. 14–17; and (3) this "new man" has access to God through the Holy Spirit and is "a dwelling place of God in the Spirit" (v. 22).

Because Ephesians 2:11–22 states that Jew and Gentile were created into one new body by the cross of Christ, Ryrie argues that "the new man, the one body, was not in existence in Old Testament times" (DT 134). Indeed, Paul's words clearly affirm that this "one body" and "new man," in which Gentiles are on an equal footing with Jews, has come into being only after the cross of Christ. Surely this is the Church that Christ, during his earthly ministry, had said he would build (Matt. 16:18).[5] Walvoord also argues that since Paul emphasizes the work of the Holy Spirit in connection with this new body (Eph. 2:18, 22), the Church "did not exist before Pentecost," and that since "the concept of the

---

[5]Note the future tense, "I will build" (Matt. 16:18).

body is foreign to the Old Testament and to Israel's promises," therefore "something new had begun" (MK 226). Likewise, since Israelites who had been saved before the cross and had heartily concurred with the apostles' preaching the Gospel were made members of the body of Christ, therefore the Church which began to be formed at Pentecost, Walvoord insists, could not be a continuation of the Old Testament people of God but a wholly new entity. Otherwise, why would Paul refer to these Jews as becoming members of a *new* man (Eph. 2:15)? Walvoord concludes that, "In virtue of these significant truths, it becomes apparent that a new thing has been formed—the body of Christ" (MK 226).

The Church, however, is not only a new entity existing from Pentecost on but also a mystery which was not foreseen by the prophets, for one of its most essential qualities—the equal standing of Jew and Gentile—"was not made known to the sons of men in other generations, as it has now been revealed to his holy apostles and prophets by the Spirit" (Eph. 3:5). To the extent that this equal standing was unknown to the Old Testament prophets (and this extent depends on how the "as" of Ephesians 3:5 is construed), it can be argued that the Church is totally separate from God's dealings with Israel in the past and in the future. If the prophets did not foresee this equal standing, then they did not foresee the Church. The equal standing of Jew and Gentile in enjoying blessings from God is an essential aspect of the Church, and so if what is essential to the Church is not foreseen by the prophets as they describe Israel's future, then the Church itself is not envisioned by them and plays no role in God's future for Israel. Therefore, the Church is totally distinct from Israel.

Unquestionably, Paul did regard at least part of the knowledge of the equal standing of Jew and Gentile to be unknown, for he calls it a "mystery which was not made known to the sons of men in other generations as it has now been revealed. . . ." (Eph. 3:4–5), and the word "mystery" here connotes the idea that at least some knowledge was not hitherto revealed. But if some knowledge of this was given in the Old Testament, and the mystery consists only in the added clarity provided for the first time by New Testament spokesmen, then it follows that, to the extent the Old Testament prophets did have some knowledge of these essential features of the Church, they had some knowledge of the

Church itself. Therefore, knowledge of it is not totally excluded from the Old Testament prophetic picture. In order to avoid this conclusion, dispensationalists have tried to argue that the two clauses "which was not made known ... as it has now been revealed" should be construed to read, "The mystery which was not made known in other generations *having now* been revealed to his holy apostles and prophets."[6] Walvoord cites Acts 2:15, "These are not drunk, as you suppose," as an instance where a comparative clause introduced by "as" totally enforces the negation of the main clause: all of what the Jerusalem populace regarded as the cause of the apostles' speaking in foreign languages (viz., that they were drunk) is to be negated. Likewise *all* of what is known from the revelation of the mystery through the New Testament apostles and holy prophets is what was *not* made known to the sons of men before this recent revelation. Obviously the intended meaning of Acts 2:15 is to exclude drunkenness as making any contribution to the apostles' behavior. "These are not drunk to the extent you suppose them to be drunk" is not the meaning of Acts 2:15. But the circumstances surrounding the wording of Ephesians 3:5 do not rule out the *possibility* of construing it to read, "The mystery was not made known to the extent that it is now made known. ..." The verse could mean this, but does not have to. The wording of Ephesians 3:5 does not, by itself, settle the question of just how it is to be construed.

But Ephesians 3:4–6 alludes to two other facts which are relevant. It encourages the reader (1) to examine the Old Testament prophecy to see whether or not it had anything to say about Jews and Gentiles' being on an equal footing. It also encourages the reader (2) to look at what other apostles and prophets in the New Testament era had to say about the matter.

Surely the James who cites Amos 9:11–12 in Acts 15:16–18 in order to prove to the Jerusalem Council that Gentiles are on an equal footing with the Jewish believers is one of "the apostles and prophets" whom Paul regarded as having authority to speak on this subject. Before James spoke, Peter had recounted how God had given the Holy Spirit to uncircumcised but believing Gentiles "just as he did to us" circumcised, believing Jews. From this he

---

[6]Ryrie, *Biblical Theology*, p. 189 n.

concluded, "We [Jewish apostles] believe that we [Jews] shall be saved through the grace of the Lord Jesus, just as they [the Gentiles] will" (Acts 15:7–11). Afterward Paul and Barnabas related how God had also unequivocally demonstrated, during the first missionary journey, his purpose to give the blessing of the Holy Spirit to uncircumcised Gentiles simply on the basis of faith (Acts 15:12). Then James, the acknowledged leader of the Jerusalem Church, supported the conclusion of Peter and Paul,. not from any experience he had had with Gentile evangelism (he had had none), but from "the words of the prophets" which, he affirmed, agreed with Peter and Paul (v. 15). He then cited words which were drawn largely from Amos 9:11–12:

> After this I will return, and I will rebuild the dwelling of David, which has fallen; I will rebuild its ruins, and I will set it up, that the rest of men may seek the Lord, and all the Gentiles which are called by my name, says the Lord, who has made known these things from of old. (Acts 15:16–18)

From these words he concluded that the Church should regard uncircumcised Gentile believers as on an equal footing with believing Jews.

How James understood Amos 9:11–12 to agree with the conclusion of Peter and Paul is quite obvious. Amos is very clear in stating that in the future God will accept Gentiles as fully as anyone else. Hence from Amos, an Old Testament prophet, as well as from James, who was a New Testament prophet and an apostle, the affirmation is explicit and unambiguous that God had revealed enough to the Old Testament prophets to support the conclusion that Gentile believers were to have the same status as Jewish believers.

This being so, we must conclude that the equality of Jews and Gentiles in the people of God was by no means totally foreign to Old Testament prophecy, unless we have reason to regard Paul's statement in Ephesians 3:5 as contrary to the teaching of James in Acts 15:13–18. But since Paul's language in Ephesians 3:5 can cohere with James' point in Acts 15:13–18, and since Paul says there that what he teaches about Gentile and Jewish equality is in concert with what another recent revelational spokesman has said, therefore we understand Ephesians 3:5 to mean that the revelation of the equal standing of Jews and Gentiles was not made known to the Old Testament prophets to the full extent that it is now made known. All that constituted this completed revelation was the fact that Jews and Gentiles should be *fellow heirs*.

But dispensationalists do not go along with what is obviously James' intended meaning in Acts 15:13–18. Most commentators construe the word "first" in James' statement, "Symeon has related how God *first* visited the Gentiles to take out of them a people for his name" (v. 13), to echo Peter's statement in verse 7, "Brethren, you know that *in the early days* God made choice among you that by my mouth the Gentiles should hear...." But Walvoord understands it to mean that

> it was God's purpose to bless the Gentiles as well as Israel, but in their order. God was to visit the Gentiles *first*, "to take out of them a people for his name." James goes on to say that this is entirely in keeping with the prophets for they had stated that the period of Jewish blessing and triumph should be *after* [cf. "After this"—v. 16] the Gentile period. ... Instead of identifying the period of Gentile conversion with the rebuilding of the tabernacle of David, [this period] is carefully distinguished by the *first* (referring to Gentile blessing), and *after* this (referring to Israel's coming glory). The passage, instead of identifying God's purpose for the church and for the nation Israel, established a specific time order. (MK 205–206)

This interpretation derives some plausibility from the "first" and "after this" of verses 14 and 16, but the great objection to Walvoord's interpretation is that it "does not have a word to say as to its bearing upon the point at issue,"[7] which is whether or not Gentile believers can remain as such and be on an equal footing with Jewish believers. In fact, if Walvoord's interpretation were James' intended meaning, the only way it could conceivably have a bearing upon the point at issue would be that there was an *analogy* between the future millennial age (outlined by Amos) in which Gentiles will be blessed along with Jews, and the present Church age. This was the only way Darby could understand James'

---

[7]Oswald T. Allis, *Prophecy and the Church* (Philadelphia: Presbyterian and Reformed Publishing Company, 1945), pp. 147–148.

use of Amos to have relevance to the issue before the Jerusalem Council:

> Verses 11, 12 of [Amos 9] are quoted in Acts 15, not for the purpose of showing that the prophecy had come to pass; but to prove that God had all along determined upon having a people from out of the Gentiles; and that, therefore, the language of the prophets agreed with that which Simon Peter had been relating of what God had done in his days. It is not the accomplishment of a prophecy, but the establishment of a principle by the mouth of the prophets, as well as by the word of the Spirit through Simon Peter.[8]

The *New Scofield Bible* follows Darby in its interpretation of Acts 15:13–18. The editors say, "James showed that there will be Gentile believers at that time [after Christ's return, during the millennium] as well as Jewish believers; hence he concluded that Gentiles are not required to become Jewish proselytes" (p. 1186). But the "hence" in this note introduces a conclusion which does not follow from the premise. According to dispensationalists, Gentiles will be blessed during the millennium but will always have a somewhat inferior status; they feel this is reflected in whatever the prophets say about Jew-Gentile relations in the future Messianic kingdom. Ryrie, for instance, says, "The Old Testament does predict Gentile blessings for the millennial period (Isa. 61:5–6; 2:1–4), but the specific blessings do not include equality with the Jews as is true today in the Body of Christ" (DT 134). Walvoord declares that "the thought of equality of Jew and Gentile is never mentioned in the great kingdom passages of the Old Testament" (MK 236). If James also believed this—and a dispensationalist would affirm that he did—then the point to be gained from his quoting of Amos 9:11–12 would be not to grant the Gentiles equal status with the Jews but only a status like that which they would have in the millennium. The result would have been that those who argued that Gentiles must be circumcised to be saved (Acts 15:1) would have been strengthened, and the truth of the gospel (cf. Gal. 2:5) would have been endangered.

But James did not quote Amos 9:11–12 for this reason. The meaning which James did derive from these verses involves his

---

[8]J. N. Darby, "The Hopes of the Church of God," *Collected Writings*, II, 555.

understanding that the Gentile mission, reported by Peter and Paul, was a fulfillment of Amos 9:11–12 and other passages in the prophets (cf. "the prophet*s*"—Acts 15:15) which speak of God's blessing the Gentiles along with the Jews. Therefore, since another New Testament "prophet" (James) understands the mystery of Ephesians 3:4–6 as being partially known to the Old Testament prophets, we argue that Paul also believed that this mystery was partially known. So we construe the "as" of Ephesians 3:4–5 to mean, "This mystery was not made known to the sons of men in other generations as—to the extent that—it is now made known. . . ." If the Old Testament prophets had partial knowledge of the mystery of Ephesians 3:4–6, then this passage (and Eph. 2:11–22) does not support the conclusion that the Church itself is wholly unknown to Old Testament prophecy.

Paul and the other New Testament spokesmen, by virtue of being farther along in the sequence of progressive revelation, added many pieces to the jigsaw puzzle, in addition to those provided by the Old Testament. Thus they could speak of Gentile and Jewish equality in the Church (the New Testament name for the people of God) with a greater completeness and within a clearer context than the Old Testament prophets. But the Old Testament prophets made a very real contribution to the mystery, which in the last analysis is all summed up in Christ (Col. 2:2) and in God's purpose to sum up all things in him (Eph. 1:9–10). Hence we conclude that what Paul intended to communicate by the "mystery" of Ephesians 3:4–6 is not something as radical as labeling the Church a "*new* person" in the sense of its having no continuity with Old Testament prophecy and the people of God who existed before the cross. Indeed, the New Testament people of God—the Church—are new in the sense that now, in distinction from Old Testament times, Gentiles in general as well as Jews comprise this people. (For this reason it is not fitting to call Old Testament people of God, the Church.) It is also true that through the cross of Christ the enmity that existed between Jew and Gentile is broken down. The chief cause for that enmity was the sense of superiority which the Jews felt in the mistaken notion that they, unlike the Gentiles, had qualities and were doing things which met a need in God so that he was obligated to bless them. The meaning of the cross of Christ, however, underscored what Moses and the prophets had been saying all along, namely, that God would bless only those who pled for mercy and entertained no delusions that they could provide for God's needs.

But it was through his cross that Christ also propitiated God's wrath against men, whose greatest sin was presuming they could earn God's blessing. The benefits of this propitiation, as we have seen, extended backward from the cross to make possible the salvation of Old Testament saints, and forward to make possible the salvation of the people comprising the "new man" which is the Church.

The mystery that "we shall all be changed" (I Cor. 15:51)

As the "mysteries" of "Christ in you" (Col. 1:27) and "the Gentiles are fellow heirs" (Eph. 3:6) are used by dispensationalists to argue that the Church is a "mystery," and thus distinct from God's working with Israel in the past, so this third mystery is the basis for arguing that the Church is distinct from God's working with Israel in the future. "Lo! I tell you a mystery," Paul says. "We shall not all sleep, but we shall all be changed, in a moment, in the twinkling of an eye, at the last trumpet. For the trumpet will sound, and the dead will be raised imperishable, and we shall all be changed" (I Cor. 15:51–52). That saints will be translated, given immortal, imperishable bodies when Christ returns is a mystery, a truth of which the Old Testament prophets knew nothing:

> the Old Testament in its prophecies of the second coming of Christ shows life as continuing on earth, and the saints surviving the great tribulation are seen entering the millennial earth and continuing in their natural state. It is for this reason that the apostle declares that the translation of the church is a mystery. (CP 97)[9]

In seeking to relate this translation of the saints to other events that are predicted in Scripture, Walvoord concludes there is no way for this event to occur at the time when Jesus returns to

---

[9]Much data could be gleaned from the Old Testament to show that there was some understanding—though somewhat obscure—that there would be a resurrection of the dead. We shall not attempt to detail the data here but merely point out that Walvoord's statement vastly oversimplifies the picture. Furthermore, it comes dangerously close to denying Jesus' teaching of the resurrection of the dead from Exodus 3:6 in Matthew 22:32 et par.

establish his millennial kingdom on earth. Prior to this return, there will be the time of great tribulation, as Jesus predicted in his Olivet Discourse (Matt. 24:21, 29). During this great tribulation, the Anti-Christ will reign and all men will be required to wear the mark of the beast and to worship his name (Rev. 13:8). The Anti-Christ will have such power over the world that he will cause "all, both small and great, both rich and poor, both free and slave, to be marked on the right hand or the forehead, so that no one can buy or sell unless he has the mark . . ." (Rev. 13:16–17).

But God will condemn all those who worship the Anti-Christ and wear his mark. "If any one worships the beast and its image, and receives a mark on his forehead or on his hand, he also shall drink the wine of God's wrath . . . and he shall be tormented with fire and brimstone. . . . And the smoke of their torments goes up for ever and ever" (Rev. 14:9–11). So the only people who will survive this judgment are those who did not wear the mark of the beast. "Only a few, both Jews and Gentiles, will escape the awful hatred of Satan and the world ruler [Anti-Christ]. . . . The possibility of one who is identified as a believer in Christ at its [the tribulation's] beginning, surviving to its end is indeed quite remote" (CP 131).

Nevertheless some will survive, and these will be the ones over whom Christ and the Church rule when he comes to establish his millennial kingdom. To those who believe that the translation of I Corinthians 15:51 occurs at the end of this tribulation period, Walvoord replies that if this were the case, there would be none left on earth for Christ and his saints to rule over. All those who had somehow survived the reign of Anti-Christ would be translated and, meeting Christ in the air, would return immediately with him to earth to rule with him for a thousand years. Over whom, then, would they rule? All those who had worn the mark of the beast would have been consigned to everlasting punishment, as Revelation 14:9–11 affirms. Thus Walvoord argues:

> If all the wicked are put to death and if all the saints are translated, it leaves no one in their natural bodies to populate the millennial earth. Hence, the simple fact that everyone will be transformed who believes in Christ on the occasion of the rapture of the church makes it necessary to move this event forward [i.e., earlier] and leave a sufficient time period between the rapture and Christ's coming to

establish His kingdom to raise up a whole new generation of saints from both Jews and Gentiles to populate the millennial earth. (CP 106–107)

With the rapture of the Church moved back from the second coming when Jesus establishes the millennial kingdom, there is a period of time during which a sufficient number of Jews and Gentiles respond to the Jewish remnant who resume the preaching of the gospel of the kingdom which John the Baptist and Jesus had initially preached. These people refuse to take the mark of the beast, and though many of them are martyred, enough survive to enter the millennium with the natural bodies that are described in Isaiah 65:20–25. It is over these people that Jesus and his Church rule when he comes "with his saints" and establishes the millennial kingdom. For some time the millennial kingdom consists only of righteous people. But finally some of the posterity of these godly people apostatize and, joining forces with Satan, who is released from the bottomless pit at the end of the millennium, make war (unsuccessfully) against the saints (Rev. 20:7–10).

Dispensationalists argue from the mystery in I Corinthians 15:51–52 to the pre-tribulation rapture of the Church in this manner. Seven years is the timespan of the tribulation, it seems, because the time periods in the book of Revelation (Rev. 11:2; 12:6; 13:3, 5) during which there is great tribulation on earth, seem to correspond to the second three-and-one-half-year period mentioned in Daniel 9:27 when the reign of one like Anti-Christ will become particularly oppressive. According to Daniel 9:27 this sinister ruler, who will oppress Israel and establish some sort of abomination to symbolize his rule, will reign seven years, that is, the last of the seventy weeks of years. Major events in Israel will occur during these seventy weeks of years referred to in Daniel 9:24–27.

The events commence in 445 B.C. with the decree of Artaxerxes to rebuild Jerusalem. Sixty-nine weeks of years later (A.D. 29 if the years are counted as having only 360 days) the Messiah is cut off, as Daniel 9:26 predicts. No sinister ruler appears, however, during the next seven-year period. But since Jesus referred to the "abomination of desolation" which this ruler would establish as happening shortly before his second coming (Matt. 24:15), and since Daniel speaks of this seventieth week as existing by itself, it is concluded that between the sixty-ninth and seventieth week of Daniel there is a gap which corresponds to the time when God calls out his heavenly people, the Church. When the Church is raptured from the earth, the seventieth week of Daniel commences, and the earth enters the period of great tribulation under the reign of Anti-Christ.

Dispensationalists support the concept of the pre-tribulation rapture by arguing that the final seven years comprising Daniel's seventieth week "is specifically the time of Jacob's trouble (Jer. 30:7) and coincides with the last seven years of Israel's program as outlined in Daniel 9:24–27. It is God's program for Israel, therefore, rather than God's program for the Church that is primarily in view." Walvoord continues:

> It is also specifically the consummation of the times of the Gentiles foreshadowed in Daniel's visions in Daniel 2 and 7, the progress of which was interrupted by the interposition of the present purpose of God in the church. The dual purpose of God to fulfill Israel's program and the times of the Gentiles culminating in the second coming of Christ are quite different than His purpose for the church in this present age. (CP 129–130)

Thus dispensationalists begin their argument with the "mystery" of I Corinthians 15:51–52, and find corroboration from what is said about Anti-Christ's reign during the great tribulation that climaxes the seventy weeks of Daniel which concern not the Church but Israel and the Gentiles. On this basis dispensationalists conclude that the rapture of the saints described in 1 Thessalonians 4:13–18, or the translation of the saints described in I Corinthians 15:51–52, takes place prior to the commencement of the great tribulation and Anti-Christ's reign. By this insistence on the pre-tribulation rapture of the Church, the dispensationalist is able to regard the Church as separated from God's dealings with Israel which commence again with Daniel's seventieth week and with the Jewish remnant who resume the preaching of the "gospel of the kingdom" preached by John the Baptist and Jesus himself during the first part of his earthly ministry. Since the Church is so disconnected from what happens on earth after she is raptured, as well as from God's dealings with Israel before Pentecost when

she was first begun, the third "mystery" in I Corinthians 15:51–
52, along with the other two, helps the dispensationalists to argue
that the Church itself is wholly a "mystery"—a parenthesis between God's dealings with Israel before and after the Church age.
The Church in the dispensational view of things is an intercalation
between what God was doing with Israel up through the sixty-
ninth week and what he will resume doing during the seventieth
week of Daniel.

It is beyond our purpose to enumerate the secondary arguments which the dispensationalist advances in support of the pre-
tribulation rapture and to discuss the objections which have been
raised against this concept. We shall instead limit ourselves to a
consideration of the validity of this argument from the "mystery"
of I Corinthians 15:51–52 which Walvoord, it would seem, regards as the most compelling. One essential facet of his argument
is that neither Christ's second coming at the end of the tribulation
nor his subsequent presence on the earth functions to effect the
conversion of any Israelite, or Gentile, for that matter. All that
Christ's second coming does is to *ratify* the spiritual condition
of both Jews and Gentiles at the end of the great tribulation
period. Those who have responded positively to the preaching of
the Jewish remnant during the previous seven-year period will be
allowed to enjóy the blessings of the millennial kingdom. The
Gentiles who thus qualify would be the sheep in the judgment
described in Matthew 25:31–46 (MK 289). The Jews would be
those gathered from other nations of the earth from whose midst
the rebels and transgressors would be purged before the remainder would be allowed to join the third of the Jews that are already
in the land (Ezek. 20:33–38).[10] Hence Walvoord concludes:

---

[10]We recall, however (supra, pp. 183–184), that the power of Anti-Christ to
make people wear the mark of the beast would be so great, and God's judgments
against those who submitted so final, that (to use Walvoord's words) "the possibility of one who is identified as a believer in Christ [which the Jewish remnant
and their Gentile converts would be] at [the tribulation's] beginning, surviving
to its end is indeed quite remote" (CP 131). So the pre-tribulation rapture
theory has no little difficulty in populating the millennium over whom Christ
and his Church will rule. But it is conceivable that many people will resist
submitting to Anti-Christ for any number of non-Christian reasons, and that some
of these will survive to populate the millennium as mortal human beings. This
supposition would help solve the post-tribulationist's problem.

The subjects of the millennial rule of Christ at the beginning of the millennium will consist in those who survive the searching judgments of both Israel and Gentiles as the millennial reign of Christ begins. From many Scriptures it may be gathered that all the wicked will be put to death after the second coming of Christ, and only saints who have lived through the preceding time of trouble will be eligible for entrance into the millennial kingdom. This is demonstrated in the judgment of the Gentiles in Matthew 25:31–46, where only the righteous are permitted to enter the millennium. According to Ezekiel 20:33–38, God will also deal with Israel and purge out all rebels, that is, unbelievers, permitting only saints among Israel to enter the millennial kingdom. The parables of the wheat and the tares (Matt. 13:30–31) and of the good and bad fish (Matt. 13:49–50) teach likewise that only the wheat and the good fish, representing the righteous, will survive the judgment. Confirmation is also found in Isaiah 65:11—66:16; Jeremiah 25:30–33. (MK 302)

This understanding of the effect of Christ's second coming is consistent with the passages that were just cited. There is another group of passages, however, in which the effect of Christ's coming upon the earth is something beyond simply ascertaining people's spiritual condition and dispatching forthwith the rebels among the Jews and the goats among the Gentiles into perdition. Concerning the third of the Jews in Palestine who survive the tribulation God says, "I will ... refine them as one refines silver. ... They will call on my name, and I will answer them. I will say, 'They are my people'; and they will say, 'The Lord is my God' " (Zech. 13:9). Here it would seem that Christ is working actively to convert these survivors. Then too, Zechariah 12:10 describes how *God will work* to effect a change of heart in Israel when Christ returns:

> I will pour out on the house of David and the inhabitants of Jerusalem a spirit of compassion and supplication, so that, when they look on him whom they have pierced, they shall mourn for him, as one mourns for an only child, and weep bitterly over him, as one weeps over a firstborn. ... The land itself shall mourn, each family by itself ... and all families that are left, each by itself, and their wives by themselves. (Zech. 12:10, 12, 14)

Walvoord says nothing about this passage in his *Millennial Kingdom*. Lewis Sperry Chafer, however, does say that this passage described what would happen to Israel at Christ's return (ST, V, 126). One conceivable reason that Walvoord omits it is that it speaks of Christ's *active* work in effecting Israel's conversion at his second coming, but if Christ can work to convert rebels after he has returned to earth, then unbelievers can enter the millennium and be saved after they respond favorably to Christ.

The time of the inauguration of the new covenant with Israel also gives dispensationalists a problem. According to them Jesus inaugurates it at his second coming. But according to Jeremiah 31:33, what is central in this inauguration is the *regeneration* of a significant number of Israelites. Consequently, prior to the second coming, these Israelites must have been rebellious and unresponsive to the preaching of the Jewish remnant. It is hard to see how at least some of them could have avoided wearing the mark of the beast. Nevertheless, they were not sent to perdition at the second coming, but were regenerated in that they received a new heart. This, it seems, is why Walvoord mentions God's radical new covenant with Israel only with the mild term "spiritual revival" which will come to the Israelites who have successfully survived both the preceding tribulation period and Christ's judgment after his return:

> Along with the deliverance of the godly [!], the Scriptures predict that at the second coming Israel will experience spiritual revival. This is intimated in Romans 11:26–27 and is involved in the fulfillment of numerous Old Testament passages of which Jeremiah 31:31–34 may be taken as representative. (MK 274)

But these "numerous Old Testament passages" which predict the inauguration of the new covenant with Israel refer to conversion more than revival. In Jeremiah 32:37–41 and Ezekiel 36:26–27 there is the implantation of a new heart through the work of the Holy Spirit, and according to Jeremiah 31:34, sins will be forgiven. Deuteronomy 30:6 states that God must circumcise the heart in order for Israel to love him and keep his commandments.

Even though Isaiah 59:20 says, "And he will come to Zion as Redeemer, to those in Jacob who turn from transgression," Paul regarded the second coming of Christ to be so active in converting Israel that he quoted this verse as saying, "The Deliverer will come from Zion, he will banish ungodliness from Jacob" (Rom. 11:26). Then he immediately cited Jeremiah 31:34 as saying, "And this [the promise of Isaiah 59:20] will be my covenant with them when I take away their sins" (Rom. 11:27).

Therefore, since such Scripture passages stress Christ's active work in effecting Israel's conversion at his return, we conclude that people do enter the millennium (in their natural bodies) who up to that time had not repented and believed. If this is the case, then a fundamental premise in Walvoord's argument for the pre-tribulation rapture is destroyed, and the "mystery" of I Corinthians 15:51–52 does not help prove that the Church itself is a "mystery." We now turn to what is an essential part of still another Pauline "mystery" which, we believe, argues against the concept of the Church as a "mystery" and a "parenthesis."

II. The Olive Tree of Romans 11

In Romans 11:25–26 Paul sets forth the "mystery" that "a hardening has come upon part of Israel, until the full numbers of the Gentiles come in, and so all Israel shall be saved. . . ." Prior to this statement he used the analogy of an olive tree to describe certain aspects of redemptive history from the call of Abraham down to the inclusion of the Gentiles as a part of God's people and then to the conversion of the entire nation of Israel. The roots of this olive tree are the patriarchs Abraham, Isaac, and Jacob, and in particular, God's promise to be their God and the God of their seed. In Romans 11:28–29 Paul speaks of how the election of the nation of Israel remains valid for the sake of the "forefathers" to whom God made irrevocable promises. For a part of redemptive history this olive tree primarily represented the nation of Israel. But then God broke off many of the branches because of the unbelief of large segments of Israel (Rom. 11:17, 19–22).

In place of these branches, God engrafted shoots from a wild olive tree, which represented the Gentiles' becoming one with the believing Jews in sharing the blessing that God would be their God. Later on when the nation of Israel is converted at Jesus' second coming he will, as it were, engraft into the cultivated olive tree shoots that once were from the cultivated olive tree. Then both Israel and the Gentile nations of earth will enjoy together the promises that God made to Jew and Gentile (Gen. 12:2–3; 17:4–8).

One of the points Paul draws from the analogy of this olive tree is that Gentile believers, who are now so obviously included in the blessings that hitherto had been limited to Israel, should not become proud and self-confident (as many Israelites had) in thinking that they would automatically come into the full enjoyment of the blessings that were promised to the patriarchs. Indeed, there was a partial truth in a Gentile's saying, "[Jewish] branches were broken off so that I might be grafted in" (v. 19). But these Jewish branches were broken off because of unbelief, and the same fate will befall the Gentile who does not persevere in faith but trusts instead in some distinctive, or lack of it, which he thinks will obligate God to bless him. Paul warns his Gentile readers:

> [20]So do not become proud, but stand in awe. [21]For if God did not spare the natural branches, neither will he spare you. [22]Note then the kindness and severity of God: severity toward those who have fallen, but God's kindness to you, provided you continue in his kindness; otherwise you too will be cut off. [23]And even the others, if they do not persist in their unbelief will be grafted in, for God has the power to graft them in again. (Rom. 11:20–23)

But Paul's primary point in this analogy of the olive tree is the mystery that God will graft back into the original tree natural branches representing Israelites alive at the time of Jesus' second coming, all of whom will turn to God. "How much more will these natural branches be grafted back into their own olive tree [!]. . . . And so all Israel will be saved, as it is written, 'The Deliverer will come from Zion . . .' " (vv. 24, 26).

Dispensationalists correctly stress this fundamental point in discussing Romans 11:24–27. But much more is intentionally taught and necessarily implied by this analogy. When Paul says that Gentile believers "were grafted in their place to share the fat root of the olive tree," his only possible meaning is that Gentile believers come to share jointly, along with Jewish believers who still remain in the tree, the blessing of Abraham, which Paul equates elsewhere (Gal. 3:14) with the promise of the Spirit received through faith. Since this analogy is very much akin to the theme of Ephesians, chapters 2 and 3, that "Gentiles are fellow heirs, members of the same body, and partakers of the promise in Christ Jesus through the gospel" (Eph. 3:6), it makes explicit some aspects of Paul's thinking which show exactly what he meant by

Gentiles' becoming fellow heirs. In that he said that Gentile believers share "the fat root of the olive tree," he could not have subscribed to the dispensational interpretation of Ephesians 3:6 that Gentiles as members of the Church belong to "a wholly new thing" (NSB 1275). But Paul could have subscribed to Ryrie's note on the olive tree analogy of Romans 11:17–24 if Ryrie would have included the material I have placed in brackets:

> The olive tree is the place of privilege [i.e., of enjoying God as one's God] which was first occupied by the natural branches (the Jews) [who were of the remnant]. The wild branches are Gentiles who, because of the unbelief of Israel [and because they have repented and believed], now occupy the place of privilege [along with the remnant of believing Israelites with whom they are one]. The root of the tree is the Abrahamic covenant which promised [the] blessing [of having God as their God] to both Jew and Gentile through Christ. (RSB 1718)

The meaning is plain that Gentile believers come to enjoy the *same fatness* from the root which Jewish believers had been enjoying.

Dispensationalists make scarcely any comment on this statement in Romans 11:17 that Gentile believers "were grafted in [the Jewish non-remnant's place] to share the fat root of the olive tree." The *New Scofield Bible* (p. 1226) devotes three lines to this verse: "The olive tree represents the blessings promised to Abraham's seed. Though Gentiles do not, by faith in Christ, inherit Israel's particular promises, they do receive the blessing promised to 'all families of the earth' " (Gen. 12:3; cf. Gal. 3:6–9). This note is obviously intended to fit in with the insistence that "the predicted future of the true Church is translation and glory" (NSB 1299), and that "the Christian is a heavenly man, and a stranger and pilgrim on the earth" (NSB 1272), whereas Israel's future, as certified by the Abrahamic covenant, "is not the gospel of salvation" nor "the covenant of redemption, ... the promise of forgiveness of sin, the promise of eternal life or any of the elements of salvation" (MK 142–143). In the dispensational view, Gentiles are indeed grafted into the tree whose root is Abraham, but it is as though the branches by which they are represented have a special pipeline down through the tree trunk to a part of the

Abrahamic root which nourishes them with the soteriological blessings, while the Jewish branches are blessed only from the sap coming up from the root promising the general providential blessings of a land, membership in a large and prosperous nation, and having God as their God "in the general and providential sense" (MK 142).

But any thought of such a division of blessings must be rejected on the basis that Gentiles are *joint heirs* (Eph. 3:6), and *share* the fat root of the olive tree (Rom. 11:17). To the dispensationalist objection that believers today are not going to inherit the land of Palestine in the future, it need only be replied that all such prosperity means nothing according to the Old Testament unless it is enjoyed in the context of the assurance that God is one's God, which assurance carries with it such other blessings as forgiveness and the guarantee of eternal life. But also, since believers are going to reign with Christ during the millennium, they will no doubt have access to Palestine and will surely be a part of those who will "sit at table with Abraham, Isaac, and Jacob in the kingdom of heaven" (Matt. 8:11).

Dispensationalism, however, insists on perpetuating the distinction between Israel and the Church in the millennium and even in the final new heavens and earth. Naturally, Christians will be reigning with Christ during the millennium in resurrected, immortal bodies, and so they may, on occasion, rub shoulders with those who became converted subsequent to Christ's return and who, like us today, have bodies that are still earmarked for death (these will be resurrected or translated at the end of the millennium). According to dispensationalists, Old Testament saints, as well as those martyred during the great tribulation, will also be resurrected at the end of the tribulation (NSB 1250), so people like Abraham, Isaac, and Jacob will be with Christ in the millennium in immortal bodies. But these Old Testament and tribulation-period saints will be in a class that is distinct from the Church during the millennium. Walvoord explains:

> the church will reign with Christ [in the millennium] in a different sense than saints of other ages. . . . The church will follow her typical position as the bride of Christ while other saints will have other responsibility in the government of the millennium. There is no real need, however, for a sharp distinction between the church and saints

of other ages in the eternal state, though the Scriptures seem to indicate clearly that each group of saints will retain its identity throughout eternity. (CP 156–157)[11]

Nevertheless, since both the saints of the Church and those of
other ages will have immortal bodies, Walvoord finds it difficult
to conceive of their living on earth during the millennium, just
like believers today who still have mortal bodies:

> there is no particular reason why the New Jerusalem should not be
> in existence throughout the millennium and suspended above the
> earth as a satellite city. . . . If the heavenly Jerusalem is hovering over
> the earth during the millennial reign, it would be a natural dwelling-
> place not only for Christ Himself but for the saints of all ages who are
> resurrected or translated and therefore somewhat removed from or-
> dinary earthly affairs. (CP 159)

Walvoord believes that the components of this New Jerusalem
are listed in Hebrews 12:22–24, which speaks of believers coming
to "the city of the living God, the heavenly Jerusalem, and to
innumerable angels in festal gathering, and to the assembly of the
first-born who are enrolled in heaven, and to a judge who is God
of all, and to the spirits of just men made perfect. . . ." He comments:

> This important passage teaches that the saints of all ages will be in
> the heavenly Jerusalem. The inhabitants of the heavenly city are item-
> ized as an innumerable company of angels, the church, God, Jesus,
> the Mediator, and the spirits of just men made perfect, the latter
> designation seemingly referring to all Old Testament saints. (MK 326)

This heavenly city, which hovers over the earth during the
millennium and is therefore spared the destruction at the end of
the millennium, is the New Jerusalem of Revelation 21:9 through
22:5, which comes down from heaven and dwells upon the new
earth that is created along with the new heavens. The saints who
lived on earth during the millennium are resurrected or translated

---

[11]Chafer thought the distinction would be great. The Church would always
relate to Christ as a bride to her husband, whereas the other people of God
would relate to him as subjects to a king (D 404). So while Christ is ruling Israel
and the Gentiles, "she [the Church] will still be under the heavenly teachings
of grace, and her home will be in the bosom of the Bridegroom in the ivory
palace of the King" (ST, IV, 207).

at its end, and these are the ones who are already upon the earth when the heavenly Jerusalem is established there. And so in the final state of things in the new heavens and earth, the distinctions between Jew, Gentile, and Church, which are so crucial for the dispensational scheme, are retained. Walvoord comments on Revelation 21:24, which speaks of the "nations" or "Gentiles":

> in the eternal state the racial and spiritual background of different groups of saints will be respected and continued. Old Testament saints will be classified as Old Testament saints [in their separate category in the New Jerusalem], the Church will still be the body of Christ, and Israelites will still be Israelites as well as Gentiles [the saints who lived on earth during the millennium]. (CP 163)

To regard these groups as remaining distinct entities throughout the eternal ages to come is consistent with dispensationalism's fundamental principle:

> The various purposes of God for Israel, for the church which is His body, for the Gentile nations, for the unsaved, for Satan and the wicked angels, for the earth and for the heavens have each their contribution. How impossible it is to compress all of these factors into the mold of the [one] covenant of grace! (MK 92)

Because it sees God's purpose in history and Christ's death on the cross as accomplishing manifold purposes, dispensationalism claims that it is better able to display the richness of scriptural revelation than a so-called "idealism" like covenant theology, which regards God as doing one thing in redemption and creation so that everything in Scripture is either an elaboration on this one thing or a means for its accomplishment. In maintaining throughout the eternal ages the distinction between Old Testament and tribulation saints—the Church, and Jews and Gentiles who lived during the millennium—Walvoord believes that he is at once providing "for the unity and diversity in God's program, the unity in the common salvation experienced by all the saints, the diversity in their peculiar character and dispensational background" (MK 326).

But in dispensational thinking the Church is always the body of Christ and as such it presumably has a greater blessing throughout eternity than any other saints. Walvoord insists:

> While Israel as a nation was joined to God in a spiritual union, the new entity of the body of Christ in this age is *never* [italics added] contemplated in such a relationship. It is therefore a revelation of the union of love binding Christ and the church in addition to the union of life indicated in the figure of one body. (MK 246–247)

As long as dispensationalists conceive of the union with Christ enjoyed by the Church as something superior to the spiritual union enjoyed by other saints, their emphasis on the unity of Scripture, which they never want to deny, is problematical. Is God's purpose to unite one people to himself in the closest and most vital fashion, but others—Old Testament and tribulation saints and Jew and Gentile saints from the millennium—in a less vital, inferior way, intended to show, by contrast, the greatness of the blessing that God has bestowed upon the Church? If this is the answer, they can speak coherently of the unity of God's purpose in redemptive history. But such an understanding of the Bible's unity would be contrary to Hebrews 11:40, which affirms that Old Testament saints will not be made perfect apart from us New Testament saints. The double negative ("not made perfect"—"apart from us") is thus making the positive affirmation that Old Testament saints will be made perfect along with New Testament saints. If dispensationalism, however, views God's purpose for the other saints to be coordinate with his purpose for the Church, and not subordinate to show the Church's exalted position, then the Bible cannot be a unity. Instead it is a composite whole in which God reveals separately and coordinately various aspects of his glory in order to show the sum of all that he is. But does not the sum of all God is finally become a unity? If these various purposes of God were not finally all for one thing, then God himself is bifurcated, and that would raise serious problems in understanding the unity of God.

Since, however, there is one olive tree in Romans 11 which includes both Old Testament saints, New Testament believers, and Jews who will be re-engrafted in the millennium, dispensationalism's maintaining of separate distinctions is contrary to Paul's express teaching. Their teaching also clashes with Ephesians 3:10, which affirms that "through the church the *manifold* wisdom of God might be made known. ..." By talking of the "manifold" wisdom, Paul makes it clear that *all* of God's wisdom and thus *all* of his purpose becomes represented, manifested, and revealed in the Church. The Church which Christ builds beginning at Pentecost differs from the Old Testament people of God—the faithful remnant (Rom. 11:1–6)—only in that it comprises Gentiles as fellow heirs with Jews. This newness which begins a few years after Pentecost (Acts 11) continues on without reverting back, as in the dispensational view (which we have noted) of the tribulation period and the millennium, to where Jews again have something of a better standing than Gentile saints. Henceforth Gentiles, who are now part of the people of God, partake of the *same* fat root of the olive tree of Romans 11, just as the remnant among the Jews were doing before Pentecost. When New Testament saints are perfected at the resurrection, then Old Testament saints will be resurrected and perfected as well (Heb. 11:40). So the "manifold" wisdom of God (Eph. 3:10), which was manifest when Gentile believers were included in the Church as well as Jews, will be evident from the final glorified state of all the saints. Since Old Testament saints (mostly Jewish) are going to be made perfect along with New Testament saints, the group that will emerge at this perfecting will be an enlarged Church which shows the manifold wisdom of God in, among other things, having Jews and Gentiles on the same footing. Paul, then, is saying that God's plan, which has now become evident with the inclusion of Gentiles into the people of God and which is now best represented by the word "Church," is the unfolding of that model which from here on in for the rest of redemptive history is going to show forth the *manifold* wisdom of God.

In his reply to my unpublished dissertation of 1957, Ryrie correctly criticized me for assuming, a priori, the unity of Scripture and then using this assumption to argue against dispensationalism. I am glad for his criticism. One of the objectives of this book has been to banish all a priori assumptions regarding the unity of the Bible and to allow this concept to arise of its own accord from an inductive handling of such exegetical data as the olive tree of Romans 11 and the "manifold" of Ephesians 3:10. But this book, like the dissertation, does conclude that the Bible is a unity consisting of the one basic thing God is doing throughout redemptive history. Dispensationalists are incorrect in regarding God as doing more than one thing which necessitates their dividing Scripture into compartments that represent these several things. Dispensationalists, as we have seen, claim that this compartmentalizing is inescapable if one wants to follow a literal method of interpretation which alone honors the Bible as the Word of God. Our evidence, however, has demonstrated that dispensationalism's real concern is to keep the Church in the grace of God and separate from the supposed legalism of God's dealings with Israel. Because this, rather than a genuine concern for a "face-value" hermeneutic, controls the exegesis of the crucial passages in both Testaments, dispensationalism is refusing to let the Bible speak for itself and thus be Lord over the Church. We join with dispensationalists in wanting to reject all works in which men can boast. But we regard distinguishing between the "works in which men boast" and the "works of faith" (chapter four) as the correct way to do this rather than dispensationalism's attempt to do it by compartmentalizing Scripture.

Appendix on Galatians 3:18

A major objection against the interpretation of Galatians 3:10–12 given on pages 88 through 105 can be drawn from Galatians 3:18, "For if the inheritance is by the law, it is no longer by promise; but God gave it to Abraham by promise." Here "law" is unmistakably placed in antithesis to "promise," and by implication to "faith," which Paul linked so closely to his understanding of "promise" (cf. Gal. 3:14, 22). In order for our interpretation of Galatians 3:10–12 to be valid, we would have to understand "law" in verse 18 as the legalistic frame of mind which had twisted around the revelatory law's intended meaning so that it no longer enjoined the works of faith, in which God alone gets the credit, but rather enjoined the works in which men can boast.

An apparently insurmountable objection, however, against understanding "law" in verse 18 to have this meaning comes from the immediately preceding verse, which speaks of the law given at Sinai 430 years after the covenant made with Abraham. This, it would seem, would make the law spoken of in verse 17 the revelatory law, rather than the Pharisaic, legalistic misinterpretation of Moses. Certainly, when Paul in the very next verse pits "law" against "promise," it would seem that it is the revelatory law that is regarded as antithetical to the promise of the Abrahamic covenant and thus to the gospel.

Such an understanding of "law" in verse 18 would also seem to be supported by Galatians 3:15–17, where Paul explicitly speaks of the Mosaic law as standing in such sharp contrast to the Abrahamic covenant as to annul that covenant, were it possible (it is not!) to attach the Mosaic covenant to it as a codicil or an amendment. If these considerations led to the conclusion that the law of verses 17 and 18 is the revelatory law, then the crucial thesis of this book would be invalid.

But there are two other facts which must be carefully considered in answering the question of whether the "law" in Galatians 3:18 is the revelatory law or the Pharisaic misunderstanding of it. The first is that all the evidence indicates that the Judaizers at Galatia never would have agreed with Paul's statement that the Mosaic covenant was antithetical to the promise of the Abrahamic covenant. The way the Judaizers and the Pharisees thought can be reconstructed from the Rabbinical teachings of the early centuries of the Christian era, as well as from certain writings of the Old Testament Apocrypha and Pseudepigrapha. Every allusion to this subject in these writings understands Abraham to be the epitome of one who lived according to the Pharisaic understanding of the law. According to II Baruch 57:2, ". . . the unwritten law was named amongst [Abraham, Isaac, and Jacob], and the works of the commandments were then fulfilled." Likewise, according to Kiddushin 4:14 in the Mishnah, "We find that Abraham our father had performed the whole Law before it was given, for it is written [Gen. 26:5], 'Because that Abraham . . . kept my [God's] charge, my commandments, my statutes, and my laws.' " From such citations Strack-Billerbeck conclude that in the old Rabbinical understanding, "All promises were made to Abraham exclusively on the basis of his having lived righteously according to the law."[1]

So the probability is that the Judaizers, with whom Paul was locked in a life-and-death struggle in writing Galatians, understood Abraham as the perfect exemplar of one who lived uprightly according to the law and therefore received promised blessings from God. Consequently, they would have been totally unimpressed by Paul's mere assertion that the Mosaic law was totally opposite to the promise made to Abraham. But it is highly unlikely that Paul was simply pitting his word against theirs in contrasting the Mosaic law with the promise made to Abraham. It can be demonstrated that for every other point Paul makes in Galatians, there is a supporting argument which begins with what is authoritative for both the Judaizers and Paul. Genesis 12:3, for ex-

---

[1]Strack-Billerbeck, *Kommentar zum N.T.*, III, 204.

ample, was authoritative for both, and on pages 99 through 103 we demonstrated how Paul's argument from it in Galatians 3:8–9 would inescapably lead a reasonable person to the conclusion that all ethnic groups in the world would, like Abraham, be blessed simply by faith and not by following a certain set of distinctives like circumcision and the Jewish dietary regulations.

Thus when Paul says in Galatians 3:15–17 that the law cannot annul the righteousness of faith set forth 430 years before in God's dealings with Abraham, he is writing as one who believes that he has already established that the Judaizers' way of interpreting Abraham as the exemplar of Pharisaism is patently false. So when he alludes in Galatians 3:17 to the Mosaic law as that which cannot annul the righteousness of faith exemplified in Abraham, he is not necessarily affirming that the law taught what was opposite to faith. What he is saying is that even if the Judaizers were right and the law enjoined the doing of good works in which men can boast, it could not annul that righteousness attained through the obedience of faith, which according to the argument of Galatians 3:8 is undeniably taught in God's dealings with Abraham.

In construing Galatians 3:17 this way, Paul would, for argument's sake, be assigning not his, but the Judaizers' meaning to the law given by Moses. It would be natural, then, for that meaning to be carried over into verse 18 so that the word "law" there would not mean the revelatory law, but the legalistic way in which the Judaizers falsely understood Moses. Paul's strong affirmation in Galatians 3:18 that "God gave [the inheritance] to Abraham by promise [and not by law]" echoes the argument in Galatians 3:8 that the promises came to Abraham by faith and not by "law" in the sense of works or distinctives in which he could boast. So when one remembers that early Rabbinics interpreted Abraham's life in terms of Pharisaic legalism, then it becomes understandable how the "law" mentioned in Galatians 3:18 refers to the legalistic interpretation of it, even though the preceding verse had talked about the law given at Sinai.

A second fact which supports this interpretation of verse 18 comes from Paul's firm declaration in Galatians 3:21 that the revelatory law is not at all contrary to the promises of God. That Paul would make this strong affirmation in verse 21 indicates his concern to forestall the conclusion that could plausibly be drawn

both from verses 15–17 and verse 18—that the revelatory law
was antithetical to the promise made to Abraham. The vehement
denial in verse 21 of any contrariety between the revelatory law
and the promise lends support to our conclusion that the antitheses between "law" and promise that were made in verses 15
through 18 arise not from the nature of the law itself but from
the way the law had been misinterpreted by sinful men. Indeed,
it is significant that the power of sin figures strongly in the reason
Paul gives in Galatians 3:22–24 for why there is a "law" operative
in this world which is so at odds with the promise, while the
revelatory law itself (v. 21) is one and the same with the promise.

In verse 21 Paul affirms that the content and thought structure
of the law is just as capable as the promise of making a man
righteous before God. The law is a law of faith (Rom. 3:27; 9:31–
32) whose commands call for an obedience of faith (Rom. 1:5;
16:26) that produces the works of faith (Gal. 5:6; I Thess. 1:3;
II Thess. 1:11). It is not a law of works in which men could boast
of their compliance with its conditions or commands (Rom. 3:27).
The revelatory law was only deficient in that it lacked the power
to make a man righteous. "If a law had been given," Paul says,
"which could make alive, then righteousness would indeed be by
the law." This means that, in general, the recipients of the Mosaic
law did not receive along with it the supernatural, regenerative
power of the Holy Spirit to keep the law.

A number of Old Testament passages affirm that the Mosaic
law, for the most part, lacked the power to make a person righteous and alive to God. After hearing the Israelites promise, in
Deuteronomy 5:29, that they would gladly comply with all that
the Lord wanted them to do, God then laments, "Oh that they
had such a mind as this always, to fear me and to keep my commandments. . . ." This lack of a persevering disposition to keep
the law stems from God's decision, as Deuteronomy 29:4 makes
clear: "To this day the Lord has not given you a mind to understand, or eyes to see, or ears to hear."[2]

---

[2]The case was different, however, with the remnant, e.g., the seven thousand
people who did not bow the knee to Baal (Rom. 11:4; cf. I Kings 19:18). Like
Joshua, *in* whom God's spirit dwelt (Num. 27:18), and Caleb, who walked according to a "different spirit" (Num. 14:24) from the others, this relatively small

It should be noted, however, that the time would come when ethnic Israel would have the God-given disposition to comply with the law. Deuteronomy 30:6 tells of a future time when God would circumcise Israel's heart so they would keep his commandments. Likewise, according to Jeremiah 31:33, God promised, "I will put my law within them, and I will write it upon their hearts...." God also said in Ezekiel 36:27, "I will put my spirit within you and cause you to walk in my statutes and be careful to observe my ordinances." So according to these verses, when Israel is supplied with power to please God, the standard which will control her conduct will be nothing more nor less than the revelatory law, and this lends support to our thesis that Paul regarded the revelatory law and the promise as one and the same. The promise was the same as the law, because the conditions for receiving the promise were the commands of a law of faith, which enjoined nothing but the obedience of faith and the works of faith. Far from encouraging works in which men could boast, it enjoined a humility in which God received all the credit (Lev. 26:41; Deut. 10:21).

Why then does Paul use the same word "law" (as in Galatians 3:18) to represent what is totally opposite to the promise? The answer to this comes from the train of thought introduced at Galatians 3:22, a literal translation of which could read, "But the scripture has shut up [or boxed in] all things under sin...." Since Paul then proceeds in verses 23 and 24 to speak of how the *law* also "shut up [or boxed in]" Israel, it becomes clear that, apart from the regenerating power of the Holy Spirit, sin's power caused men to take the revelatory law, which is "holy and just and good" (Rom. 7:12), and "through the commandment [make them] sinful beyond measure" (Rom. 7:13). Therefore, when people who are under the power of sin interpret the revelatory law, the result is a body of teaching which encourages them to boast of their works before God rather than make the Lord their praise (cf. Deut. 10:21). This is why the "works of the law" which such men perform are so sinful that they are under a curse (cf. Gal. 3:10). The life they

---

remnant had a prevailing disposition to obey God's law. The delight of these people in the law (e.g., Psalm 19:7–10 and Psalm 119) was radically different from the majority of Israel, who boasted in their possession and supposed keeping of the law (Rom. 2:17–20 and Luke 18:9–12).

live is contrary to the revelatory law as well as to the promise and the gospel.

The conjunction "but" which introduces Galatians 3:22 represents the Greek *alla*, a conjunction which unambiguously signals to the reader that the forthcoming line of thought will proceed in a direction that is opposite to the preceding one. In the preceding thought of verse 21 Paul had spoken of how the revelatory law was one and the same with the promise. By commencing verse 22 with the use of the strong conjunction "but" (*alla*), Paul gives the reason why the Pharisaic teaching, which claims to be a faithful interpretation of the law, is totally opposite to the law's intended meaning: "all things are shut up under sin." Unless a person is under the power of the Holy Spirit, he will twist around the revelatory law's intended meaning until it caters to his ego.

Paul's use of "law" in Galatians 3:18 signifies such a misinterpretation of the revelatory law, but since it is a *misinterpretation* of that law, Galatians 3:18 cannot, as Calvin claimed, be used to prove that Paul "so often opposes the promise to the [revelatory] law, as things mutually contradictory: 'If the inheritance is by the law, it is no longer by promise' [Gal. 3:18]; and passages in this same chapter that express this idea" (*Inst.* III, 11, 17). Calvin never sensed, as biblical theology has begun to perceive, that Paul used the same term "law" in two ways that are very opposite to each other because of the complicating factor of the power of sin.

Bibliography

Allis, Oswald T. "Modern Dispensationalism and the Doctrine of the Unity of Scripture," *The Evangelical Quarterly*, 8 (January 1936), 22–35.
_____ "Modern Dispensationalism and the Law of God," *The Evangelical Quarterly*, 8 (January 1936), 272–289.
_____ *Prophecy and the Church*. Philadelphia: Presbyterian and Reformed Publishing Company, 1945.

The Apocrypha and Pseudepigrapha. 2 vols. Edited by R. H. Charles. Oxford: at the Clarendon Press, 1913.

Arndt, William F., and Gingrich, F. Wilbur. *A Greek-English Lexicon of the New Testament and Other Early Christian Literature*. 4th ed.; Cambridge: at the University Press, 1952.

Barth, Karl. "Gospel and Law," *God, Grace, and Gospel*. Translated by J. S. McNab. Scottish Journal of Theology Occasional Papers No. 8. London: Oliver Boyd, 1959, 1–28.

Bear, James E. "Dispensationalism and the Covenant of Grace," *The Union Seminary Review*, 49 (July 1938), 285–307.

Berkhof, Louis. *Principles of Biblical Interpretation*. 2nd ed.; Grand Rapids: Baker Book House, 1952.
_____ *Systematic Theology*. 3rd ed.; Grand Rapids: Wm. B. Eerdmans Publishing Co., 1946.

Blass, F., and Debrunner, A. *A Greek Grammar of the New Testament and Other Early Christian Literature*. Translated and revised from the 9th and 10th German editions by Robert W. Funk. Chicago: The University of Chicago Press, 1961.

Bornkamm, G. *"mystērion," Theological Dictionary of the New Testament*. Edited by Gerhard Kittel. Translated by Geoffrey W. Bromiley. 9 vols. Grand Rapids: Wm. B. Eerdmans Publishing Company, 1967. IV, 802–827.

Bowman, John Wick. "Dispensationalism," *Interpretation*, X (April 1956), 170–187.

Bring, Ragnar. *Commentary on Galatians*. Translated by E. Wahlstrom. Philadelphia: Muhlenberg Press, 1961.

Bullinger, E. W. *The Foundations of Dispensational Truth*. London: Eyre & Spottiswoode (Publishers) Ltd., 1931.

Calvino, Iojanne. *Institutiones Christianae Religionis*. Geneva: Apud Iohannem, le Preux, 1606.

Calvin, John. *Institutes of the Christian Religion*. Translated by Ford Lewis Battles. 2 vols. The Library of Christian Classics, vols. XX, XXI. Edited by John T. McNeill. Philadelphia: The Westminster Press, 1967.

Chafer, Lewis Sperry. "Dispensational Distinctions Challenged," *Bibliotheca Sacra*, 100 (July 1943), 337–345.

——————. "Dispensational Distinctions Denounced," *Bibliotheca Sacra*, 101 (July 1944), 257–260.

——————. "Dispensationalism," *Bibliotheca Sacra*, 93 (October 1936), 390–449.

——————. *Systematic Theology*. 7 vols. Dallas, Texas: Dallas Seminary Press, 1948.

Cranfield, C. E. B. "St. Paul and the Law," *Scottish Journal of Theology*, 17, 1 (March 1964), 43–68.

——————. "Some Notes on Romans 9:30–33," *Jesus und Paulus*, Festschrift für Werner Georg Kümmel zum 70. Geburtstag, 2nd ed.; Göttingen: Vandenhoeck & Ruprecht, 1978, 35–43.

Dallas Theological Seminary, *Doctrinal Statement*. Dallas, Texas: Dallas Theological Seminary, 1952.

Darby, John Nelson. "The Apostasy of Successive Dispensations," *The Collected Writings of J. N. Darby*, 2nd ed. Edited by William Kelly. 34 vols. London: G. M. Morrish, n.d. I, 192–202.

——————. "Lectures on the Second Coming of Christ," *The Collected Writings of J. N. Darby*, 2nd ed. Edited by William Kelly. 34 vols. London: G. M. Morrish, n.d. XI, 313–512.

——————. "On 'Days' Signifying 'Years' in Prophetic Language," *The Collected Writings of J. N. Darby*, 2nd ed. Edited by William Kelly. 34 vols. London: G. M. Morrish, n.d. II, 48–61.

——————. "The Hopes of the Church of God," *The Collected Writings of J. N. Darby*, 2nd ed. Edited by William Kelly. 34 vols. London: G. M. Morrish, n.d. II, 420–581.

Diem, Hermann. "Luthers Predigt in den zwei Reichen," *Theologische Existenz heute*, N.F. 6, 1947, 5–40.

Edwards, Jonathan. "Inquiry Concerning Qualifications for Communion," *The Works of President Edwards*. 4 vols. 8th ed.; New York: Leavitt & Allen, 1858. I, 85–192.

English, E. Schuyler. "The New Scofield Reference Bible," *Bibliotheca Sacra*, 124, 2 (April–June 1967), 125–132.

"E. Schuyler English Looks at Dispensationalism," *Christian Life*, XVIII, 5 (September 1956), 24–27.

Flückiger, Felix. "Christus, des Gesetzes *telos*," *Theologische Zeitschrift*, 11 (1955), 153–157.

Forde, Gerhard O. *The Law-Gospel Debate*. Minneapolis: Augsburg Publishing House, 1969.

"The Formula of Concord," *The Creeds of Christendom*. 4th ed. Edited by Philip Schaff. 3 vols. New York: Harper & Brothers, 1877. III, 93–180.

Friedrich, Gerhard. "Das Gesetz des Glaubens Röm. 3, 27," *Theologische Zeitschrift*, 10 (November 1954), 401–417.

Fuller, Daniel P. "The Hermeneutics of Dispensationalism." Unpublished Doctoral Dissertation, Northern Baptist Theological Seminary, 1957.

_____ "Paul and 'The Works of the Law'," *Westminster Theological Journal*, 38 (1975–76), 28–42.

Gaebelein, Arno Clemens. *The Acts of the Apostles*. New York: Publication Office of "Our Hope," 1912.

Gifford, E. H. *The Epistle of St. Paul to the Romans*. London: John Murray, 1866.

Godet, F. *Commentary on the Epistle to the Romans*. Translated by A. Cusin. Revised and edited by Talbot W. Chambers. Grand Rapids: Zondervan Publishing House, 1970.

Harrison, Everett F. *Romans*. The Expositor's Bible Commentary. Edited by Frank E. Gaebelein. 12 vols. Grand Rapids: Zondervan Publishing House, 1974–. Vol. 10.

Heppe, Heinrich. *Reformed Dogmatics*. Edited by E. Bizer. Translated by G. T. Thompson. London: George Allen & Unwin Ltd., 1950.

Hodge, Charles. *Commentary on the Epistle to the Romans*. New edition. Grand Rapids: Wm. B. Eerdmans Publishing Company, 1953 (reprint of 1886 edition).

_____ *Systematic Theology*. Reprint ed., 3 vols. Grand Rapids: Wm. B. Eerdmans Publishing Company, n.d.

Holy Bible. New Scofield Reference Edition. E. Schuyler English, chairman of the editorial committee. New York: Oxford University Press, 1967.

Holy Bible. Pilgrim Edition. Edited by E. Schuyler English. New York: Oxford University Press, 1948.

An Intermediate Greek-English Lexicon. Founded upon the 7th edition of Liddell & Scott's Greek-English Lexicon. Oxford: at the Clarendon Press, 1964.

Ironside, Harry A. *The Mysteries of God*. New York: Loizeaux Brothers, 1908.

Keller, Walter E. et al., "A Review Essay of *A Statement of Scriptural and Confessional Principles*," *The Cresset*, XXXVI, 7 (May 1973), 6–20.

Kelly, William. *Lectures on the Gospel of Matthew*. New edition. New York: Loizeaux Brothers, 1943.

Kümmel, Werner Georg. *Römer 7 und die Bekehrung des Paulus*, Untersuchung zum N. T. Hrsg. von Hans Windisch, Heft 17. Leipzig: J. C. Hinrichs'sche Buchhandlung, 1929.

Letters of J. N. D[arby]. 3 vols. Kingston-on-Thames, England: Stow Hill Bible and Tract Depot, n.d.

Luther, Martin. *Selections from His Writings*. Edited by John Dillenberger. Garden City, New York: Doubleday & Company, 1961.

MacInnis, John. "Is Fundamentalism Being Redefined?" *The King's Business* (September 1928), 517–518.

M[ackintosh], C. H. *Notes on the Book of Exodus*. New York: Fleming H. Revell, n.d.

Mauro, Philip. *The Gospel of the Kingdom*. Boston: Hamilton Bros., 1928.

McClain, Alva J. *The Greatness of the Kingdom*. Grand Rapids: Zondervan Publishing House, 1959.

Meyer, H. A. W. *The Epistle to the Romans*. 5th ed. Translated by J. C. Moore et al. New York: Funk & Wagnalls, Publishers, 1884.

Moore, George Foote. *Judaism*, 3 vols. Cambridge: Harvard University Press, 1927.

Moule, C. F. D. "Obligation in the Ethics of Paul," *Christian History and Interpretation*: Studies Presented to John Knox. Edited by W. R. Farmer et al. Cambridge: at the University Press, 1967, 389–406.

Murray, John. *The Covenant of Grace*. London: Tyndale Press, 1953.

———————— *The Epistle of Romans*, 2 vols. The New International Commentary on the New Testament, 17 vols. Grand Rapids: Wm. B. Eerdmans Publishing Company, 1975.

Pentecost, J. Dwight. *Things to Come*. Findlay, Ohio: Dunham Publishing Company, 1958.

Pieters, Albertus. *A Candid Examination of the Scofield Bible*. Swengel, Pennsylvania: Bible Truth Depot, n.d.

Ralston, Holmes III. *John Calvin versus the Westminster Confession*. Richmond: John Knox Press, 1972.

Ramm, Bernard. *Protestant Biblical Interpretation*. 2nd ed. Boston: W. A. Wilde, 1956.

"Report of the Ad Interim Committee on Changes in the Confession of Faith and Catechisms," *Minutes of the Eighty-Fourth General Assembly of the Presbyterian Church in the United States, 1944*. Richmond, Virginia: Presbyterian Committee for Publication, 1944, 123–127.

Ryrie, Charles Caldwell. *Biblical Theology of the New Testament*. Chicago: Moody Press, 1959.

———————— *Dispensationalism Today*. Chicago: Moody Press, 1965.

———————— *The Grace of God*. Chicago: Moody Press, 1963.

———————— *The Ryrie Study Bible*. New American Standard Translation. Chicago: Moody Press, 1978.

Sandeen, Ernest R. *The Origins of Fundamentalism*. Facet Books, historical series 10 (American Church). Edited by Richard C. Wolf. Philadelphia: Fortress Press, 1968.

Schmidt, Karl Ludwig. *"basileia," Theological Dictionary of the New Testament*. Edited by Gerhard Kittel. Translated and edited by Geoffrey W. Bromiley. 9 vols. Grand Rapids: Wm. B. Eerdmans Publishing Company, 1964. I, 579–593.

Scofield, C. I. *Rightly Dividing the Word of Truth*. Findlay, Ohio: Fundamental Truth Publishers, 1940.

The Scofield Reference Bible. Edited by C. I. Scofield. New York: Oxford University Press, 1917.

Strack, Hermann L., and Billerbeck, Paul. *Kommentar zum Neuen Testament*. 6 vols. Münich: C. H. Beck. 1961[3].

Suggs, M. Jack. " 'The Word is near you,': Rom. 10:6–10," *Christian History and Interpretation*: Studies Presented to John Knox. Edited by W. R. Farmer et al. Cambridge: at the University Press, 1967. Pp. 289–312.

Terkel, Studs. *Working*. New York: Avon Books, 1972.

Tertullian, *The Five Books Against Marcion*. Vol. III, 271–474. Translated by Peter Holmes. Ante-Nicene Fathers. Edited by Alexander Roberts and James Donaldson. 9 vols. Grand Rapids: Wm. B. Eerdmans Publishing Company, 1951.

Walther, C. F. W. *The Proper Distinction between Law and Gospel*. Translated from the German edition of 1897 by W. H. T. Dau. St. Louis: Concordia Publishing House, 1928.

Walvoord, John F. "The Abrahamic Covenant and Premillennialism," *Bibliotheca Sacra*, 108 (1951), 414–422; 109 (1951), 37–46; 136–150; 217–225; 293–303.

——————— *The Church in Prophecy*. Grand Rapids: Wm. B. Eerdmans Publishing Company, 1964.

——————— Letters to Daniel P. Fuller, dated November 5 and November 23, 1956.

——————— . *The Millennial Kingdom*. Findlay, Ohio: The Dunham Publishing Company, 1959.

"The Westminster Confession of Faith. A. D. 1647," *The Creeds of Christendom*. 4th ed. Edited by Philip Schaff. 3 vols. New York: Harper & Brothers, 1877. III, 598–673.

Wilckens, Ulrich. *Rechtfertigung als Freiheit*. Neukirchen: Neukirchener Verlag, 1974.

Winer, Georg B. *Grammar of the Idiom of the New Testament*. 7th ed. Translated by H. Thayer. Andover: Warren F. Draper, 1897.

Zahn, D. Theodor. *Der Brief des Paulus an die Römer*. 2nd ed. Leipzig: A. Deichert, 1910.

Index of References

Index of Names

216

Printed in the United States
22591LVS00004B/306

9 780960 263813